The McGraw-Hill
Internet Training Manual

The McGraw-Hill Internet Training Manual

Ronald L. Wagner
Eric Engelmann

Internet Home Page
http://www.marketing-coach.com/mh-guide

McGraw-Hill

New York   San Francisco   Washington, D.C.   Auckland   Bogotá   Caracas   Lisbon   London   Madrid
Mexico City   Milan   Montreal   New Delhi   San Juan   Singapore   Sydney   Tokyo   Toronto

McGraw-Hill

A Division of The McGraw-Hill Companies

© 1996 by **Ronald L. Wagner**.
Published by the McGraw-Hill Companies, Inc.

pbk 1 2 3 4 5 6 7 8 9 BBC/BBC 9 0 0 9 8 7 6

Library of Congress Cataloging-in-Publication Data
Wagner, Ronald L.
     The McGraw-Hill Internet training manual / by Ronald L. Wagner &
Eric Engelmann.
       p.   cm.
     Includes index.
     ISBN 0-07-066937-6 (pbk.)
     1. Internet (Computer network)—Handbooks, manuals, etc.
I. Engelmann, Eric.   II. Title.
TK5105.875.I57W37   1996
004.6'7—dc20   95-48893
                                                             CIP

Acquisitions editor: Brad Schepp
Editorial team: Robert E. Ostrander, Executive Editor
                        Aaron G. Bittner, Book Editor
Production team: Katherine G. Brown, Director
                        Lisa M. Mellott, Layout
                        Jodi L. Tyler, Indexer
Design team: Jaclyn J. Boone, Designer
                     Katherine Lukaszewicz, Associate Designer

0669376
TNG1

Dedications

From Ron:
To Lisa, Michael, Rich and Jamie for the summer of 1995.
To Dick Connor for everything.
And to Jeff Davidson for being an extra "ace" in my deck.

From Eric:
To my wife, Linda, for her patience
during my many hours in front of the PC
(and complaints about ILFMT).

Acknowledgments

Bill Adler, Jr., Adler and Robin Books
Dick Connor, cmc
Jeff Davidson, The Breathing Space Institute
Bruce Gnatowski, Mobil 1 Racing
Alan Chung, Digiweb
Theda Parrish, BTG Corporation
Joe Littely, BTG Corporation
Bridget A. Robey, BTG Corporation
Jessica Johannes, The Benjamin Group (Qualcomm PR)
Roy Ang, Qualcom Technical Support
Joe Bresler, Poppe-Tyson (Valvoline Oil PR)
Ellen Elias, O'Reilly & Associates
David J. Hark, Hark Internet Help
Russ Rosenzweig, Round Table Group
Sally Davenport, FedEx
Steve Kelley, Cybertours
Michael Morrison, Internext
Brett Sawrie, Internext
Brad Templeton, ClariNet Communications
Keith T. Cruickshank, NetExpo/Internet Business Events
Tom Perrine, San Diego State University
Ken Outcalt, Evan Kemp Associates, Inc.
Harvey Brydon, Dowell Tulsa, (WinVN)
Kathleen Smyth, Case-Western Reserve University
Barbara Pearson, NetBill
Bob Asleson, The Library Corporation
Ron Hipschman, The Exploratorium

Contents

▶

Foreword

Your timing is perfect. This is a terrific time to learn the Internet, because it's never been easier and it definitely is not too late to be starting.

The Internet has changed so rapidly, it's done the equivalent of advancing from open-cockpit, fabric-covered biplanes to modern jet airliners in just two years. We won't even cover the use of most of the standard Internet tools because—though they served with valor for many years—most of them are passé. You'll never know the agonies you've missed.

It's astounding how many massive tomes about the Internet we've found that are practically comical in the way they tell you "how to use the Internet." By the time most Internet books make it into the public libraries, they probably are not worth checking out, because so much of the information they contain is outdated. The books on store shelves are fresher, but still they often feature fading Internet practices.

Many Internet books will do you about as much good as trying to learn about home entertainment systems by reading books about vinyl records and turntables. You always will be able to play vinyl records, but you'll have to be content with "golden oldies." The Internet has created the same problem of obsolescence as we recently experienced in the music industry, and the change-over will happen at the same hyper-speed pace. One day we had thousands of record stores that each had a couple of aisles of CDs—then a few months later vinyl records vanished. Now, everything has been transferred over to CD—even the golden oldies—and that's what's happening to the Internet as you read this. The World Wide Web is the CD of the Internet and is quickly replacing the traditional methods that the Internet previously used to deliver information.

It may be impossible to write a book that truly tells you exactly how to use the Internet. But we've solved the obsolescence problem by leaving out of this book a great deal of material that quickly would go stale. Because we don't expect this book to be the final word on how to use the Internet profitably, we close each chapter by pointing you to Internet sites that will enable you to keep the latest technology at your fingertips. Consider this book as a starting point on what will be a journey of continuous learning in cyberspace.

Ron Wagner   Eric Engelmann
                    http://www.marketing-coach.com/mh-guide

Introduction

THIS BOOK is a training manual that will enable employees to use the Internet to dramatically increase their organization's productivity. Internet providers, trainers, and consultants find a common theme within organizations that are new to the Internet: They want to know how their employees are going to use the Internet to improve the organization's bottom line. This book will provide a two-fold bonus: Besides being an Internet training guide, its value starts before training and extends beyond it.

First, employees often don't apprehend what the Internet is and what it is not. They need to learn about its powerful features and to learn to beware of its faults. They need ideas on how they can help their organization, and pointers that can keep the organization out of cyberspace trouble. They need a knowledge base that will put the Internet in perspective. We'll give them a foundation that will be grounded in the business world and enable them to focus on the Internet tools that can benefit their organization.

Second, managements know that they can send employees to Internet classes or that they can buy Internet guidebooks so employees can learn to use their Internet software—but what do employees do *after* the class? To bring value to the company, employees need follow-up lessons to refine the technical skills they pick up in a classroom session. We'll cover the essential information that employees need to make the Internet a blessing to the bottom line instead of a burden.

This book handles *all three* phases of Internet training:
- Preparing students before the classroom training;
- Giving actual classroom guidance;
- Ensuring that the Internet training provides value to the organization long after the class sessions.

We'll present the three phases of preparation, lessons, and follow-up guidance in three sections of the book.

PHASE 1 *First things first*

Employees should read this section before classroom training, because it will prepare them for the dramatic transformation that the Internet will bring to their work styles. We'll give them a treasure trove of exciting stories of organizations that currently are booming on the Internet, and we'll separate facts from fiction by showing that the Internet isn't perfect.

We'll give students an Internet map and a five-cent tour of their new business environment, so they'll know the lay of this new cyber-land before class. We'll include a lesson on netiquette that will contain a potpourri of tips students can use in the lessons on Internet mail and Newsgroups.

We'll quell some of the fears that our training experience routinely uncovers in people when they face changes and new technology. We will close by preparing students to accept change as a way of computer-life so they can come to class excited and hopeful about the future, and not be anxious and fearful.

PHASE 2 *Hands On*

This section is for hands-on student learning. We'll begin by giving students a jump on using Windows to the max—it's called "Windows Wide Open"—that teaches what we call "advanced basics" to ensure that students get top performance out of the software they're going to use. The second lesson teaches Internet mail using Eudora for Windows.

The third lesson will use some popular Internet software to teach the basic tools of Internet access—making sense out of the alphabet soup of Internet acronyms by showing what they do. The last two lessons will teach students how to use Internet indexes to quickly target the information they want to find.

PHASE 3 *The rest of the story*

We'll devote most of our follow-up lessons to the World Wide Web. We'll show how to plan, design, and manage a good Web home page. We'll discusss how to leverage an organization's Internet presence so that the organization will reap multiple, cascading benefits from the work of its employees.

We'll cover setting up customer ordering systems, how businesses collect money via the Internet, and how the Internet can be used to save money.

Once an organization's computer system is opened to the Internet security becomes a critical issue, so we'll discuss how organizations can safeguard their priceless internal data and company secrets. We'll close this section with a lesson on the technical aspects of actually creating a World Wide Web site.

Bonuses: Continuing education

We'll close each chapter with a module called "Continuing Education"—a listing of Internet sources that will keep students up-to-the-second-informed on the topic. The business world is changing faster right now than ever before—and we've only just begun; but this book will ensure that students stay abreast of the topics that affect their profession and their company.

NET TIP You don't need to manually type any of the links you find in the Continuing Education sections. This book has its own site on the World Wide Web and on that site you'll find a hypertext jump entitled "URL Links" that will bring up all the links, chapter by chapter, including the Glossary and Appendices. You then can scroll through the complete listing of all of our URLs and click on any of them to see the featured site.

The home page also has a link entitled "Glossary" that will jump you to an online version of this book's glossary. You will be able to search this document for any term you want to look up.

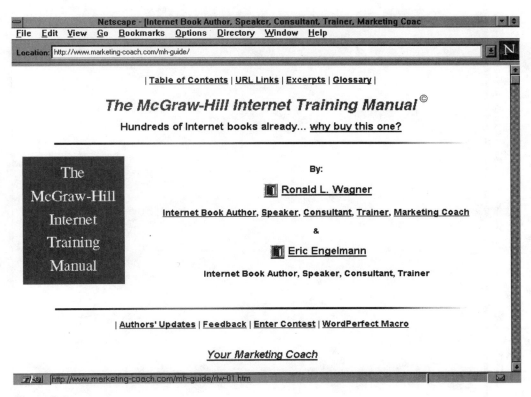

Figure I-1

Appendices

We'll close the book with a glossary and some appendices that will present a gold mine of helpful reference sources: Internet terms, electronic copyright issues, and computer and workplace ergonomics. Then, just for fun, we'll tell you how the authors created this book using the Internet—we'd better practice what we preach, right?

XX

▶

PHASE 1
First things first

IN PHASE 1, we'll truly put first things first by giving you a preparatory overview of the ethereal realm of cyberspace. You will not need a computer for Phase 1, and you should complete it before the Hands On phase of your training. Here's a run-down of what you'll get as this phase lays the foundation for Phase 2, Hands On.

Inspirational stories

We'll show you how some organizations have achieved success on the Internet. While vast areas of the Internet still remain in the category of "Not Ready For Prime-Time Players," there are success stories and the Internet is having a positive impact on organizations around the world.

A reality check

We'll show you "the dark side" of the Internet so you'll know how to avoid a cyberspace black hole. Keep in mind that you are a pioneer in a developing territory. Even if you believe that you're woefully behind, you soon will discover that the Internet is not nearly as advanced as you may have been led to believe.

Technical overview

This is a little history of the Internet and a quick overview of some essential Internet jargon. Without knowing these terms, you'll drown in the alphabet soup—a thick composition of more acronyms that you can imagine—that fills the Internet.

Netiquette

We'll give you the highlights of Internet business Netiquette that will help you steer clear of any electronic faux pas. The Internet is a new communication tool and you need to know the rules of the road to keep from being blasted out of cyberspace by irate fellow travelers.

Breathing space

The Internet can make you feel that you're hopelessly behind. To ease that pain we'll give you some *Breathing Space* tips by Jeff Davidson, founder of The Breathing Space Institute, so that you never again will believe that letting the world pass you by is bad for business. Most of the world *will* pass you by—especially on the Internet. Once you see the futility of trying to access more than a tiny slice, you'll be happy to let, intentionally, the world pass you by.

The future of the Internet

Here's a peek at some of the things that we believe lie ahead in the near future on the Internet. You'll see that the so-called information superhighway is but a winding farm road compared to the electronic byways that you soon will be traveling. And where is this superhighway taking us all? Here's one "Deep Thought" quotation before you begin the training:

> *"A human being is a part of the whole, called by us 'Universe,' a part limited in time and space. We experience ourselves, our thoughts and our feelings as something separated from the rest—a kind of optical delusion of our consciousness. This delusion is a kind of prison for us, restricting us to our personal desires and to affection for a few persons nearest to us.*
>
> *Our task must be to free ourselves from this prison by widening our circle of compassion to embrace all living creatures and the whole of nature in its beauty."*
> **Albert Einstein**

Once we fully have integrated the Internet into our consciousness, we no longer will be restricted to our personal desires and to affection for a few persons nearest to us. As we widen our circle of compassion, the optical delusion of being something separated from the rest will vanish forever.

Internet express to success

THE INTERNET has created the ability to get clients and customers physically involved with your business. People love to explore cyberspace, testing uncharted new worlds with their mouses. The magical attraction of the Internet is that your clients and customers can manipulate their environment—and that opens up new ways in which your organization can serve them.

While people are accustomed to passive participation in ads in newspapers, magazines, and on television, practically no one is interested in sitting in front of a PC and reading a static screen-full of plain text—they can do that more conveniently with a newspaper or a magazine. Your company easily can create a static Internet World Wide Web site with text, a graphic image, and an e-mail address, but the Internet express to success rides the highway of valuable information, interactivity, and engaging fun for your customers and clients. That's what generates repeat visits.

The Web sites that generate the most traffic include buttons to push, images to download, sound clips, video clips, or some activity that involves the site visitor and that provides value. Good Internet sites usually include links to other enticing and related sites. Another factor that fosters repeat visits is a site that changes frequently, rewarding those who return by giving them something new.

The Internet success stories in this chapter embody the principles of success we've outlined so far. Each of these examples has brought major benefits for either the organizations that created them or for their users. We've selected successes from a wide range of organizations, from a small business to one of the largest corporations in the U.S., as well as nonprofit community successes that have created benefits greater than anything money can buy.

These examples also will give you a broad overview into ways the Internet provides benefits and into ways those benefits can have far-reaching follow-up effects. Reading about the organizations chronicled here likely will kindle your creativity and encourage you to embrace your Internet training with enthusiasm as you see some of the possibilities for using what you can learn in this book.

The Alzheimer's Disease Support Center (ADSC)

Cleveland area families, professionals, and others caring for persons with Alzheimer's disease or related dementias (ADRD) use personal computers or terminals and a host computer to share information and support through the Alzheimer's Disease Support Center (ADSC). The ADSC is a 24-hour telecomputing project that provides information and support to families, health and social service professionals, and others helping to care for persons with ADRD. The ADSC is a joint project of the University Hospitals of Cleveland/Case Western University Alzheimer Center and the Cleveland Area Chapter of the Alzheimer's Association.

Through grants to the Alzheimer's Association from the Cleveland Foundation and the Alzheimer Center from the National Institute of Aging, families have access to computers, special phone lines, training classes, and instruction manuals—all free of charge. By supplying all the necessary computer equipment and training, the ADSC has created a new community of computer users.

Even this basic equipment can appear complicated to a generation to whom computers were not available at school, work, or home. Most ADSC users had no prior experience with computers, yet the ADSC has been embraced even by elderly users with no prior computer experience. They surprise even themselves with how easily they learn the system and become proficient.

Before using the ADSC, it is unlikely that most of its users—especially those who are elderly—would have seen much relevance of the Internet to their lives. Since joining the ADSC, many users have indicated that they can't imagine their lives without the ADSC. The ADSC is a compelling example of the benefits of personal empowerment through the Internet.

How the ADSC works

Users register on the Cleveland Free-Net (see Figure 1-1) telecomputing system, which is sponsored by Case Western Reserve University (*http://www.cwru.edu*). Users then can reach the ADSC via menus and simple commands to post comments or questions and read others' postings or information files.

Users communicate at their convenience and get responses tailored to their specific needs. Both public and anonymous communication are supported, but the public communication has grown to the point that users have become a cohesive group who call themselves a "computer family."

ADSC users have access to a full array of telecomputing options via the Cleveland Free-Net: e-mail for private communications; a "Caregiver Forum" bulletin board for public postings emphasizing peer-to-peer support that is monitored by a professional from the Alzheimer's Association; a Question and Answer module whereby user questions are answered by clinical experts from the University Alzheimer Center; and information files containing annotated bibliographies, detailed information on community services, and other pertinent and timely information.

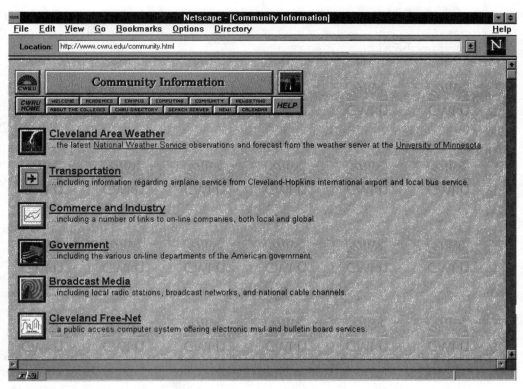

Figure 1-1

How the ADSC has helped

Many ADRD caregivers do not participate in traditional support groups or education programs because of barriers they encounter. They may be overwhelmed by the responsibilities of caring for a person with ADRD; they can't arrange for alternative care; they don't have transportation; there isn't a group located near their home; they are reluctant to share personal problems face-to-face with strangers; or they are unable to attend at the times when meetings are held in their area. The ADSC provides a way for full-time caregivers to remain intellectually active and connected to the community even though their physical access may be limited.

One of the most powerful features of this system is around-the-clock access to information and support. This feature complements caregivers' and professionals' hectic and variable schedules, which are a major barrier to the more traditional forms of help. By linking family caregiver to family caregiver, caregiver to professional, and professional to professional, the ADSC brings the entire caregiving system together in a way that effectively transcends many traditional communication boundaries.

From the heart

The ADSC has united a community of family caregivers and professionals. Participants represent a range of geographic, age, education, income, and cultural boundaries unparalleled by more traditional approaches. As a group, they share a collective caregiving knowledge that spans a wide variety of topics. They have initiated monthly lunches at a local restaurant to build upon relationships formed on the ADSC.

But enough details. Let's hear from the hearts of the people who use the system:

- *The computer family is the best source for help and sharing...*
- *My husband wants to know if I'm getting any information out of this thing or if it's just interesting. I can't really explain the kind of help you get just being able to talk with someone who has the same problems.*
- *Whenever I get frustrated and need to talk to someone, I come to this forum. It has never let me down. Although I am only typing my feelings, it is the same as talking, and this starts the process of relieving my tension.*
- *This computer has also become an important part of my day.*
- *What makes this board so great is that it relates* real life *experiences and not a text-book dissertation of some untested ideas.*
- *This* family *is closer in many ways than blood family. Certainly you won't experience a lack of understanding from this family. They are eager to lend a hand in any way they can.*
- *This computer family has been my most important support from the day I signed on.*

The ADSC primarily serves the greater Cleveland area, yet they receive international messages expressing interest in the project, and with the increasing availability of the Internet, use of this system will expand. The Internet has far-reaching implications in the delivery of information and support services to persons such as these by eliminating many of the key barriers to using support services. And the ADSC proves that the Internet is not limited to the younger, more computer-literate generation—it is intergenerational.

The Wine Rack

A small Gaithersburg, Maryland, beer/wine and specialty store in a Washington, D.C. suburb might seem an unlikely candidate for success on the Internet. But the Wine Rack illustrates the potential that retail stores have to exploit global communications. The manager of the Wine Rack, Linda Engelmann, is the wife of co-author Eric Engelmann. After looking over Eric's shoulder one evening as he surfed the Net, Linda asked to see if he could find anything on "wine" on the Internet. She was hooked in minutes and thought it "might be fun" to have her store on the Internet (see Figure 1-2).

Eric was teaching Internet publishing courses at the time and Linda attended one, bringing information about her store on a diskette. After three hours of training and a half-day of fine-tuning, the Wine Rack went online (*http://www.wdn.com/ems/rack*). Eric was developing another course on Internet publishing and soon worked through the exercises by posting information on the Wine Rack on various search engines, such as Lycos, Yahoo, and Web Crawler.

Almost immediately, Linda got a call from the United Kingdom from someone who ordered Champagne delivered to a Maryland address. The next day a walk-in customer said that though she had worked nearby for years, she never knew the Wine Rack existed until she saw its Internet home page. Linda's farthest

Figure 1-2

outreach has been to a customer in Japan who requested air-freight delivery for several cases of high-end wines.

 NET TIP A key to the success of The Wine Rack's site lies in its highly descriptive title. We'll cover more about this later in chapter 13, "Client-centered Interneting."

Because the Wine Rack carries one of the area's largest micro-brewery beer selections, it soon added its micro-brewery line to its Web site. Within days, three customers asked when new micro-brewery shipments would arrive, and inquired about additional products. Many customers purchase gift baskets and use the Wine Rack's shipping services. At least one customer a day mentions that he or she saw the Wine Rack on the Web. Wholesalers, wineries, and micro-breweries discover the page and inquire about distribution. A recent customer mentioned he had seen the Wine Rack being discussed in several Internet newsgroups.

Linda now is excited about the Net and is pushing other merchants in her shopping center to get aboard. The shopping center always has used conventional mailings for advertising, but that is an expensive undertaking that has generated almost no sales for the Wine Rack in the last five years. The Internet enables Linda to reach far beyond a limited geographic area—with more detailed information than with printed coupon books—and at far less cost. And Linda's Web page still lets her offer discounts and online coupons to attract new customers.

The Internet permits flexible, up-to-the minute ads. Printed coupons, in contrast, forced Linda to make a decision six weeks in advance to run a special on a particular item. The Internet enables the Wine Rack to respond quickly to the rapid price and availability fluctuations that are common within her industry. She now easily responds to trends and seasonal price variations. For example, Octoberfest beers arrive with as little as one week's notice. But because the selections and prices can be put online instantly, the Wine Rack's customers can sample the new selections right away and advise fellow Netizens on the new crop of brews.

 NET TIP If your Web site is maintained on-site, then instant updates are a breeze. If you use a Web service provider, however, updating your Web site still will be a breeze if you catch our lesson in chapter 9, "Internet tools," on how to transfer files anywhere in the world. Any organization easily can keep the information on its Web site up-to-the-minute fresh.

If the Internet can create an international presence for a local beer and wine shop, what can it do for a major corporation that already is known around the world? Ironically, one answer is that the Internet can create a local presence for a major corporation.

The Valvoline company

The world of auto racing roared onto a whole new road over the Memorial Day weekend of 1995 when Valvoline included in its Indianapolis 500 advertisements the address of its Web site: *http://www.valvoline.com*.

The Lexington, Kentucky-based oil company was the first major oil manufacturer to tap into the information superhighway, providing motorsports fans with late-breaking information and results leading up to the Indy 500, May 28, 1995. In such a climate, a competitive edge and marketing leadership take on added importance. The fact that there were more than 500,000 hits during the three weeks prior to and during the 1995 Indy 500 race indicates that Valvoline's site established them as a marketing leader on the Internet (see Figure 1-3).

After seeing the excitement generated by its Indy presence—at its peak the site was being hit an average of 50,000 times per day—Valvoline added during the summer of 1995 new features to its home page that focus on product news and general consumer information. The site's racing area has expanded substantially to include results from IndyCar, NASCAR, NHRA, and other major racing circuits.

"It's really exciting for us at Valvoline to be the first of the major motor oil marketers to venture onto the Internet," said Jan Robert Horsfall, Valvoline's Advertising and Marketing Vice President. "We decided to lead with our strong suit and that was racing. Our motorsports marketing effort is the envy of the industry, we support top teams, and we have been quite successful in transferring high-performance imagery to our products."

Here are some services that Valvoline has brought to the Internet:

- A locator service that helps people find oil recycling centers in their communities—a local service from an international corporation!
- Consumer advice columns by Norm Hudecki, Valvoline's technical services director and a syndicated newspaper columnist. Users can ask Hudecki for automotive advice.

▶ *First things first*

Figure 1-3

- A forum that enables automotive technicians to talk to Valvoline and to each other.
- Information on Valvoline's "family of brands," which includes Valvoline motor oil and lubricants, Zerex antifreeze, and Pyroil automotive chemicals.

The Valvoline site has some direct, commercial features as well, including an online racing merchandise retail store from which fans can purchase polo shirts, T-shirts, and hats that feature race driver Robby Gordon (driving Valvoline-sponsored cars, Gordon has become one of the hottest drivers on the IndyCar circuit today). Fans even can get information on joining the Robby Gordon Fan Club.

The Valvoline site embodies all of the best Internet principles that define a good Web site. It's interactive, it delivers photos, sound, video, and news that has no other source, and it gives every visitor the possibility of creating his or her own unique trip through cyberspace.

Joe Bresler of Poppe-Tyson (the advertising firm that created Valvoline's Web site) says that three months wasn't enough time to measure a hard-number profit boost from the Internet site, but Poppe-Tyson believes that soon Valvoline's site will have a positive impact on the company's bottom line. Nonetheless, with the establishment of its own address in cyberspace, Valvoline is positioned to speak directly to customers, consumers, and key audiences such as mechanics, and to attach all the high-performance imagery available today to the company and its brands. It is a competitive advantage upon which to build in this computer-based age that now is being transformed by the Internet.

If you'd like more information on how Poppe-Tyson can help your organization, you can e-mail Joe Bresler at *jbresler@sv.poppe.com*. Mention that you read about Valvoline's Web site in this book.

FedEx

Here's a success story with a different perspective: This one comes from a client's point of view. In 1995 the Fourth of July fell on a Tuesday, and most of the U.S. shut down on Friday, June 30 for a four-day party. That Friday, however, Jack Littely was doing anything but shutting down. Jack's company, BTG Incorporated, is a major government contractor and one of the original builders of ARPANET, the system that has evolved into the Internet you're using today. BTG recently had completed a proposal for a 926-million-dollar government contract—or, at least, he *thought* the proposal was complete. At about 4 o'clock Friday afternoon, while nearly everyone else was celebrating, Jack got the news that some crucial contract specifications had changed. Their proposal now was worthless, but they had ten days to respond. Not business days, but *days*! And the four-day holiday hadn't even begun.

Jack didn't mind too much that his holiday was out the window but if he couldn't immediately get the new specifications, the whole contract—and 926 million dollars—would be out the window. Jack used BTG's FedEx account to have the updated information sent to him that afternoon with a Saturday delivery the next morning.

Saturday morning, while the rest of us were playing, Jack and his team were in their office awaiting the FedEx delivery. The package didn't show up on time.

But Jack is a savvy Internet user and he connected with the FedEx home page at *http://www.fedex.com* to check the status of the package. FedEx gives its customers direct access to package tracking via their Web site (see Figure 1-4). The Web site helped Jack quickly discover the problem: The package had been addressed incorrectly and had gone to the wrong BTG office. Worse, that office was closed for the entire holiday weekend so the package was in limbo out there in FedEx Land.

But the FedEx Web site also helped Jack quickly discover that the package was in a nearby FedEx office that was open even on this holiday-weekend Saturday. Jack drove to the office for the package and his team had the full ten days to rewrite their proposal using the new specifications instead of being forced to wait until the following Wednesday morning.

Okay, so the FedEx Web site helped one organization—although it was a 926-million-dollar deal. Still, we wondered if FedEx's Web site had helped its bottom line, so we asked them. Sally Davenport, FedEx Media Relations said, "We generally do not estimate what savings we may have experienced due to the home page, because no one has been able to track the exact derivation of who hits our site. We feel that the online presence is part of our overall strategy to

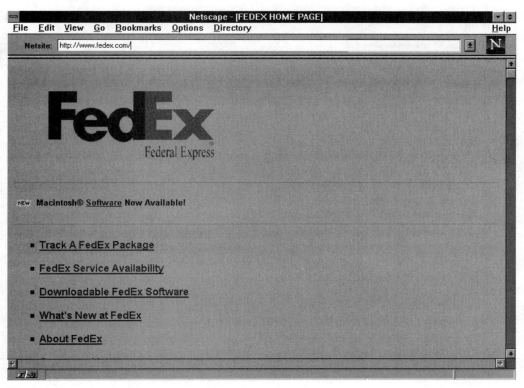

Figure 1-4

have a ubiquitous presence for our customers—whenever and wherever they choose to conduct business."

For now, merely increasing your organization's presence for your clients and customers is a sound goal for your own Web site. Sure, for a long time to come, most FedEx customers will track packages by calling the FedEx toll-free number. But the Web site will help FedEx to better serve individual needs. Similarly, the Web will bring a new level of service to your organization and help you reach your clients and customers on their terms. As Sally said, "whenever and wherever they choose."

Meeting clients and customers on their terms is an important factor in any successful organization. The Internet certainly will help you make resources available in ways that serve peoples' needs—on their terms. Here's an excellent example of a Web site that is enabling a lot of organizations to meet the needs of a large segment of our population for whom having their needs met on their terms is more than just a polite business etiquette—it's the law.

Evan Kemp Associates, Inc.

The disability resources listing located at *http://disability.com/cool.html* is a comprehensive listing of disability-related sites on the Internet. People with disabilities and those in the disability field often use the Evan Kemp Associates, Inc. (EKA) site (see Figure 1-5) as an excellent research tool on many topics including careers, children's issues, cognitive/developmental disabilities,

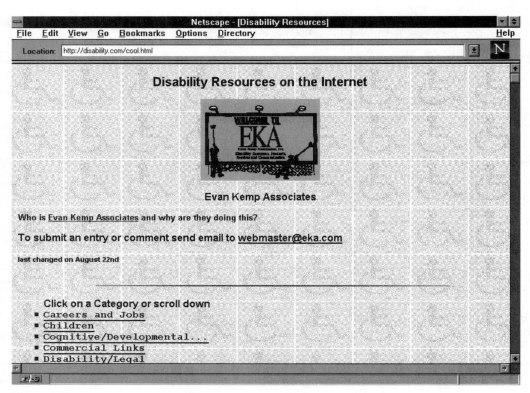

Figure 1-5

commercial links, legal resources, government sites, medicine and health, mobility impairments, nonprofit organizations, recreation and lifestyle, university sites, and visual/hearing-impaired resources. The EKA home page is well-organized and user-friendly, allowing users to find the information they are looking for in an efficient manner.

A large number of frequent visitors are from companies looking for information about compliance with the American Disabilities Act (ADA) and other disability-related laws. The Disability-Related Legal Resources portion of the EKA site contains many links that lead users to a vast wealth of information, helping them wade through these seemingly insurmountable and complex laws. All of the links to this site are thoroughly browsed by EKA staff before being added to the list, ensuring that each link represents a high-quality disability resource. EKA frequently adds new links, and they ensure that any site with which they link also links to EKA's home page.

The Honorable Evan J. Kemp, Jr. was Chairman of the Equal Employment Opportunity Commission under President Bush, and was the leading political figure who pushed the ADA through Congress. He is known as a leader of the civil rights movement for people with disabilities, and founded EKA as a way to bring economic empowerment to individuals with disabilities. A key to this objective is providing disability information to the public. His organization's Web home page is one of many methods Evan Kemp employs to accomplish his long-term mission.

Mr. Kemp summarizes this organization's Web presence by saying, "We feel that disseminating disability-related information via the Internet is a logical and effective way to meet special needs and to further empower this market of consumers. At the same time, our home page has helped companies comply with the ADA and other disability legislation. The Internet has been a very useful tool for our firm."

The National Information Infrastructure (NII)

Those are all the Internet success stories we're going to include for now, but your organization could benefit if you regularly read more success stories. We've found at least one Web site that is an outstanding, ongoing resource for finding worthwhile ways to use the Internet. The site is run by Access Media Incorporated (see Figure 1-6).

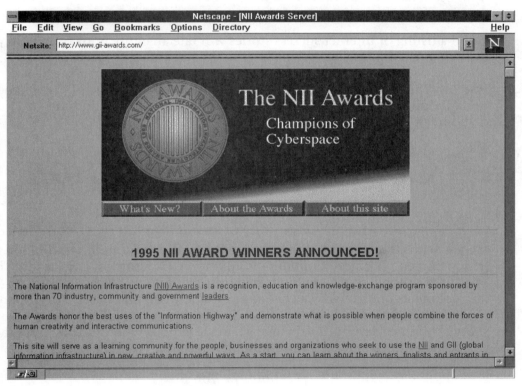

Figure 1-6

Access Media regards the Internet as critical to our future well-being. They believe that the Internet will bring an unprecedented explosion in human creativity and expression, but they had observed that relatively few people were aware of the Internet's potential. This lack of awareness created a barrier to realizing the Internet's benefits: If Internet awareness remained low, people would miss its benefits.

So, in February, 1994, Access Media created the National Information Infrastructure (NII) Awards to create broad public awareness of how the Internet can benefit people, businesses, communities, and organizations of all kinds. In turn, they expect that the realization of benefits will stimulate the creation of new applications, services, and uses. Access Media envisions their NII Awards program as a way to:

- Gather the stories and identify examples of excellence that could be used in education and awareness efforts.
- Engage people and organizations that could serve as the core of a learning community.
- Establish a program with enough national visibility to increase general Internet awareness to a level that will permit the Internet to make a measurable contribution to society.

Access Media is a for-profit corporation (part think-tank, part new-media company) in Santa Monica, California. Founded in 1987, Access Media's mission is to accelerate the adoption of concepts and technologies that improve the quality of life.

Soon a listing of Internet success stories will rate an entire book, not merely a first chapter. Still, as you will discover in the remaining chapters of Phase 1, the Internet is not yet fully developed—and not all of its stories are about success. The next chapter will give you a look at the downside of the Internet today, though many of the adverse aspects on which we'll report are temporary.

 # *Continuing Education*

The National Information Infrastructure (NII)
http://www.gii-awards.com

Access Media, Incorporated presents its NII Awards in six categories: Arts and Entertainment, Business, Community, Education, Government and Health. This may be your top resource on Internet success stories. Stay abreast of developments on this Web site because you surely will find here a treasure trove of quality ideas, inspiring anecdotes and heartening personal experiences. Our story about the Cleveland Alzheimer's Disease Support Center (ADSC) was the 1995 NII Award winner in the Community category.

Tenagra Top 5
http://arganet.tenagra.com/Tenagra/awards94.html

Do you want to read about the latest "Top 5 Internet marketing successes?" Then check out this page (see Figure 1-7). The Top 5 listing changes regularly, so the exact URL listed above presents only the 1994 awards. In early 1996, you might try the same URL but substitute "awards95" for "awards94." As a minimum, once you get there, you'll be able to browse around and find other interesting topics about businesses on the Internet.

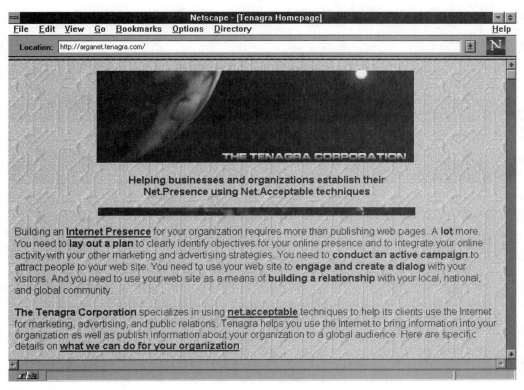

Figure 1-7

CommerceNet backgrounder

http://www.commerce.net/information/background.html

CommerceNet is a nonprofit consortium of companies and organizations whose goal is to create an electronic marketplace where companies transact business spontaneously over the Internet. CommerceNet is promoting a communications infrastructure that will be easy-to-use, oriented for commercial use, and able to expand rapidly. The net results for businesses will be lower operating costs and a faster dissemination of technological advancements and their practical applications. Regular visits to this site also will help you track Internet success stories.

Meckler Web's iWorld™

http://www.mecklerweb.com

Internet users have expressed a need for a Web site that caters to their specific information needs and interests. MecklerWeb's iWORLD provides a solution with what they call the Internet users' "First Stop on the Internet," where users can find the latest Internet news, tips, how-to, product reviews, resources, directories, and expert commentary. iWORLD draws upon Mecklermedia's expertise on the Internet through Internet World and Web Week magazines, Internet Books, and the Internet World Fall and Spring Expositions. You're likely to find many more Internet success stories behind the links on this Web site.

Internet reality check

NOW THAT you've read in the first chapter the Internet's good news, we'll give you a glimpse of the other side. The Internet has success stories, but it has horror stories as well. Some companies have watched cyberspace literally suck up huge chunks of investment capital without increasing profits. We're going to make sure that the success stories you've read don't draw you into a black hole in cyberspace.

This chapter is not a chronicle of negativity. We simply don't want you to drop everything else you're doing for your company to join a gold rush to a non-existent mother lode. You'll see that the Internet is not one giant, electronic get-rich-quick scheme.

Over the long term, money is attracted to value. So, for the Internet to increase your company's profits, you'll need to use the Internet to create increased value that will attract money. The best way to ensure that the Internet makes a positive contribution to your company is to understand what the Internet truly does best.

Information distribution

The Internet was designed more than 30 years ago to be an information distribution system, but it has evolved far beyond the wildest dreams of its originators. Once the exclusive realm of government contractors, universities, and the military, the Internet now is available to everyone. Conceived as a system to ensure communications for the U.S. military during a global thermonuclear war, the Internet today ensures communications for a rapidly growing global community.

Despite undergoing such an incredible transformation, one of the Internet's original functions remains unchanged: It is primarily a communications tool. It was not designed as a sales tool.

Many users connect to the Internet because they have heard it is going to revolutionize overnight the foundations of all successful business principles. Some users are motivated by a fear that their competitors will set up an Internet presence and dominate their industry. Some people expect that putting their business on the Internet will enable themselves to dominate their industry. A few expect that an Internet site will effortlessly skyrocket their business to new sales records.

Such ideas are founded upon the very definition of "hype." There's a lot of hype on and about the Internet.

HYPERJUMP

Hype
Excessive publicity and its ensuing commotion. Exaggerated or extravagant claims, especially in advertising or promotional material.

So far most of the publicity about money being made via the Internet is about computer companies and companies that supply Internet access and services. Other than that, much of what you've heard about the Internet simply is hype, often promoted by those who most will profit if you buy into the siren song of quick Internet riches. Keith Cruickshank, the chairman of NetExpo/Internet Business Events, says, "The so-called 'enablers' are making most of the Internet money today. I have been keeping my eye open for end-users who are making money. I know of a couple of companies that claim their Internet presence is profitable, but few who would say they could base their business on the Internet alone."

We can confirm Keith's experience. When we began this book project, we put out feelers on the Internet asking for success stories for chapter 1. We proceeded slowly at first, expecting to be inundated with e-mail if our request circulated widely. We were not inundated. In fact, the anecdotes you read in chapter 1 actually required research to uncover. There's a simple explanation: Few businesses yet have any idea of how to use the Internet to benefit people outside their own business.

The Internet will reshape global business and the winners will be the organizations who discover and employ ways to use the Internet to benefit people outside their own business.

Client-centered Interneting

The foundations of successful business principles haven't changed in thousands of years and the Internet isn't going to change them now. People want value before they part with their money. Most of the value that the Internet has provided so far has been in providing the Internet itself.

Now, however, the Internet is beginning to offer value beyond itself and the computer industry. The Internet is a spectacular information distribution system, and we're living in an era in which information is a prime industry—seems like a perfect match for the times.

Indeed, the Internet has the potential to create a revolution in the ways that businesses use information distribution to provide value, and you are poised to be a part of that revolution. Always regard the Internet, though, as an additional tool that you can use to provide value to your customers and clients.

In chapter 13 ("Client-centered Interneting"), we'll cover ways to use the Internet to provide value. *Client-centered Interneting* (CCI) is derived from Dick Connor's *Client-centered Marketing* (CCM). CCM is a client/customer service system that has been the topic of several of Dick's books, and a topic that he's taught for more than 30 years. The whole concept of using the Internet to serve your clients and customers will make more sense after you've finished the Hands On phase in this book, so we'll return to this topic after that phase.

Until then, consider what you want when you are surfing the Net. Carefully note the good, the bad, and the ugly. If something you find on the Internet annoys you, most likely it will annoy millions of other people. If something you find on the Internet is valuable to you, most likely millions of others would agree.

When you encounter some other company's Web page that brings you valuable information, then you've encountered some Client-centered Interneting principles in use. To learn how to satisfy your clients and customers on the Internet, study the services that satisfy you. The knowledge you gain by using valuable Internet resources can help you create ways that your company can provide similar value.

For now, however, we're looking at cyberspace projects that have not proven to embody Client-centered Interneting principles.

You can lose a fortune online

Are you excited about using the Internet as a replacement for your local shopping mall? If not, you've got a lot of company. Online shopping has been available for more than a decade and has yet to prove to be a gold rush. Here's a strong case for reining in any dreams of easy riches on the Internet:

> The online service Prodigy—which in 1984 teamed IBM, Sears, and CBS—has yet to turn a profit. Someone at CBS must have been a Kenny Rogers fan and took to heart his advice in *The Gambler*, that said, "You've got to know when to fold 'em." After gambling nearly $20 million by 1986 and facing the prospect of anteing at least $80 million more, CBS wisely folded 'em. The total stake on the Prodigy table now is up to about $1 billion without a winning hand.

The Prodigy joint venture teamed giants in retailing, computers and communications. Sears, IBM, and CBS haven't turned a profit with online shopping after investing $1 billion. Is your company going to do better than these three? Perhaps so, but we've seen that even a billion dollars may not be enough to transform consumers into online shoppers.

"Of course we'll do better," you may say, "Prodigy started many years ago. Few people had computers. The ones they had were slow. The connections were slow, especially when delivering the graphic images that are featured on Prodigy. Besides, the system forced users to waste a lot of time waiting for and viewing commercial messages. Just wait until someone properly sets up a shopping service on the Internet."

Well, they have. It's called the Internet Shopping Network (ISN). Let's see how it's fared.

Better, but where's the value?

The Internet Shopping Network looks well done. When it first appeared, it featured a full-color graphic of a small shopping mall. It was much like the TV game show "Let's Make a Deal." Potential buyers could see what was behind Door Number 1 by clicking their mouse. It looked terrific.

There was, however, a serious problem: the time it took to download the graphic image of its store front. The average user at the time had only a 9600 baud modem that could require up to five minutes to deliver the shopping mall graphics display. They since have changed the opening screen, but even with a 28.8-Kbps modem and a direct PPP account, the opening screen you see in Figure 2-1 consumes only a few seconds of connect time.

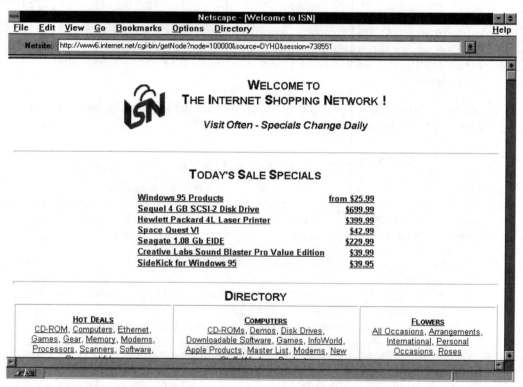

Figure 2-1

If people will surf TV channels during commercial breaks while they could watch exciting, expensively produced commercials flash on their screen, do you believe they'll wait more than a few seconds for your Internet system to slowly draw a single, silent, still image?

Techy stuff on modems and graphics

Elaborate, creative graphics images are a staple of our modern-day cable TV era, but graphic images demand more than the Internet was designed to deliver. The Internet itself and the modems we use to tap its resources were designed to transfer text. Here is some techy stuff that will help you understand why the graphics images you'll be seeing are going to take so long to display.

Modems transfer data in units called "bits." A bit in a computer is a microscopic, electronic switch: If the switch is off, the bit equals zero, and if the switch is on, the bit equals one. Because a single bit only could represent one of two values—zero and one—computers must group eight bits together to form one character.

A group of eight bits is called a byte. Every letter you see in this book was at one time one byte in a WordPerfect for Windows 6.1 file. One page of text might be about 2,000 bytes (16,000 bits). A typical book is between 500,000 to 1,000,000 bytes in length (4,000,000 to 8,000,000 bits); this book was a 911,000-byte WordPerfect file.

Modem speeds

PC modems are electronic devices that are able to transfer electronic bits across telephone lines. About ten years ago, PC modem transfer rates were only 300 baud. What's a baud? Who cares—baud is the buggy whip of the information superhighway. Today, modem transfer rates are measured in bits per second, which is easy to understand.

Today, the fastest PC modems transfer data at 28,800 bits per second. For shorthand, this is called 28.8 Kbps (kilobits per second). Remember, that's *bits* per second, and your word processor's file sizes are measured in bytes. Thus, 28.8 Kbps comes out to about 3,600 letters per second, or approximately two pages per second.

You might imagine that you could estimate a file's transfer time by dividing the file size by the transfer rate. Let's say we're transferring a typical chapter from this book with a file size of 72,000 bytes. Some quick division tells us to expect the transfer to take about 20 seconds. But it's not that simple. Through some intricate trickery, a 28.8-Kbps modem can transfer data as rapidly as 115 Kbps. Sounds good, doesn't it? That's about four times as fast as we figured—only about 5 seconds.

The reality of transfer rates

But that's under ideal test conditions and, unfortunately, not much about the Internet is ideal. There are so many users competing for lanes on the same electronic highway that no one ever even approaches ideal speeds. The technical term for the cause of this traffic problem is *bandwidth*, the transmission capacity of a computer communication connection. Connections with higher bandwidth can carry more traffic, just as an eight-lane superhighway can carry more traffic than a narrow dirt road. More bandwidth is coming—and it's coming fast—but today the Internet has a serious bandwidth problem.

How long will downloads really take?

The reality? Using a 28.8-Kbps modem to transfer a 72,000-byte chapter from this book to our editor at McGraw-Hill across the Internet and into his CompuServe mail box actually required three and a half minutes!

There's another reason that transfers take much longer than the estimate you'd get merely from simple division. Files that travel the Internet are broken up into blocks of bytes called *packets*, and each packet is wrapped in a "shell" of other bytes that do the work of an addressing label on a package you ship. The bytes that comprise the packet shell add size to your message, and thus require additional bandwidth, much as a box and packing material add to freight charges you pay to ship a physical object.

So, there's only one rule that you can apply with certainty to estimating transfer times for various file sizes: *Small files will transfer more quickly than large files.* Beyond that, it's hard to estimate. Remember, though, this is temporary—in a couple of years or so, transfer time will be nearly instantaneous.

A Web page example

Now let's consider an example of what you routinely will encounter on the Internet: a page on the World Wide Web that has several thousand bytes of text and several graphic images that each require 20,000 to 200,000 bytes. You could wait from a few seconds to several minutes for this Web page to display a single color image.

That same Web page also may include a sound file. With today's sound-file technology, expect about 10,000 bytes per second of telephone-line quality sound. Thus, a relatively low-quality, 20-second sound clip (see sound icon in Figure 2-2) could require several minutes of connect time to download.

Figure 2-2

Compare these times to modern-today television cable systems that transfer across a single cable up to 120 individual channels of full-motion video and high-fidelity stereo sound. The Internet has a long way to go in the speed race, but wait until you read chapter 6, "2001: A cyberspace odyssey." It's going to get much better very quickly! For now, though, be prepared to wait... and wait... and wait...

Is it worth the wait?

Wasting the time of your clients and customers is not client-centered in the slightest bit. One five-minute graphics download—or even a *one*-minute download—might scare away someone forever. But that's not the only serious problem that might keep a potential Internet Shopping Network buyer from using the service to find your product. There's another. Little on the Internet today rewards those who are willing to wait.

A recent perusal of the ISN uncovered the "bargain" of a VCR that was "on sale." Its suggested retail price was $599.95. Its sale price was $549.95 and the ad boasted, "A savings of $50.00!"

Electronics equipment routinely sells in many stores and via mail order at a 30-percent discount. Wouldn't you expect even lower prices on the Internet? After all, there is no retail store rent to pay and no store clerks to hire. Utilities and insurance costs are insignificant compared to those incurred in maintaining a retail store front. Those savings should result in lower prices that would reward the buyer's trip through cyberspace. Instead, this VCR was discounted far less than those in most stores. Where is the client-centered incentive to return to this Web site?

Not ready for prime time

Check out the ISN and some other Internet shopping sites and see how many times you return. An exercise in a later chapter in our Hands On phase will list the contact information for a few online shopping sites. You'll discover that Internet shopping services appear to have been designed to serve the vendors better than the customers.

Does this mean that you can't turn a profit with online selling? Of course you can sell profitably online—but it will require effort, as making a profit always has.

There is much you can do to encourage people to surf through cyberspace to find your site. But you'll discover that the Internet is not a gold mine waiting to deliver to your company easy riches. Selling on the Internet, as it does everywhere else, requires a client-centered approach. You've got to provide value to your customers and give them an incentive to track down and visit your Internet site. Keep in mind that cable TV is in their face all day with high-quality, fast-paced graphics images.

As promised earlier, we'll give examples later. For now, though, let's close this chapter by looking at other problems that your clients and customers may face on the Internet.

Internet shopping, games and business ethics

When you take your first "step" into an electronic mall like the ISN, you'll be crossing into an uncharted area in cyberspace that raises a lot of business ethics questions. One of them is their knack for drawing people away from getting any work done on the Internet. The Internet has a powerful, attractive charisma that can lure almost anyone to while away hours exploring its engaging features. We've seen in companies some astounding sights of these temptations working their magic. Here's a recent example that was witnessed in a family-owned business:

> Company "X" is owned by Mom and Dad and employs two of the owners' "children." (Both children are married adults with families of their own.) One day, the daughter was playing a computer game during business hours. Down the hall, the son also was totally absorbed in a game, aggressively hacking at something out there in cyberspace with his mouse. What would Mom and Dad say if they knew that their own children were playing computer games on company time? Not much. A quick trip around the office revealed that Mom and Dad both also were playing computer games. All four of them at the same time—in a family-owned business! The temptations are that compelling! (See Figure 2-3).

We've mentioned these electronic shopping malls because so many companies believe they're going to use the Internet to construct a global, self-managing retail store. It's important for your success to see some of them so you know what they can and cannot do for your organization. But stay focused when you're working—do the research that you require to analyze their Client-centered Interneting principles—then *get out*.

Above all, resist the allure of computer games until you're on your own time. Everybody at Company "X" may have been playing games at the same time, but you're not competing against Company "X." Your competitors probably aren't using the Internet to win a cyberspace game, they're using it to win your share of the market. Beating your competition on the Internet is the best computer game you'll ever play.

Superhighway traffic jams

As with most of our concrete roads, our information superhighway was not designed to handle its current traffic demands (see Figure 2-4). The result is that you may encounter some truly aggravating Internet speed problems. The causes are two-fold: Too many users and too many slow modems. Let's examine the impact on the people who will use your Internet site that each of these problems will have.

Too much traffic

You and your customers and clients are part of an information explosion that is overwhelming the Internet's resources. Internet traffic patterns are much like vehicular traffic patterns: There are slow times and there are rush hours. The rush

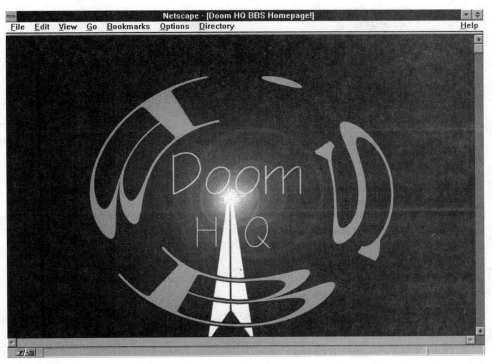

Figure 2-3

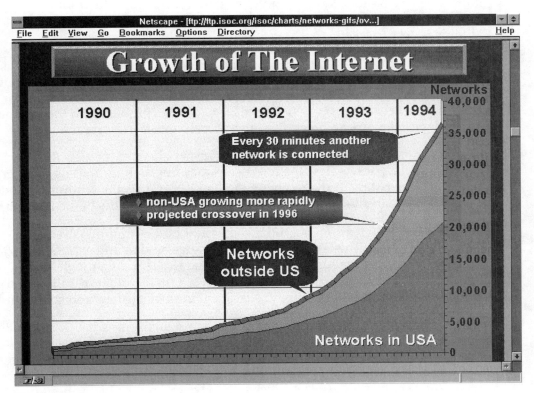

Figure 2-4

Internet reality check ◀

hours already can be horrendously slow, and yet the number of users is increasing more rapidly than ever. One day the Internet's traffic speed problems will be solved, but as pioneers on this new road, you and your clients and customers need to be willing to rough it a bit right now.

If the information your company distributes via the Internet is consumer-oriented, remind customers and clients that accessing your site during evening hours or on weekends will be faster. Internet traffic begins to peak as lunch-time arrives on the East Coast of the U.S. Traffic demands remain high as lunch-time sweeps across the country. Internet traffic makes a significant drop after 1 p.m. Pacific Time.

Suggest to customers that they avoid weekday business hours if at all possible. Suggest that they use the "text-only" version of your Web page to reduce the traffic burden that your graphic images place on the Internet. If they must use the Internet only during peak hours, remind them to use the fastest connection they can afford. That brings us to the second factor in Internet traffic problems.

Too many slow modems

When you access information on the Internet, it travels to your computer in a series of many, perhaps millions of, electronic packets—we mentioned these earlier. These packets enter your computer system through a modem link. Here's a quick analogy of how they work. Do you remember when resort developers in Arizona bought the London Bridge? They disassembled it block-by-block, coded each piece with a number, and shipped the blocks to Arizona. Builders used the numbers on each block to reassemble the London Bridge at the resort. Information travels over the Internet in much the same way—in small, coded building blocks (packets) that are reassembled at their destination.

Each packet is absorbed much as a digestion process. The information you want is encased inside an electronic shell. Your computer first must crack the shell and then digest the seed of information that remains. If modems could absorb the electronic packets instantly, we would have few traffic problems on the Internet, but modems take time to digest the Internet's electronic information packets.

Because your modem and computer cannot instantaneously process the packets they receive, the packets slow the Internet as they linger about waiting to enter your computer system. If the receiving modem is too slow, the sending computer may have to retransmit some packets, adding even more traffic to the Internet.

Modem speed is increasing, but today the typical home computer user has a 9600-baud modem. The fastest personal computer modem today (28.8 Kbps) is approximately three times as fast as a 9600 baud modem. As a rough comparison, cable television signals are processed on the order of a thousand times as fast. But cable television was designed to carry pictures and sound and, as you know, the Internet was designed to carry text.

The satisfaction that the Internet brings to your customers and clients will increase if they upgrade older, slow modems to the fastest available. Prices on the fastest modems are dropping rapidly, making upgrading affordable for most users. While chapter 6, "2001: A cyberspace odyssey," will tell you about new technologies that will result in quantum leaps in Internet transfer speed, keep in mind during all your Internet planning and work the fact that your customers and clients may be using old, slow modems. Offer a text-only version of your Web home page—more on this in a later chapter—and test it yourself, if possible, using a 9600-baud modem.

Do your share to boost Internet speed

Speed problems, however, could be on your end of the system. If you discover from clients and customers that performance is a serious problem for your users, see what you can do to improve the speed of the Internet services you provide.

If your Internet site is maintained by an Internet service provider (ISP), make sure they're providing the fastest data transfer methods. Check with other ISPs about the speed of their Internet access. Some providers may have difficulty keeping their systems abreast of the massive changes that are coming. If your provider is lagging behind the leaps in technology, it may be time to switch services.

 NET TIP Be sure you're using the latest version of connection software. Technically, we're getting ahead of ourselves here, but service providers tend to package old versions of the critical software that manages your Internet connection (WinSock). We've witnessed dramatic speed improvements by upgrading from the old stuff that a service provider included free. We recommend you use the latest, fully-registered versions of all of your prime software—these usually cost only about $20 to $30.

If your organization maintains its own Internet information servers, check with your computer professionals. Make sure they understand what your organization is providing to clients and customers via the Internet. When your organization's Internet connection was established, perhaps no one had any idea how much traffic your new initiatives would generate. Your system could be creating a bottleneck for your own clients and customers.

The topic of Internet speed involves some rapidly changing technology. Knowing that, we're not covering details here about all the different connections such as 56K, T1, T3, and ISDN. Those terms—and other such technical jargon—are defined in the Glossary. Your success on the Internet will depend on you staying abreast of service capabilities so that you always use whatever level of service is best for your organization at the time.

For now, though, speed is not the forte of the Internet. Today, try to be satisfied that an Internet connection quickly can bring you cyberspace information from anywhere on the planet. Cyberspace is an amazing new territory, and we've devoted the next chapter to outlining exactly what it has in store for you.

 **Continuing Education**

Is anyone really making money on the net?
http://www.intuitive.com/taylor/#books

Here's a sample chapter from a business book on the Internet. The book is by David Taylor, who runs the Internet Mall. The chapter is entitled, "Is anyone making money on the net?" and can give you another perspective on the reality of what's really happening on the Internet.

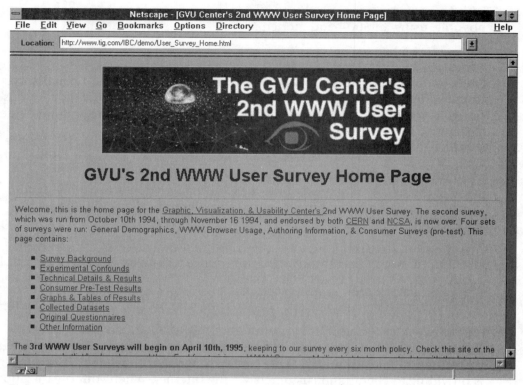

Figure 2-5

Track the Internet
http://www.tig.com/cgi-bin/genobject/statsdex

Here's a Web page (see Figure 2-5) that will keep you abreast of Internet demographics, including average age, gender ratios, education levels, income averages, and market segment information. From this page you can jump to a vast collection of maps, charts, and tables that will enable you to track the explosive growth of the Internet. The information you'll find here comes from WWW user surveys conducted by the Graphics, Visualization & Usability Laboratory at Georgia Institute of Technology.

Matrix Information and Directory Services
http://www.mids.org/mids/index.html

Matrix Information and Directory Services (MIDS) conducts ongoing investigations about the size, shape, and other characteristics of the Internet and other networks. MIDS publishes the monthly newsletter Matrix News and the color Matrix Maps Quarterly, both on paper and online, and also sells maps and other information. MIDS has on-staff experts in the field of understanding how to handle growth in all types of computer networks. Their expertise is not limited to the Internet, but encompasses a wide variety of network resources.

An overview of cyberspace

IN THIS CHAPTER we'll give you a quick overview of how the Internet is laid out. You'll learn just enough of its origin, history, and current status to be comfortable, but we're not going to burden you with a lot of details. After all, you probably have been driving for years without reading former President Eisenhower's original proclamation to build our interstate highway system. Of course, if you want to, you could find it on the Internet. The Internet also can point you to lots of information on its own origins if you want details. But let's not worry about details now; we're just out for a scenic drive to see the highlights.

The end of this chapter lists a wide selection of Internet sites that each can give you a comprehensive, online glossary. After all, there's no reason to include in this book an extensive glossary when it's available on the Internet. But we will define one term now, the term "internet" itself.

internet versus The Internet

There are internets and then there is The Internet. A small "i" internet could be any two computer *networks* that are interconnected so that users on both networks can share resources on either network. A network is at least two computers connected locally to each other—but some single networks have thousands of computers. An internet is at least two connected networks—regardless of the size of either one (see Figure 3-1).

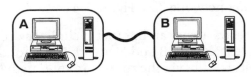

Figure 3-1

If more networks are interconnected, they all may be directly connected to each other (see Figure 3-2). Notice that each network in Figure 3-2 has a direct connection to every other network on the internet. It's easy to see that directly connecting each computer would severely limit the size and area that an internet could cover. Even if the numbers remained small, direct connections may be impractical, so they could be linked in series to limit the number of lines (see Figure 3-3).

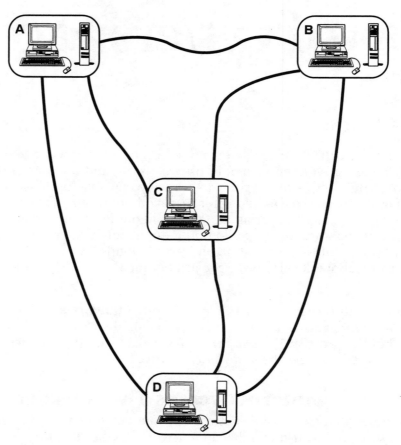

Figure 3-2

If all networks on an internet are not directly connected, however, then communications between all networks only is possible if the middle networks act as relays for the outer networks (see Figure 3-4).

Networks that act as relays across an internet include devices called routers. In Figure 3-4, for example, Network B and Network E are not directly connected, so they can communicate only via the routers in intermediary networks. If Network A has a router, then communications could be routed from B through A to E. If Network A does not have routing capability, but Network C and Network D do, then Network B still could communicate with Network E

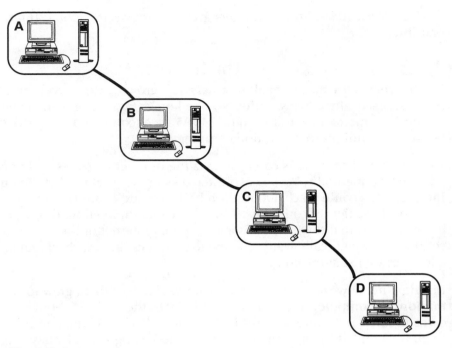

Figure 3-3

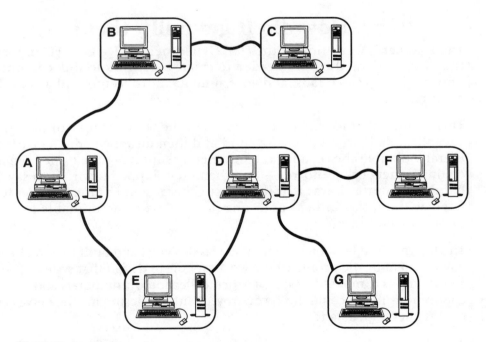

Figure 3-4

through Networks C and D. Routers are what makes the global Internet possible.

The Internet

The Internet is the master of all internets. It is growing explosively and has become practically a living entity. No one knows for sure how many networks the Internet interconnects, but in July 1995 we encountered estimates ranging between 20 million to 30 million computers.

The number of computers connected via the Internet increases daily, and is growing exponentially. We've encountered estimates that predict the number of Internet users could reach 100 million by 1998, and could reach 500 million by 2001; or those figures could be off by a large margin in either direction. The bottom line is that the Internet is a vast, global internet of literally countless computers. If you really want to know the latest estimates, check out some of the addresses we list at the end of this chapter.

Imagine the network models depicted above if one of them grew to connect millions of computers around the world. That's the capital "I" Internet. No one owns it. It has no central controlling authority. No one could control it if they tried. It's simply too large and too complex to be reigned in by any single group or government. As you may be surprised to discover, however, it was planned that way.

How did it get built, then?

The Internet is a creation of the U.S. Department of Defense (DoD). During the Cold War era, the DoD needed to create a network to link computers in universities, research labs, and government control centers all across the country.

This requirement led the DoD to do us all the wonderful favor of being a "deadbeat dad" who fathered a child and then disappeared. The DoD literally planted the seed for the Internet by supplying the basic "genetic coding"—network protocols— and then they skipped town, so to say. This hands-off approach was a brilliant tactic, because it left the Internet to grow freely without the burdens and constraints of being accountable to an office of bureaucrats.

The Internet is at least one system that was designed and built in a totally free environment by the people who knew best how to design that system. It also is so vast and is composed of such a varied collection of computers and connections that it could not be destroyed without destroying the nerve centers of every developed nation.

And that was the plan of the DoD from the beginning. They wanted a diverse, global computer network that could not be destroyed by a strategic nuclear attack. Only global annihilation would destroy the Internet. So, the U.S. government was the parent, but no group ever has controlled the Internet.

Do you really mean there's no control?

Yes.

Practically speaking, of course, no complex system would function smoothly without some central coordination. But coordination is not control. The Internet's central coordination is provided by the Internet Architecture Board (IAB) that *ratifies* the communications standards on the Internet.

The IAB heads a group of volunteers called the Internet Society (ISOC) that fosters the Internet and promotes Internet usage. The ISOC is based in Reston, Virginia, has branch groups around the world and hosts an annual, global conference (see Figure 3-5). *Inet'95*, the annual conference hosted by the Internet Society in Hawaii during the summer of 1995, attracted Internet boosters from 103 countries. The ISOC's first president, Dr. Vinton Cerf, is the co-creator of the basic programming codes—called TCP/IP (Transmission Control Protocol/Internet Protocol)—that you will use as you "surf" through cyberspace.

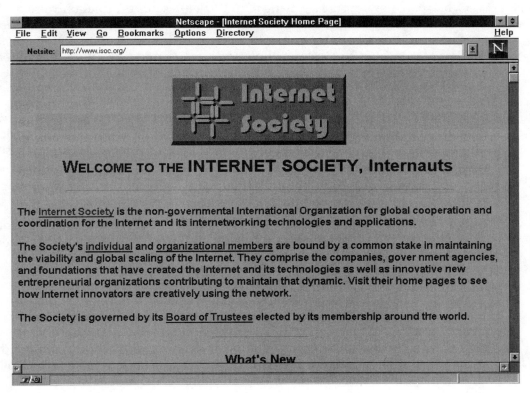

Figure 3-5

Another group of volunteers—no more groups after this, we promise—called the Internet Engineering Task Force (IETF) develops standards and resolves Internet technical and operational issues. The IETF functions as a public forum that organizes ad hoc workgroups that explore ways to keep the Internet abreast of technology changes.

How you got invited

During the Internet's first 20 years or so, the people who were building and using it did not allow any commercial usage. Its construction had been funded by a vast conglomeration of organizations and was used primarily for technical communications between those who built it.

The first major step toward you being invited to the cyberspace party occurred in the late 1980s, when the National Science Foundation (NSF) established its own network, the NSFNET, to connect several supercomputers. The NSF realized that these supercomputers had the potential to be a national treasure if they were interconnected and made available to other computer systems across the U.S. Wisely, the NSF set up a national network modeled after the existing Internet. This provided regular Internet connections and access across the U.S.

Cyberspace

Cyberspace has become a generic term that represents the total universe of all interconnected computers. The term was created by science fiction author William Gibson. In Gibson's books, cyberspace is a computer network called "The Matrix." His books foretell of a cold and forbidding future that suffers from too many people and too many computers. Mere fiction, right?

The dissolution of the Communist Party in the Soviet Union triggered some vast changes in the lifestyles of former Soviet citizens. But the collapse of the Soviet Union has had a far-reaching impact on us all and the Internet is a highly visible sign of the sweeping, global changes that have followed.

With the Cold War threat gone, the military value of the Internet all but evaporated. Blessedly for all of humankind, the people who conceived of this erstwhile military machine recognized its value as a tool for the growth of global peace and international harmony. Commercial Internet traffic quickly expanded, and now greatly exceeds military usage.

So, who is the Internet?

You are.

And *where* is the Internet? It's your computer, every other computer connected to the Internet, plus millions of miles of copper wire, fiber optic cable, microwave channels and satellite links. It's like the air you breathe; no one owns it or controls it, and it's everywhere.

Thanks—in some small way—to the fall of the Berlin wall, you now can work and play in a land that was the brainchild of the U.S. military. Originally designed to carry the communications that might have created a vast, global wasteland, the Internet now carries the communications that are creating a vast, global community.

Most assuredly, the Internet has fulfilled an ancient prophecy that said, "They will beat their swords into plowshares and their spears into pruning hooks." Amen and welcome to the party.

OK, what's out there waiting for me?

You probably have heard a lot lately about the Internet. Most of what you've heard is about one aspect of the Internet that's called the World Wide Web. You'll often see it written in shorthand—Web, WWW, and W3. There are several other aspects to the Internet, but the importance of most of the others is waning rapidly. We'll give you a short rundown of each.

World Wide Web (Web)

For all practical purposes *the Web is cyberspace*. It's become more than anyone ever dreamed. The Web was made possible by a technology called *hypertext*. When information is written in hypertext, key words can be highlighted and linked to related text. The reader merely clicks on a highlighted word to jump to the linked, related text.

Think of the end of an article in a encyclopedia that has a listing of "Related Topics." How many times have you actually dragged out all the additional volumes that would be required to see those related topics? How about never?

But in a hypertext encyclopedia (CD-ROM encyclopedias use hypertext), you simply click on the titles of the related topics to jump to the follow-on article. How many times will you actually click on a hypertext link to see a related topic? How about constantly? Hypertext is a charismatic attraction—it's like an electronic black hole that can pull you ever deeper into interesting areas in cyberspace—and that attraction is why you may have heard so much about the Web.

E-mail

The bulk of Internet traffic is electronic mail (e-mail). E-mail enables you to swap messages with anyone on the Internet anywhere in the world. The best part is that e-mail essentially is free—often there are no distance-based or per-message charges on e-mail. Some service providers still charge a per message rate, but usually only for those messages beyond a threshold number of messages included in their basic package. Whether it's free or very cheap, e-mail may completely change the way you conduct much of your business communication.

Newsgroups

Newsgroups—sometimes referred to as the Usenet—are electronic discussion forums. Newsgroups are akin to community bulletin boards upon which people can post notices but they serve the global community and have no formal membership requirements—anyone on the Internet can read and post messages. No one can accurately count their number, but estimates go as high as 15,000 public newsgroups. There also are private newsgroups, but no one can count them, either.

File Transfer Protocol (FTP)

This does pretty much as its name suggests—you can use FTP to transfer computer files between your computer and other computers on the Internet. You will use this mostly to transfer files into your computer from larger computer ·

systems (download), though you also can transfer files from your computer to others (upload). What can you get using FTP? Just about anything you can imagine that can be stored on a computer: maps, photos, a copy of the Constitution, audio sound clips, and even video clips. The Internet has thousands of FTP sites and millions of files. Perhaps you'll use the FTP directly sometime, but you primarily will encounter it as a hidden part of the Web.

Mailing lists

Here's a terrific tool to stay up-to-the-minute informed on a vast array of topics. The best feature about getting information from this system is that—unlike most of the Internet—it comes to you. Instead of providing a repository of information that can be searched and downloaded, mailing lists send automated e-mail to users who subscribe to electronic publications.

Gopher

A team of computer folks at the University of Minnesota developed in 1991 a system that enables Internet users to "go fer" stuff all over cyberspace. Can it be merely coincidence, then, that the mascot of the University of Minnesota is a gopher? The name certainly fits because this electronic rodent can burrow all over the Internet to find information you want. Once the mainstay of surfing the Net, most people now use Gopher only when it pops up on the Web.

Golden oldies

In the Introduction to this book, we told you that many aspects of the Internet already have become passé. That doesn't mean they're old—it just means that life in cyberspace moves pretty fast, and yesterday's hot technology is today's "Remember when..." The BetaMax VCRs of the Internet are Veronica, Archie, Jughead, finger, Telnet, and WAIS. In chapter 9 ("Internet tools"), we'll briefly cover some of these, but before you take time to learn them, first see if the World Wide Web leaves you crying, "More!"

Now, about defining all that jargon

Okay, so we've defined a few common terms, but the Internet involves so much technical jargon that learning it can bewilder an Internet beginner. In fact, there's even technical jargon for an Internet beginner. The term is "newbie."

Jargon is an integral part of the Internet, so, before you get to the Hands On phase of the training, you should learn the essential jargon because we freely will use the terms during our Hands On lessons. Jargon is useful, of course, because once you understand the terms, its shorthand will save time when communicating about the Internet. Besides, you're going to see it everywhere, so you might as well learn it now.

We highly recommend that you now read through the glossary that we've included. It intentionally is brief, because we only need to introduce you to terms you'll need for your Hands On training.

What about other, more technical terms? You can find all you need and more than you'll ever want in a variety of places using the Internet itself—the end of this book's glossary includes the address of an online technical glossary. Here is a listing of some other sites that can put the definition of every Internet jargon term at your fingertips.

# Continuing Education

The Internet Society
http://www.isoc.org

The Internet Society (ISOC) is the non-governmental, international organization for global cooperation and coordination for the Internet and its internetworking technologies and applications. Its members, both individual and organizational, have a common goal of maintaining the viability and the global scaling of the Internet.

For individual membership: *membership@isoc.org*
For organization membership: *org-membership@isoc.org*
Fax: 703-648-9887
Voice: 703-648-9888 (or 800-468-9507 in the USA only)
Snail mail: 12020 Sunrise Valley Dr., Suite 270, Reston, VA 22091, USA

Internet literacy consultants
http://www.matisse.net

The home page of the Internet Literacy Consultants (ILC) includes a jump to the "Internet Glossary," the best glossary we've found on the Internet. It's comprehensive and it has an alphabetical index you can use to quickly locate terms. A nice touch is that when any definition contains other technical terms, each term is italicized so you'll know you can look it up.

The jargon file
http://web.cnam.fr/Jargon/

This is a computing jargon dictionary. It was the basis for the book *The New Hacker's Dictionary*. Notice the "fr" in the address. That's France. You can get your technical jargon questions answered from a computer in Paris! Once you get to the jargon page, you can click to jump to their home page and check out other services—they even offer an English option.

Boardwatch Magazine
http://www.boardwatch.com

Originally a magazine for the Bulletin Board System (BBS) community, Boardwatch magazine (see Figure 3-6) now covers the Internet and commercial online services as well. This Web site has the full text of back issues, dating back to October 1994. The articles deal with trends, legal and social issues, and technology. Luckily, they avoid much of the hype we've warned you to expect on the Internet. We recommend this one highly if you want to stay abreast of Internet developments.

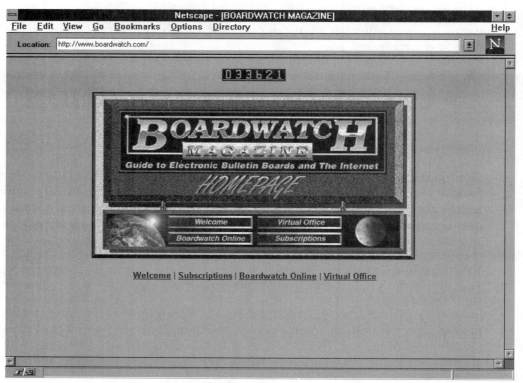

Figure 3-6

Data communications and networking links
http://www.racal.com/networking.html

From the ISDN User's Guide to the Cell-Relay (ATM) Archives, Don Joslyn's Data Communications' page surveys the Networking resources of the Net. Don is a software engineer at Racal-Datacom, which hosts the page. The page has an especially good collection of links to other specialized collections of links.

Computing oriented abbreviation and acronyms
http://crl.nmsu.edu/lists/Babel.html

This is New Mexico State University's search interface to the Babel Computing Oriented Abbreviation and Acronyms database. If you're ever stumped by gibberish like RISC, COBOL, VRAM, VDT, IMTV, or OEM, this is a good place to visit.

Computer Literacy Bookshops home page
http://www.clbooks.com/

Here's a good example of a Web page that was designed with functionality, not glitz, as the highest priority. It serves its purpose well and you won't waste time downloading unnecessary graphics. Use their search feature to locate books by topic or by author. You even can use this page to order more copies of this book for your colleagues who aren't lucky enough to have their own copy!

Internet joke book

http://www.clarinet.com:80/inetjoke.html

The Internet isn't all a bunch of boring computers, computer networks, and computer nerds. It has its funny moments. Check out this page to order an Internet joke book—although you might need to be a computer nerd to get the jokes. Just in case going online has made you and your coworkers a bit edgy, remember this book and see if you can use it to find some humor out there in cyberspace.

40

Netiquette

EVERY LAND has its own language and culture. Cyberspace has both of those, plus a whole new psychological demeanor. It's a good thing, too, because the Internet itself consists of computers and a few million humming, blinking electrical boxes that would be too cold, ugly, and boring for humans to tolerate. In this chapter, we're going to help you understand all three of these aspects of the land of cyberspace: language, culture and psychological demeanor. This discussion introduces yet another bit of Internet jargon: netiquette—Internet etiquette.

Proper netiquette—the special rules of Internet social consideration—will improve the quality of your relationships and smooth the complicated process of communication. The detached nature of Internet communication presents some serious limitations to expression and understanding that require special care.

Sociologists say that between 70 percent to 90 percent of human communication is conveyed through body language and tone of voice—only 10 percent to 30 percent is conveyed by words.

Mailed letters have expressive abilities because you can communicate a lot with your choice of paper, letterhead design, how the envelope is addressed, font size and style, your signature, plus embellishments such as color, bold, italics, pictures, charts, and even enclosures. The telephone at least lets you use tone of voice and pauses, but its role in business communication is waning. Thus, much of your business communication is at risk of becoming impersonal, because the Internet reduces our communications tools to nothing but mere words.

New communication tools

Because most of your normal communication tools are ineffective on the Internet, we'll show you some replacements. These tools will include some of the best-known "emoticons"—icons that emulate emotions—that can help you avoid misunderstandings by letting people see the feelings that are behind the mere words on the page.

We also will give you some tips on writing for the Internet. The timbre of the language is different than in business letters of the past, and that results in more misunderstandings. Our "Electronic Elements of Style" can spare your fingers a few keystrokes because rules of grammar are less rigid and time-saving acronyms abound. We'll give you enough tools so that you'll be able to understand the ones you read and quickly lose the status of "newbie."

Flaming words

We present these tools because misunderstandings abound on the Internet. The result often is something called a flame war—the Internet equivalent of a shouting match. The messages that are flung back and forth in a flame war—one of the weapons of cyberspace—are called flames. Sending flames is call flaming.

When you eventually encounter a flame war—of course we hope only as an observer of someone else's battle—be prepared to witness a return to the grade school playground. No, it's worse than that. Grade school kids have better things to do than to devote as much time to getting in the last word as some Internet users spend. Flame wars are a tremendous waste of Internet resources and usually completely unnecessary.

Apologies R painless

Often, good netiquette on the part of either combatant will stop a flame war before it starts. You can do your part for the peace effort in cyberspace. If something you send or post earns a hostile reply message, instead of firing back the first barb that comes to mind, perhaps you could reread your message.

Did you leave open the possibility for an alternate interpretation? Remember that if the other person *feels* they've been flamed, then there's no question about it—they have been flamed. Even if you're completely perplexed by their interpretation, the best professional course is to acknowledge the results and accept responsibility for the harm.

The bright side

Here's a high note in case reading all of these negative things about communicating in cyberspace is making you jittery. Not being able to see the other person has its benefits. There are no doubt countless excellent business relationships on the Internet between people who wouldn't look at each other in person. In cyberspace, bigots aren't biased. Age and gender barriers don't exist. Accents don't impede comprehension. And no one will criticize what you're wearing.

When you feel that the impersonal realm of cyberspace has cost you the good will of a business relationship, think of how many relationships you might have developed that never would have blossomed F2F (face-to-face).

You will step on a few toes in any crowd, and in cyberspace you can stomp on a lot of them fast. When you do, you'll do yourself a favor to simply reply with something like, "Sorry. Your reply showed me that I hit a sensitive spot. I didn't phrase it carefully at all. Will you accept my apology and can you accept a rephrased version of what I meant to convey?"

It's amazing, though, how a few people never can apologize or accept responsibility for their actions, even across the anonymous reaches of cyberspace. The Internet gives you the ability to insult thousands—perhaps millions—of people at the speed of light. The good news, though, is that it also gives you the fastest and most painless way ever devised to apologize and make amends—and doing so is excellent netiquette.

Let it be

Finally, consider the other side of the flame war alliance: Help prevent flame wars by being slow to come to a boil.

Few people send intentional insults, so someone may be taken aback if you blast off an immediate, flaming retort. They may feel that you have thrown the first punch and blast you back when you were certain you'd receive a humble apology. So you nail them for being so stupid as to think that you flamed them and—voilà—a flame war has been launched.

The Internet may well tromple your feelings if you are sensitive to every perceived wrong. Instead of being quick on the flamethrower trigger, give the benefit of the doubt to your e-mailing colleagues by assuming the best of their intentions and let most things slide.

There's one other good reason to let things slide. Some newsgroups are haunted by "trollers," people who troll through the Internet fishing for a flame war. Their motives, often politically based, are to start flame wars that will disrupt communications and distract other users from accomplishing their planned goals. As with most activities, when you're on the Internet, stay focused. Ask yourself if responding to flames will help you accomplish your goals. If not, then avoid the distraction, disruption, and wasted time of a flame war. If, however, your goals are to "scream" at people, then go ahead and jump into the fray—but remember, some troller may be laughing because he tricked you into wasting time on a contrived fight.

Corporate netiquette

Practicing good netiquette is even more important for you because you represent an organization. A private flame war is annoying, but a business-related flame war—even between just two individuals—can tarnish the reputation of an entire organization. Countless programs—called "sniffers"—roam the Internet, sample text in message traffic, and alert people to read messages that contain "interesting" words. Any sensitive topic might be considered interesting by someone who owns a sniffer—and they'll be excited that their sniffer made a catch. Anything you say on the Internet can be on the front page of *The Washington Post* tomorrow.

Your trusty old telephone creates fewer opportunities for misunderstanding, because you can hear each other's tone of voice. Tone of voice works to head off trouble from both ends of a conversation. You may hear words that might have sounded offensive in a transcript of the call, but on the phone you don't take offense because the tone of voice clearly signals a lighthearted context. Conversely, if you accidentally offend someone on the phone, you can sense by a change in their tone of voice that you've touched a sensitive area. You have time to recover.

The Internet brings to you the burden of double-trouble: Not only does it make you more easily misunderstood, it leaves documented proof of what you say that can span the globe in a few minutes. So, not only can your communication quickly insult vast reaches of humanity, it can create evidence for a lawsuit. And remember that the U.S. has more than twice as many lawyers as the rest of the world combined!

Spam

Adherence to some rules of netiquette will do more than create good business relations, they can keep you from being thrown off the Internet. Sending spam—the act is called spamming—is a sure-fire shortcut to getting your Internet plug pulled. Spam is universally hated, and you surely will join the crowd when you first see it. So what is spam?

The poor folks who've produced the commercial meat product Spam for all these years probably have considered a name change. Internet Spam stands for, generally, anything that nobody wants. The Internet usage actually comes from a Monty Python comedy bit in which every item on a restaurant menu was made of Spam.

Spam most often is used to refer to grossly misappropriate usage of newsgroups. Spam comes from entrepreneurs who ridiculously believe that they've got the hottest product or service ever created, and that the entire world will thank them for instantly telling every one of us about it. And it seems that they usually have a title similar to, "$$$ MAKE REAL MONEY FAST $$$." So the spammer writes a tome of breathless hype and then posts it to a vast array of unrelated newsgroups, perhaps hundreds of them and sometimes thousands.

First, advertising on newsgroups generally is considered to be horrible netiquette. So the spam annoys people who logged onto the newsgroup for some news on their favorite topic. Second, in the groups where one can post ads that are not considered spam, the ads you'll see are related to the newsgroup topic, are well-written, and convey exactly the type of information that the group's readers are seeking.

People who spam are likely to have their messages cancelled from the Internet and may find *themselves* cancelled from the Internet. Some spammers cry that this infringes on their free speech rights, but the U.S. 1st Amendment doesn't cover disturbing the peace. People have a right to express their opinions in the proper forum, but society doesn't tolerate screaming and bombarding everyone with the same message—neither does the Internet. Gross offenders usually are reported to their Internet providers, and find their Internet account quickly cancelled.

With all that said, would you like to hear about the light side of Spam? As much as people rail against how much time is wasted by this uninvited intrusion, they've devoted plenty of computing power to discussing and laughing about Spam. Check out the Web site at *http://www.ip.net/BL/blacklist.html#spam* because you'll find hypertext links to a tasty menu of Spam.

As a representative of a business, then, you definitely can benefit from learning the rules of the electronic road that make up the rest of this chapter. Let's start with some handy acronyms. These widely accepted Internet shortcuts can save you typing time and help convey what you really mean to say.

Electronic elements of style

So here, in alphabetical order, is a glossary of helpful and well-known Internet acronyms.

ADN—Any Day Now

AFAIK—As Far As I Know

B4N—Bye for Now

BBS—Bulletin Board System

BL—Belly Laughing!

BTA—But Then Again

BTDT—Been There, Done That

BTW—By The Way

CUL—See You Later

CUL8R—See You Later

DTP—Desktop Publishing

EOT—End Of Topic

F2F—Face to Face

FAQ—Frequently Asked Questions

FB—Flame Bait

FLAME OFF—Off limits for flaming

FLAME ON—Normal flaming rules restored

FUBAR—Fouled Up Beyond All Recognition

FUD—Fear, Uncertainty and Doubt

FWIW—For What It's Worth

FYI—For Your Information

<G>—Grin

GAL—Get A Life

GIGO—Garbage In, Garbage Out

GIWIST—Gee, I Wish I'd Said That

GMTA—Great Minds Think Alike

IAC—In Any Case

IC—I See

IDTT—I'll Drink To That

IME—In My Experience

IMO—In My Opinion

IMHO—In My Humble Opinion

IOW—In Other Words

IRL—In Real Life

JIC—Just In Case

LOL—Laughing Out Loud
NFW—No Way
OTOH—On The Other Hand
::POOF::—I'm gone
POV—Point Of View
PTB—Powers That Be
PTMM—Please Tell Me More
RE—Regarding
RTFM—Read The Manual
SNAFU—Situation Normal, All Fouled Up
SYSOP—System Operator
TAFN—That's All For Now
TIA—Thanks In Advance
TNTL—Trying Not To Laugh
WRT—With Regard To

Emoticon lexicon

The Internet has embraced a shorthand language called *emoticons* or *smileys* that help remedy its inability to convey tone of voice. The name smiley comes from the first emoticon, which was a little smiley-face. :-) Smileys since have evolved well beyond their simple origin, and now convey a wide range of emotions.

These little electronic writing aids are so widely used that entire books have been written about them. If you want to keep a more complete reference guide by your computer, check your local computer book store for an emoticon book—they have more smileys than you can use. Or is that *should* use? Smileys are not widely used, so if you use a smiley that is found only in emoticon books, will it convey anything other than a confused "What?"

Here's a brief listing of some of the most widely understood emoticons. The key to understanding them lies in your perspective: look at them sideways.

Positive emotions

:-)   The original smiley, conveys friendliness or kidding

:)   The original with no nose

:->   A surprised smiley

:-D   Delighted smiley

:'-)   Tears of joy

:-}   Sarcastic grin

:-]   Goofy grin

:-x   Kiss

[]   Hug

Negative emotions

:-(	Frown, sadness
:(	Same thing with no nose
:-P	Sticking out your tongue
%-(	Confused and sad
:-O	Shocked or screaming
>:-|	Frowning
>:-<	Frowning and very angry
:-<	Dejected
:-C	Very unhappy
:'-(	Crying
:-{}	Blabbermouth who won't shut up

Mixed emotions, etc.

:-\	Mixed feelings leaning toward happy
:-/	Mixed feelings leaning toward sad
:-|	Neutral
:-J	Tongue in cheek
:-@	Screaming out loud
:-$	Put your money where your mouth is
;-)	Wink

Miscellaneous netiquette

Here, in no particular order, is a collection of general netiquette that can help us all.

Use mixed case

PLEASE DON'T EVER POST OR MAIL ANYTHING IN ALL CAPS. IT'S ANNOYING TO READ, ISN'T IT?

All caps definitely rate as poor netiquette, it's the equivalent of screaming all the time and is harder to read than normal mixed case text. Save the all caps for an occasional SPECIAL EMPHASIS when needed unless you want the entire message to be ignored.

Bold, italics, and underlining

Most likely your e-mail message window won't accept any of the standard font attributes such as bold, italics, and underlining. Even if it does, expect the codes to be scrambled for your readers. If your reader needs a document with all the formatting codes intact, then create a document in your word processor and attach the file to a short e-mail message.

Nonetheless, some typing standards have emerged on the Internet that enable you to use regular characters to represent both underlining and italics. Underlining is represented by bracketing a text string with underscore characters, perhaps using it to emphasize something _that is really important_. Similarly, asterisks are used to bracket text that normally would be italicized such as a book title, *The McGraw-Hill Internet Training Guide.*

Are you beginning to feel overwhelmed with all of this new information? You're not alone. The Internet can be a huge shock to your sanity and peace of mind. The next chapter will prepare you to easily handle the overwhelming mountain of information you will encounter.

Continuing Education

Guidelines for conduct on and use of the Internet
http://www.isoc.org/policy/conduct/conduct.html

An Internet publication in which Dr. Vinton G. Cerf, President, Internet Society discusses constructive models of Internet conduct both by those who use the system and by those who provide its services. Dr. Cerf co-authored the foundational computer coding of the Internet known as TCP/IP (Transmission Control Protocol/Internet Protocol).

Everything you wanted to know about netiquette but were afraid to ask
http://www.clarinet.com:80/brad/emily.html

This URL will get you to Brad Templeton's "Dear Emily Postnews." Brad boasts that Emily is the "foremost authority on proper net behaviour, who gives her advice on how to act on the net." This is some terrific fun reading, yet it will give you a lot of good tips on netiquette—at least you'll know a lot of things *not* to do when posting to newsgroups.

Arlene Rinaldi's Netiquette home page
http://www.fau.edu/rinaldi/netiquette.html

This site includes a lot of Internet netiquette tips and guidelines. It includes links to many other Internet sites on the same topic. Also, as you browse through Arlene's site, you'll encounter information on subscribing to many mailing lists that cover a variety of Internet topics (see Figure 4-1).

The Netiquette Cybertoon
http://carbon.concom.com/dmenter/Netiquette/Prerelease_Netiquette_homepge

Netiquette is a comic about diverse electronic life on the Internet that gives the Net the opportunity to make fun of itself by examining the Internet point of view. Its creator, David G. Menter, says he hopes to provide daily "netisodes" and is in the process of accumulating enough panels to provide a little breathing room to ensure that his comic can feature a daily original.

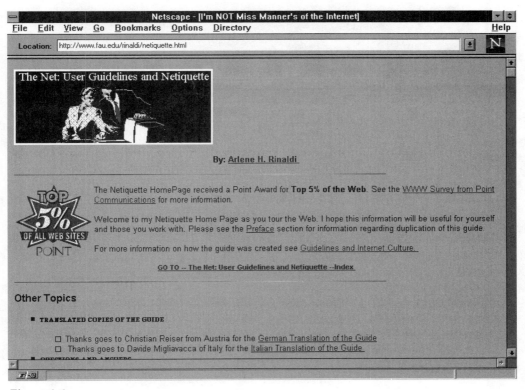

Figure 4-1

50

The over-information age

BEFORE they were 24, your grandparents probably had acquired enough knowledge or training to make a good living their entire lives. Such a deal is not available to you.

The volume of new knowledge disseminated in every field is enormous and easily exceeds anyone's ability to keep pace. As a result, everyone today fears that he/she is increasingly underinformed despite absorbing an unprecedented volume of information.

The volume of information that spewed forth to spawn the term "Information Age" is dwarfed by what's happening today. The Information Age—if it was ever here—is long dead. You now live in the Over-Information Age and the Internet is going to carry it into your life faster than ever.

Can you feel how the pace of your life has increased in the last five years? Do you fear that you are not going to be able to keep up? And you're just starting to use the Internet! But, wait, you're not alone: Nobody is keeping up!

One big blur of information

There are visible, identifiable factors that reveal why the pace of life has sped up for virtually everyone.

In this Over-Information Age, you have so much information competing for your time and attention that nearly everything is becoming one big blur. When more things compete for your attention, you feel as if the time in your life is passing by more quickly. Before delving too deeply into the Internet, your sanity may rest upon how you handle these facts:

Information

- A *single* Sunday edition of the *New York Times* contains more information than your great-grandparents may have encountered in a *lifetime*.
- Every *five years* (and dropping) half the world's technological information is replaced.

- On average, 3,000 books are published *each week* just in the U.S.—the global total is more than 2,000 new books *every day*!
- In 1970, there were three TV networks in the U.S. Now there are more than 350 full-powered networks and independent stations—and cable systems now are gearing up to bring a total of *500 or more channels* into your home.
- A single Internet Web search service (see Figure 5-1) has indexed more than *100 million* records, including more than *ten million* books and *tens of millions* of journal articles.

Figure 5-1

Paper generation

- With the advent of computers, we expected the paperless office; but we now consume *three times* the paper that we did in 1980!
- In the 1980s, *growth* in junk mail was 13 times faster than the *growth* in population.
- In the United States, each adult annually consumes 700 pounds of paper. That's a *55-foot-high* stack of regular (8×11) paper. Where do you store yours?

And you wonder why you barely seem able to remain abreast of changes in your own field? Add to your current demands your increasing amount of time online with the Internet and you may be missing a life—yours.

Cyberlock

With the increasing number of people going online to tap into the vast cache of information on the Internet, combined with the inability of the service providers to meet the increased demand, you'll be facing gridlock on the information superhighway. Jeff Davidson, author of *Breathing Space: Living and Working at a Comfortable Pace in a Sped-up Society*, calls it cyberlock.

As Jeff notes, cyberlock is in full swing. Several-minute waits for online connections are common—and that just gets you connected so you can begin waiting to download information. Often—especially during business hours—you won't even be able to logon to a favorite Internet site. Cyberlock could become a long-term phenomenon as even more people go online for longer periods of time, sending and downloading ever-larger volumes of information.

With all due respect to Al Gore, his "information superhighway" term is premature. The Internet of today is but a dirt road winding past an old farm compared to what you'll see in cyberspace by the year 2001. Yet, cyberlock isn't going to disappear. But this is the next chapter...

In the 1986 movie *Ferris Beuhler's Day Off*, the lead character played by Matthew Broderick said, "Life goes by pretty fast. If you don't slow down, you might miss it." That adage made sense even in 1986 when we had three television networks, maybe 30 cable channels, and most of us had never heard of the Internet. Today, Ferris's adage is a sound business principle.

You need an information switchboard

Adding up all the factors competing for our time and attention, we are the most distracted generation in history. We're a generation that grew up with the notion, "Take in more—there's no harm." The harm already has shown up, however, in our perception that our lives are racing by.

The Internet is going to put at your fingertips more information than you probably have imagined existed. You will become more acutely aware of an ever-increasing number of topics and areas in which you cannot keep up. Fortunately, you need not become a victim of the Over-Information Age—unless you choose to be. Here are two keys to restoring control over the information that bombards your life.

- The sooner you quit trying to keep up, the better you will feel.
- Carefully choose where you give your time and attention.

Your goal is relearning how to live with relative grace and ease. Remember the days when we all left work on time, got work done on time, did our taxes on time? You have to simplify. The quality of your life—for the rest of your life—depends on it. You can surf the Net for two hours, but you pay a price. Are the things you do on the Internet worth the price you pay?

Micro-niching

For at least the past decade, scores of business books have touted the concept of "niches." The idea was that the business world has become too complex for anyone to be a "jack-of-all-trades" and the secret to success was picking one crucial niche in which to excel and becoming an expert in it.

Today, confining your interests to a single, crucial niche is not nearly narrow enough. Suppose you had picked science—marine biology—as your niche and have ignored developments in all other fields. That won't work anymore. Within the scientific world alone more than 40,000 journals publish more than 1,000,000 articles annually!

While most of those articles aren't directly focused on marine biology, what humankind learns about the ice age, fossil fuels, sun spots, tectonic plates, and a host of other areas may impact your understanding of marine biology. And the Internet makes nearly all of these findings instantly available. Soon, merely counting new journals may be a full-time job.

Today you cannot effectively handle more than a tiny *micro-niche*. The good news is that the Internet—while massive and growing explosively—has the tools to make you an expert in the micro-niche you need while screening out what everybody else needs.

Consider the days of horse-and-buggy travel, when drivers placed blinders on their horses to keep them from being startled by things they didn't need to see. Similarly, you can choose to travel the information superhighway wearing electronic "blinders" that enable you to see only the information that affects your micro-niche.

Watch carefully in this book for tips on how to apply "kill" files that can block unwanted e-mail messages or screen bothersome newsgroup files. Be sure you understand how to set bookmarks so you easily can return to crucial information without browsing all over cyberspace. Learn to set up in your e-mail application an address book with nicknames. And, absolutely, learn Windows well enough to quickly use Cut, Copy, and Paste and to jump back and forth between Windows applications so you'll never retype anything that Windows can let you transfer.

You will need to carefully choose where you're going to give your time and attention; your time will, indeed, run out one day. Paradoxically, you can spend all the time remaining in your life logged onto the Internet and still be farther behind than you are today.

Spend time with friends. Make time for hobbies and the things you want to do. Most of all, be able to drop back at any time, take a long deep breath, and renew your spirit.

How can you do that?

Become your own information switchboard. Simply turn off your information receptors for several hours each day. Do not let new information invade your being if it doesn't promise immediate benefit to you, your family, your community, your organization, or any area of your life, or if it comes after hours. Choose to acquire only knowledge that benefits or truly interests you, not information that you simply happen to ingest, or think you must ingest.

Most importantly, at all points, recognize that there is but one party who controls the volume, rate, and frequency of information to which you're exposed: You. The notion of "keeping up" is illusory, self-defeating, and harmful. The sooner you give it up, the better you will feel.

The rise of misinformation

Unfortunately, when you do choose to absorb new information, it's difficult to ascertain what is accurate information. You see, along with the wealth of information we may tap into, also comes voluminous amounts of *misinformation*. There is no easy way to say this. We have a society in which, too often, information is false. The Internet increases this phenomenon to hyper-levels. Because of our vast capabilities for disseminating such information, the truth rarely catches up with the falsehoods. Here's an example:

> In his book, *Agents of Influence*, author Pat Choate debunks the myth that the Japanese as a whole contribute to the development of innovation and technology as evidenced by their annual lead in the number of U.S. patents they file for and obtain. As Choate explains, in a dramatic example of the way the Japanese tilt the economic playing field, they practice the ruthless art of "patent flooding."

> When a U.S. firm, for example, applies for a patent representing an innovation on which the Japanese would like to capitalize, Japanese firms will issue a flurry of patent applications that surround the technology in question. This technique can tie up an invention in the courts simply because of nuisance patents for a component or contributing element to the major patent.

> Yet most of us have heard—and fear—that the Japanese are far outpacing U.S. firms in technological advances. And most people already are working at a feverish pace. Misinformation about Japanese patent practices has hoodwinked us into believing our technology seriously lags behind the Japanese.

In *Backlash*, author Susan Faludi points out how "pop" market forecasters make a fortune by reviewing popular media such as newspapers, television, movies, and so forth, and then concluding what trends are looming in America. The extreme fallacy with this method of forecasting, Faludi notes, is that it tends to promulgate that which only a handful of editors, publishers, and directors believe or profess. Hard data supports few of these "forecasts." Similarly, vast stores of information on the Internet comprise only the opinion of someone who posted a Web page.

We rely on information in our lives, and very often it is not valid information. We, as managers, career professionals, and employees—in addition to bearing the burden of the Over-Information Age—must ensure that we act only upon quality information.

You need accurate sources

So, how do you use the Internet in a way that recognizes the informational realities we've introduced so far?

Always confirm information you've encountered on the Internet before making any decision that can impact the underpinnings of your company. Go to original sources whenever you use a statistic or data. Send e-mail back to the source asking for verification. Check informational headers in online documents. You'll learn how to implement these techniques in later chapters. But for now, beware that the Internet is teeming with misinformation called "spoof data."

Spoof data is information that is a joke or an intentional deception. Why does spoof data abound? Until very recently, the majority of Internet users have been male college students. Did you watch the movie, *National Lampoon's Animal House*? Of course Animal House was a hyper-exaggerated parody, but it's a good reminder that a few college students with an immature sense of humor can cut a huge swath of confusion and ruin.

Spoof data, of course, can come from any source. A clever junior-high student can generate spoof data that appears to emanate from the White House. Spoof data is not difficult to create and a few people think it's hilariously funny. Don't give them the satisfaction of seeing their handiwork do its intended job. Always check your sources before acting!

Conditioning your environments

In addition to controlling the amount and quality of information to which you're exposed, you need to *condition your environments*. Most people do this some of the time, but people who don't do this often say it takes too much work. "It takes work to get off mailing lists." "It takes work to learn new computer software." Sure it does, but when you take time to condition your environment, when you take time out to set up your world for the way you work and live, the payoff comes over and over again. Let's consider some specific examples.

Condition your work environment

One of the great paradoxes of our society is that to accommodate the pace of the sped-up society in which we live, sometimes—as Ferris Beuhler said—we do have to slow down. Often, that doesn't feel good, but to help you practice this principle, our first Hands On lesson—covering the advanced basics of using Windows—will slow you down to speed you up.

It might not feel good to spend the time we'll ask you to take to complete our Windows lesson. In fact, most people whom we've encountered in our roles as computer trainers believe they cannot afford the time to complete a lesson on Windows. Actually, the reverse is true. The more time-pressed you are, the more you need to be a whiz with Windows. If you're going to work all day in a Windows environment, you may as well master that environment.

Go through your file drawers—studies show that four out of five papers stuffed in files are never used again. Toss out everything you don't need to retain. Do the same on your computer. We have no studies to back it up, but we imagine that four out of five data files stored on computer hard drives are never used again. The Internet actually can lessen your own storage burden because so much now is available electronically, which means that other people store it on their computers.

Condition your personal environment

One goal worth pursuing is getting a good night's sleep. Stanford University's Center for Sleep Research conducted a study and concluded that the typical American no longer has any idea what it means to be fully awake and alert! The Internet has had an enormously negative impact on the sleep habits of countless entranced computer users. Cyberspace is a powerfully engaging world that has a charismatic attraction for most people. An all-nighter can seem like a couple of hours.

Fortunately, you have the ever-present option to make new goals, such as the number of hours you sleep, health foods you eat, great novels you read, and so on. These are just a few examples of the kinds of goals that we ignore or short-change in our fast-paced lives.

As you begin to condition your environment, you see that it's possible to choose other types of goals instead of traditional ones, such as how much money you'll make, or how big a house you want. A conditioned environment also will increase your success with other types of goals, such as reducing your weight or blood pressure.

Managing the beforehand

Managing the beforehand is related to conditioning your environments. It involves looking at forthcoming events in your life and deciding what you can handle in advance. Such a method enables you to be more rested and better prepared to encounter what enters your life—and because you're pulling onto the global information superhighway, we know that huge volumes of information soon will be crowding into your life.

Creating ad hoc piles of information you receive and don't know where to file is simply "dealing with the aftermath" of living in an over-information society. Creating space in anticipation of new information is managing the beforehand. How can you manage the beforehand electronically?

- Before you encounter mounds of new information, eliminate what you already have that is not useful to you. Throw away outdated paper documents and delete unnecessary files from your computer system.
- Create a default "download" directory on your hard drive or on the network and specify this directory in the "preferences" sections of your favorite Internet software. This way, you always will know where to find freshly downloaded files, instead of having to search your computer system.
- Create directories into which you'll transfer important files from your default download directory—after you've confirmed their long-term usefulness to you.

- Download from the Internet only the information that truly will support you. Instead of downloading a file you might use only occasionally, record its Internet address and leave the information on the Internet.
- Knowing that you'll be saving Internet addresses, create a computer file for storing and organizing them. A sidebar in the "Windows Wide-Open," chapter details the steps for implementing this technique.

It takes a little more work to condition your environment and manage the beforehand. But once you begin practicing the techniques, the payoffs are so tremendous that you can't *not* do them anymore. Sure, you already are inundated with rules, guidelines, and checklists, without us adding to them. These aren't rules, however, they are *ways of being*.

Remember: *More is going to compete for your time and attention than you ever will be able to absorb*. To keep from being overwhelmed with over-information, you must take new approaches. You could read all the best "time management" books and follow the best advice and still feel farther behind. Why? Because everything's changed, even if your perceptions haven't caught up.

Questions that can ease the crush

Ask yourself, "What would it take for me to feel good about ending work today at 5:00?" Not every day, but today. You'll strike a bargain with yourself; you'll get the most important work done in exchange for getting out of the office on time.

Next ask yourself: By the end of the work week, what do I want to have accomplished, so I can feel good about the weekend?

How many times do you take a minute—just one minute—after lunch to take a deep breath and get yourself focused? Or do you just get your lunch and jump right back to your desk? You can take that minute, can't you? In the Western world, we're caught in a trap in which we *act* like everything's important; we substitute motion and activity for results. Yet, if you're the president of a company, for example, it would be helpful to sometimes stare out your office window and just think about the direction in which you want to take the company.

Practice living and working with grace and ease, because that's when your greatest decisions and breakthroughs will come. Charles Osgood once said that we've become hostage to our "busy-ness." The way to reclaim time in your life is not through some personal revelation or cataclysmic change. The changes you need to implement can be subtle, even piecemeal, and they'll be just fine. The most important factor is to begin today.

Once you begin to adopt some of these measures, you'll see a cascading effect. One or two months from now, you'll begin to change in ways that are natural and comfortable for you. It won't be because of some set of rules; it will be because you acknowledge that there are too many choices and too much information, and it always will be that way. So put down this book for a moment and relax. After all, you deserve a little "Breathing Space!"

The Breathing Space Institute

The material in this chapter was derived from a variety of resources produced by Jeff Davidson, the Executive Director of the Breathing Space Institute, and has been used with his permission. Jeff is a popular speaker and the award-winning author of 18 books, including *Breathing Space: Living and Working at a Comfortable Pace in a Sped-up Society* (MasterMedia, $10.95).

Jeff offers presentations that we consider to be critical survival tools for almost anyone who is involved in business on the Internet. His *Marketing in Complex Times* presentation helps companies integrate the "five mega-realities" of our era: *information, media growth, population, paper,* and *an overabundance of choices.* Jeff's *Managing the Pace With Grace* seminar teaches space, time, and stress-handling techniques most people have never considered, and offers progressive methods for daily effectiveness that anyone can master.

For a free catalog of books, videos, and tapes, or for information on Jeff's availability to speak to your group, check out the Breathing Space Institute Web page at: *http://www.brespace.com*. You also can e-mail Jeff directly at *jeff@brespace.com*, or send a fax to 919-932-9982.

Continuing Education

Intentional communities

http://www.well.com/user/cmty/index.html

Now that you're working on the Internet, do you still need to live in a major city and commute to work in a glass-walled high-rise tower? Intentional communities (see Figure 5-2) have for many centuries been places where idealists have come together to create a better world. There are thousands of intentional communities in existence today and many others in the formative stages. This Web site is increasing public awareness of existing and newly forming communities. It offers information and referrals for those who are actively seeking, or simply curious about, alternate lifestyles for themselves and their families.

Communities come in all shapes and sizes, and share many similar challenges—such as defining membership, succeeding financially, distributing resources, making decisions, raising children, dividing work equitably, and choosing a standard of living. Many wrestle with questions about right livelihood, spiritual expression, land use, and the role of service in our lives. At the same time, there is limited awareness of what others are doing to meet these challenges—and much to gain through sharing information and experiences with others exploring similar paths.

Cybermind

http://lm.com/~tellis/cyber/cm.html

Cybermind is devoted to an examination of "the new subjectivities that have emerged and might yet emerge" as we all explore the new frontier of cyberspace. The articles on this Web site discuss the philosophical, psychological/

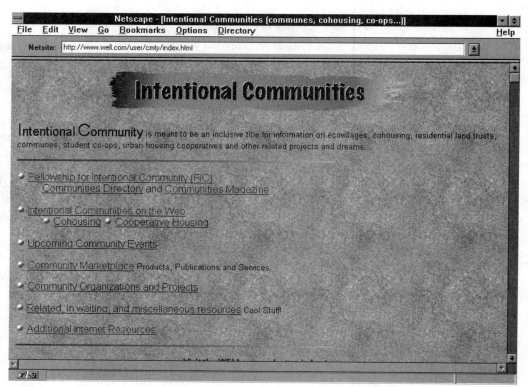

Figure 5-2

psychoanalytic, and social issues engendered by human presence in cyberspace, focusing particularly on their social impact on users.

Netsurf: the reading list

http://homepage.seas.upenn.edu/~mengwong/netsurf/contents.html

Here's a reading list of publications that can help you make sense of the onslaught of over-information brought to you by cyberspace. For example, one topic is titled "Social Psychology of Media Effects."

2001: A cyberspace odyssey

JEFF DAVIDSON, founder of the Breathing Space Institute says, "In ten or twelve years, give or take a few, smart homes with computers built into the walls—like those on *Star Trek*—will become affordable. Such computers will respond to voice commands, offer completely random-access to a global database, provide instant simulation through virtual-reality, and have the potential to free us to effectively use information, not be abused by it. We'll be able to check and cross-check information sources to help reduce the incidence of encountering misinformation."

Very soon the Internet will deliver full-motion video with stereo sound on a par with today's cable television systems. In fact, the distinction between your television, your cable system, your computer, your telephone, and the Internet will blur into a single image.

But what about today?

Today's Internet pioneers are creating tomorrow's cyberspace commodities. Your company may not survive—no, your industry may not even survive—if you wait to see how things develop. Compared to the near future, today's Internet is a telegraph system in the Wild West. Nonetheless, even the system in place today has some remarkable capabilities.

For example, today you can connect a free global video conference with up to eight users. The technology requires only a few hundred dollars of hardware, and Cornell University will give you software for free. So, if you've got a high speed Internet connection, you can begin videoconferencing right away using the CU-SeeMe system developed by Cornell University (CU).

The CU-SeeMe of 1995 sets up a black-and-white video conference with audio. The picture is a bit choppy, because the image is refreshed 12 times per second compared to the 30 times per second of regular television. The audio quality is good, except for potential signal degradation during Internet traffic jams (technical term: bandwidth limitations). Within a year or perhaps a couple of years, bandwidth problems will vanish, and full-color stereo-audio videoconferencing will become as commonplace as faxing is today.

What about the next couple of years?

We're going to give you a glimpse of what to expect within the next couple of years. We're not seers, but we've put our finger on the pulse of the industry and we'll do the best we can today to speculate on tomorrow. The best we can do is to help you to see beyond what cyberspace offers today, and to anticipate the trends so you can jump on them *before* they're a bandwagon.

A second thread in this chapter is a look at the "virtual corporation"—a company with headquarters in cyberspace—whose workers commute on the information superhighway. Today, prosperous national and international companies exist in which most workers have never seen each other, frequently have never spoken to each other, and perhaps never will. We'll give you a quick overview of how the virtual corporation works, and give you some Continuing Education information that will help you pick up business management tips on virtual corporations.

The cable connection

Until recently (January 1996), the fastest Internet lines in common use were 56-Kbps lines, which carry digital data at the rate of 56 kilobytes per second. If your company's Novell network is connected to the Internet, it likely is using a 56-Kbps line. But 56-Kbps lines are much more expensive than regular phone lines, at one point costing approximately $350 per month. The next generation of lines, called ISDN, now enable regular phone lines to carry data at 64 kilobytes per second (64-Kbps lines) and at 128 kilobytes per second (128-Kbps lines). ISDN lines offer speed increases with a substantial savings in connection fees—some are now as low as $30 per month; but the industry is changing rapidly, and you'll need to check current rates and capacities.

Unfortunately for ISDN, full-motion video with sound requires a transfer rate of about 10 megabytes per second—about 156 times what an ISDN line can deliver. The average office PC network, using common Ethernet technology, transfers data at 10 megabits per second. "Fast Ethernet" technology, which is becoming more common, has a transfer rate as high as 100 megabits per second. So, your present office network might be adequate if the Internet could provide data fast enough.

While some people are excited about ISDN, we got a different story from Jack Littely, vice president of BTG Incorporated. BTG—located in the high-tech mecca of Northern Virginia—is a major force in the emerging Internet industry (see Figure 6-1). Jack is a, well, let's say Jack is an Internet futurist. He believes that the Internet industry will blow right past ISDN lines to cable-television connections that will bring us sound, full-motion video, and world-wide full-color videoconferencing. It also will bring interactive systems and virtual reality to the Internet more quickly than you might suspect.

Cable TV connections will deliver digital data at the rate of approximately one gigabyte per second—far faster than what is demanded by full-motion video and

Figure 6-1

stereo sound. Cable TV connections will solve the Internet's current bandwidth problems that we mentioned in chapter 2, "Internet reality check."

When might you have a one-gigabyte Internet connection? We can't predict that with certainty, but consider these facts:

- Millions of homes already are wired for cable TV.
- Many Internet companies, including BTG, are cutting deals as this is written that will put the Internet on a channel of your current cable system.
- Cable modems—modems that will connect PCs to cable lines—cost today about the same as a premium 28.8 K modem.
- Cable modems will drop below the $300 level in 1996.
- Early software already is testing full, interactive Interneting methods.

Jack foresees cable TV lines bringing a major shift in the pricing structure for communication services. Today's communication lines use "bandwidth billing," which means that connections are priced on their ability to carry data—the more data, the higher the cost. But bandwidth very quickly is going to disappear as an issue and communications will switch to "content billing."

Let's look at an example that compares the two pricing concepts. On today's Internet, if you wanted to download a *Wall Street Journal* article, part of the fee you'd incur would go toward paying for the bandwidth resources required to deliver the article. But even if cable TV connections make bandwidth essentially free, there still is value in getting the article. Internet pricing may soon resemble the pricing of premium pay-per-view channels on cable TV—the cost of the connection will be insignificant, and you'll pay for what that connection brings.

Narrow-casting

Jack predicts that once the Internet has melded with cable television, we'll see the emergence of "narrow-casting." As opposed to broadcasting, narrowing-casting will bring tailored information into your home. This information tailoring will be done interactively, which means it will be done both on the receiving and on the sending ends of the system.

Information agents

Remember the last chapter: The Information Age is dead, and we're now being swamped by the Over-Information Age. With that in mind, here is some of the most comforting news about information technology that you've ever received. From the receiving end of the future's narrow-casting systems, you'll have some control over what enters the information pipeline into your home. Using technology called information agents, you'll be able to specify the information you want to receive and ignore the bulk of what's floating around out there in cyberspace.

Information agents will enable you to program your information system to gather information that interests you or that directly impacts your life. You no longer will face forced immersion into murder trials in far-away venues that have practically no impact on your life. Instead, your headlines could feature a new local regulation or a zoning plan that is poised to turn your life upside down.

Better yet, you actually will be able to create "good news" headlines that will start your day on an upbeat note. Later, after you've been heartened by reading about the positive events that are making your life more enjoyable, you can take a few minutes to brush up on the highlights of broader issues and—good or bad— you'll read them with a more optimistic perspective.

The ability to focus on what you choose to read and see and the ability to locate good news, if you want it, is one of the best features of the Internet today. In the very near future, these abilities will increase dramatically.

Tailored advertising and programming

The second aspect of narrow-casting is that the people who originate your information flow will have the ability to tailor what they send you. The benefits to you of this aspect of narrow-casting are not as clear as the benefits to you of your being able to tailor information. Narrow-casting is going to bring you advertising and programming that will have been selected for you based on how you fit into demographics patterns.

The Internet rapidly is becoming a two-way, interactive superhighway, and the agents on the other side are tracking your every move. If you cringe at the thought that a narrow-caster's computer will track your viewing and buying habits, it's too late. You already are being tracked. Your local cable company knows the shows you watch. Blockbuster knows the videos you rent. Your credit card companies know your buying habits. The Internet is going to give to all of these diverse organizations the ability to cross-reference you and bring you narrow-casting.

For an example, let's pick two people with diverse backgrounds who are watching the Super Bowl in their respective homes. Vonnie is an attorney who lives in Boston, loves a variety of sports, and is an avid skier. Charlie is a truck driver who lives in Tulsa, loves a variety of sports, and is an avid hunter. They both watch the same Super Bowl program, but during a commercial break, Vonnie sees ads about Saab automobiles pulling through snow banks, a Vermont ski resort, American Express's Gold Card, and international flavored coffee. During the same break, Charlie see ads touting Ford Thunderbirds that swept the last NASCAR season, an Oklahoma hunting lodge, VISA cards, and Budweiser beer.

Many of these ads will point the viewer to Internet sites for more information. Of course, if viewers "hit" a site, that too will be recorded and will contribute to further refining of the tailoring of the narrow-casting they'll receive in the future.

Layered information

The combination of cable television and the Internet can bring to nearly all advertising we watch a new depth that is slowly emerging on the Internet today. The ads that Vonnie and Charlie see during the Super Bowl feature "layered information" behind the glossy, quick-hitting ad that first appears.

Vonnie, for example, may perk up when she sees the Vermont ski ad and switch her system into the interactive Internet mode by clicking on the ad with her remote mouse. What will appear next will be quite similar to today's Internet Web sites. She'll be able to click on hypertext jumps for more information. She even will be able to check availability and prices, and make reservations. Sure, she may miss the next couple of ads, but those advertisers will get their share of interactive inquiries—if the ad is well-done, of course. Considering the length of some of the commercial breaks you've seen, Vonnie may be able to make her ski-trip reservation, forward the details via e-mail to her best friend, and click back to viewing mode without missing a single play.

Fortunately for us all, the Internet's capabilities extend well beyond commercial uses. The original usage envisioned for the Internet was more or less as a public service tool. That role will continue to be important and its value to all of us will expand. Let's consider how the Internet of the near future might provide some public services.

Easing the damage from natural disasters

The Internet's Byzantine connection structure features instant rerouting of communications that compensates for damaged connections. After all, it was designed to provide high-speed computer communication even after a global thermonuclear war had blown away large chunks. Natural disasters—compared to nuclear war—are hardly more than a sneeze to the Internet's redundant routing capability.

Someday the Internet will be an important factor in disaster response and recovery, lessening the suffering and trauma brought on by earthquakes, tornadoes, hurricanes and floods. Battery-operated notebook computers connected to the Internet via satellite uplink will ensure that damaged ground lines won't be a factor in helping disaster victims.

Disaster response

Once the Internet is fully developed, it will greatly enhance the abilities of disaster response managers. For example:

- Fewer people will be cut off during disasters from the rest of the world.
- Damage details will be disseminated more quickly and with more detailed accuracy.
- Lists of the needed emergency response personnel can be posted quickly and updated instantly as needs for new types of specialists are discovered.
- Lists of needed equipment and supplies can be posted so response teams will know what to bring. People in the disaster area might be able to search the Internet to locate equipment and supplies themselves.

Disaster recovery

The Internet will help disaster victims long after immediate survival needs are met. Hundreds and perhaps thousands of Web pages may spring up online to coordinate rebuilding efforts with available workers. The Internet will permit spontaneous emergence of temporary, multilevel consortiums to aid in disaster relief work (see Figure 6-2).

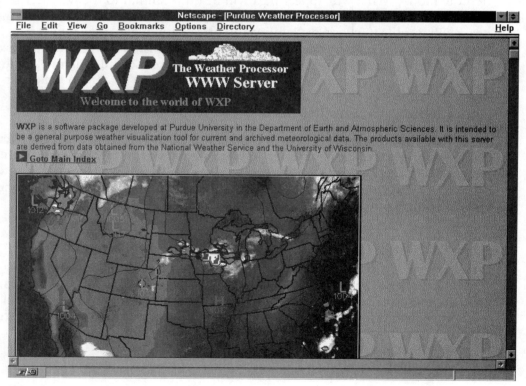

Figure 6-2

For example, a roofing company a thousand miles away might respond with word that it has extra roofers and materials, but that it can't spare the trucks with which to transport the men, equipment, and supplies. That posting could be read by a shipping company with idle trucks. With but a few minutes of online time, trucks could be on the way to pick up the needed relief help, workers would know to pack for a trip, and some company whose roof is lying in a farmer's field in the next county would know that they soon will be back in business.

While the Internet will help speed rebuilding programs, disasters always will bring disruption and inconvenience. During the rebuilding period, however, the Internet quickly will get schools back in session even if their building is destroyed. Long-distance learning will permit students to monitor—via Internet videoconferencing connections—classrooms in nearby jurisdictions that escaped damage. Students even could "attend" studies at home if their community had no buildings large enough to house classes.

None of these uses will require any special setup, either. For example, videoconferencing will be so commonplace that connecting to a distant school will require no more than standard interneting equipment.

Online education

Speaking of online education—don't wait for a disaster! Jack Littely says that his personal favorite hope for the Internet is that it someday will enable him to take a course at Harvard University—without leaving Virginia. Video-teleconferencing, large display screens, and interactive, multiwindowed environments soon will make the virtual classroom a serious learning tool that will be on par with "being there."

For example, if each student had a videoconferencing connection, the professor could see each student on a large multiwindowed monitor. Students also will be able to hear each other, and to see each other draw on the professor's screen. The advertising slogan used by Memorex tapes, "Is it live... or is it...?" may be elevated to a much loftier context. While the Internet soon may engender virtual universities, it already has brought us the virtual corporation.

The virtual corporation

For centuries, business practice has depended upon location: Interested parties were required to be in a common area. For example, during the Middle Ages, if the Vikings wanted to sack a town on the coast of Britain, they had to actually go to the location themselves to get the loot. The importance to business relationships of proximity declined with the advent of the Information Age.

And during the last few decades, as the railroad, airplane, telephone, fax machine, and computer technologies have been developed, commerce has been able to take place on an ever-larger, more effective scale. Businesses now may operate wherever is most convenient and economically feasible, working hand-in-hand with clients and branch offices located anywhere in the world. Nowadays, the Vikings can just call FedEx and have the loot delivered right to their door.

This is part of a natural progress toward being able to service more clients and customers more efficiently. The virtual corporation (see Figure 6-3) carries this progression another step farther by offering an increasingly broad range of services without the burden of recruiting and paying additional staff. Since the employees of virtual corporations do not need to sit behind a certain desk at a certain office in a certain city, they can do whatever they need to do, even maintain full-time employment at other professions. The capabilities of the Internet mean that no organization is limited to employing only what talent lives nearby, is unemployed, is willing to quit a current job, or is willing to relocate.

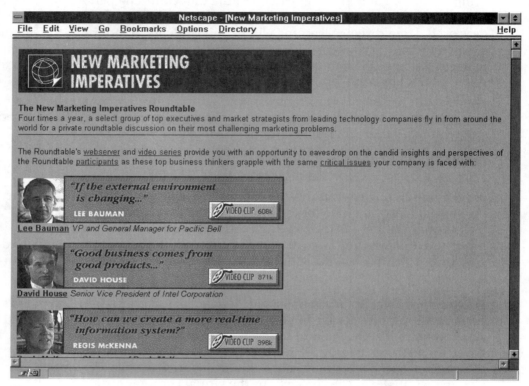

Figure 6-3

For example, from its main offices overlooking Lake Michigan, Round Table Group (RTG) uses the Internet to coordinate world-wide connections between staff scholars and clients. RTG was conceived by Russ Rosenzweig while a student at Northwestern University. Russ realized that he had instant access to the ideas and opinions of the world's most respected scholars, but that corporate leaders, policy makers, venture capitalists, and decision makers in general did not have the same access to information as the average college student.

Russ's solution was to bring together professors, decision makers, corporate leaders, and policy makers by creating a database of hundreds of professors spanning the breadth of the academic and professional disciplines, including economics, management, business, marketing, political science, international relations, government, sociology, criminal justice, and history. Individually, the Round Table Scholars are among the most respected and authoritative in their fields, publishing in prestigious journals, consulting for public and private firms, and teaching at more than 100 of the world's finest colleges and universities—Northwestern, Harvard, University of Chicago, Yale, Brown, Emory, Oxford, Cambridge, Cornell, the Universities of California, Georgetown, and Columbia among them.

Some RTG scholars are not university faculty, but nonetheless are noted experts in their fields. Because of their association with government agencies, law firms, management consultants, news media and other private corporations, RTG scholars are invaluable sources of current information and advice. Collectively, the RTG scholars comprise one of the most learned think-tanks ever assembled— except that they aren't assembled at all. Only a few years ago the RTG alliance would not have been possible, but in a few more years similarly constructed virtual organizations will be common.

But how do clients use a virtual corporation? Let's use RTG as an example.

Clients use the Internet to contact RTG with a query. RTG then contacts the professors with the relevant expertise who will produce a written report addressing the query. RTG charges the client a fee for the service and compensates its scholars. The fee is determined prior to the engagement, and is based on the client's response-time needs—one to ten business days—and the nature and length of the query. Thus, by spending but a few minutes online, anyone can quickly receive a tailored report on nearly any topic.

Using virtual corporation techniques will enable your organization to select highly qualified and experienced personnel for projects of all sizes with no geographic limitations. Airline fares, hotel and meal expenses, and research and project costs are minimized by the lack of administrational bureaucracy found in large organizations. Also, a project team is able to produce work much more rapidly than if diverse schedules had to be juggled to get a team assembled at the same time at one site.

A vast array of management problems dissolve when a virtual corporate structure is employed. Travel and vacation schedules may have little impact on a project, because team members can work anywhere in the world. Sick leave, disabled workers, and working around the school schedules of the children of your employees may no longer present barriers to completing projects.

In short, the very near future will bring dramatic changes to the basic structure of your organization. To remain competitive and efficient, you will need to read more about virtual corporations, and you will need to use all of the Internet skills you'll acquire in the next phase of this book. To reiterate the opening sentence of this book: Your timing is perfect. So, jump into cyberspace with us now and learn how to enjoyably and productivity use the Internet.

 *Continuing Education*

The Virtual Corporation

http://www.siva.com/nmi/nmdavidow.html

"Modular, flexible, committed to total quality management and hyper-responsive to customers' needs through the most advanced electronic communications media." That's the organization of the future as described in the book *The Virtual Corporation* by Silicon Valley's Bill Davidow and Mike Malone. This site includes a biographical sketch and a video clip of one of the book's authors, Bill Davidow.

Real Audio™

http://www.realaudio.com

RealAudio Server delivers "Audio on Demand" through the Internet to a RealAudio Player. The system permits continuous audio playback over just about any connection, including a 14.4-Kbps modem with standard phone lines. Organizations of all kinds can use the RealAudio Server to deliver audio programming in real-time over the internet. You can use the RealAudio Server to enhance your existing Website with RealAudio programming for marketing, commercial, entertainment, and educational purposes.

CEST-WEB

http://www.demon.co.uk/cest/welcome.html

CEST-WEB is a corporate service designed to deliver consulting services and support for consultant members. New members are welcome to apply for membership of the network, which is designed to provide the facilities, contacts, and support to generate new business in Europe. CEST-WEB should be able to help you make business sense out of the dramatic changes that Europe faces, so that you can plan an Internet strategy to serve the opportunities that are arising out of those changes.

Round Table Group

http://www.history.rochester.edu:80/rtg/

Round Table Group Incorporated (RTG) is a virtual corporation that matches corporate leaders and policy-makers with scholars and experts by maintaining a database of the world's foremost professors. RTG will market the collective wisdom of this expert community, contact relevant Round Table Scholars with a client's questions, and transmit the short replies to the client, making a prearranged payment to the scholars.

The Year 2000 Information Center

http://arganet.tenagra.com/cgi-bin/clock.cgi

Here's an entire Web site devoted to the issues related to our transition into the next century. Computer system accuracy may be particularly affected by faulty programming logic that will not adequately handle twenty-first century dates. Check out the link to "The Year 2000 Issues List."

EMS Consulting Services

http://www.wdn.com/ems

Eric Engelmann, one of this book's co-authors, is the president and founder of EMS Consulting Services, based in Olney, Maryland. EMS is a virtual corporation that provides Internet services and produces CD-ROM packages. Eric has several members of his organization whom he has never seen and one with whom he has never even spoken on the phone. Yet, the company runs smoothly despite its members being scattered across the country.

Future directions

http://homepage.seas.upenn.edu/~mengwong/netsurf/

Under the home page entitled, "Netsurf: the Discussion Seminars," you'll find this link (Future Directions) to publications that can help you sort out and prepare for the changes that cyberspace will bring to your life.

PHASE 2
Hands On

IN PHASE 2, "Hands On," we hope to transform the way you regard yourself as a computer user. You work in a high-performance world and you have a high-performance computer running high-performance software. To keep up, you need to be a high-performance, expert computer user.

To achieve high productivity on the Internet, users need what we call the "advanced basics" of Windows. In our training experience, we have encountered few Windows users who have been exposed to the Windows features that enable them to work at maximum efficiency. Learning the features in these lessons will give you the edge you need to be an expert computer user with any Windows application.

Anyone can be an expert computer user

Becoming an expert computer user is not about intelligence or about computer knowledge. You don't need a knack for technical genius. You need an aggressive attitude, a desire to excel, and a frame of mind that sees your computer as a powerful business tool that enables you to express yourself in innovative ways that have never before been available.

An expert computer user can perform on-the-job miracles and enjoys enormous productivity advantages over a casual computer user. An expert user can tap into the knowledge base of the world, transfer information into his or her system, and use it productively. An expert user quickly can move text and graphics between a word processor, a drawing package, a spreadsheet, or an Internet resource tool. An expert user can quickly and accurately create large or complex documents. An expert user can instantly begin using the basic functions within a new software package without extensive training.

You can't spare the time to skip the Windows lesson

Few computer users are expert users, however, because most believe that their busy work schedules do not include the time required to become an expert user. We've seen all types of computer users working at all types of jobs and our observations have convinced us that the opposite is true. Anyone with a busy work schedule *cannot spare the time to remain a casual user*. The tighter your work schedule, the more you need to be an expert user.

Expert computer user versus computer expert

You don't need nuts-and-bolts computer expertise. An expert computer user turns the machine into a powerful productivity tool after the computer technican is through. It's similar to the difference between a race car driver and a race car mechanic. Technical computer work is a full-time job and you have a different full-time job: You're a high-performance computer driver.

Few computer users are high-performance; most do the equivalent of driving race-tuned Ferraris on mundane around-town errands. Your job is to take a race-tuned computer out on the fast-track of the information superhighway and extract the maximum performance from the equipment that your company has provided for you.

High-performance computing

You can extract maximum performance only if you understand how to use all the controls in your high-performance machine. Software provides those controls. For most Internet users that software is based on Microsoft Windows; hence these lessons will be based on Windows.

The principles of extracting maximum performance from a PC are the same, however, for Windows, OS/2, or Macintoshes. The key principle is having a frame of mind that drives you to learn to aggressively use the power levers that tap into the hidden power of your PC. While the controls appear different on the dashboard of a Macintosh or an OS/2 machine, the functions of all three of the major graphical-user-interface (GUI) operating systems are the same.

The wonderful thing about Windows, OS/2, and Macintoshes is that they have standardized controls within all software that runs under them. If you fully understand how to use all the controls on any of these operating systems, you'll quickly become a high-performance, expert computer user. So let's get started.

Windows wide open— advanced basics

THIS FIRST Hands On lesson will be the foundation of everything else you'll do on the Internet. When touring cyberspace, you will encounter a potentially bewildering assortment of windows all over your screen. To be highly productive, you're going to need to be able to quickly and easily transfer information between any two windows.

If you don't know the principles in this lesson, you may constantly be scribbling notes on the side and doing a lot of retyping. We've seen many people do that. With the expertise this lesson can give you, however, you may never need to retype anything that you can see on your screen.

Windows wide-open

Have you noticed that race cars have their windows wide open all the time? It helps the drivers be intimately engaged with their cars. They can hear and even feel every sound. They can hear the tires biting into the track in the corners. A driver with closed windows would not have the same performance abilities as a driver with open windows. A lot of information comes through those open windows. A lot of information can come through *your* Windows if you really open them up.

To keep up with the speed of the information superhighway, you need to run with your Windows wide-open and enjoy full contact with (and control over) your computer. We'll help you think of Windows controls and techniques generically. When you regard them as general principles that apply to all the Windows software you use, you'll be ready for anything.

Simplifying your computer work

Windows has made the controls in software similar to the controls in cars. You probably have rented cars and have noticed that while the controls vary a bit from one car to the next, the basic functions remain common. When you rent a car, do you look for the common controls? The heater controls in a rental car are not exactly the same as the ones in your car, but you know that you'll find controls that adjust the temperature, select heat, defrost, or vent, and select a fan speed.

Windows has a term for this principle. It's called Common User Access (CUA). CUA is the principle under which all Windows programs provide common user access by using common user controls. You can be an expert Windows user only if you know how to use the Common User Access controls.

Apply to your Windows software the principle of operating its common controls and you will be an expert Windows user. When using Windows software, focus on the commonality, not on the differences.

Ergonomics common sense

The Internet can be a hassle. It can frazzle your nerves. But we've discovered some helpful tips that can enable you to maintain your high productivity standards and finish even a long workday less hassled and frazzled than you might expect. Check out Appendix B. It's a treasure trove of valuable tips that will help you with relaxing, stretching, and saving your eyesight as you spend increasingly longer periods of time attached to a PC.

In this lesson we are going to cover what we call "advanced basics." We will cover features that we consider to be basic, but that we find often have been overlooked. We regard them as important productivity-enhancing features. Some people have used Windows for years without knowing these advanced basics. They have paid—usually many times over—for the time it would have taken to learn the features when they first learned Windows.

Window types

You and your computer communicate constantly. You communicate what you want, the computer tells you what it's doing. When you use Windows, all communications with your computer pass through a window. There are three basic types: Application Windows, Document Windows, and Dialog Boxes. For this lesson, start Windows on your computer. We'll begin with the Program Manager.

Application window

Every application runs inside its own window. The Program Manager is an example of an application. The easiest way to identify an applications window is by the size of the hyphen in the control-menu box in the upper-left corner. Application windows have a large hyphen in the control-menu box (see the mouse arrow in Figure 7-1).

Most application windows can cover your entire screen. There are exceptions, but remember, we are focusing on common principles.

All application windows can be closed by pressing ALT+F4 or by double-clicking on the large hyphen. Shortly, we'll show you how to access a list of all of your

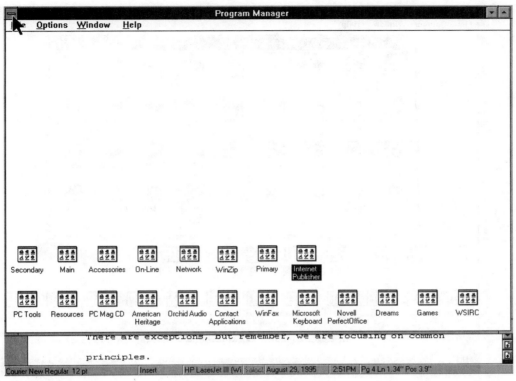

Figure 7-1

open applications windows and give you a variety of ways to switch between them, enabling you to easily run multiple applications.

Document window

A lot of applications have windows within them that are called document windows, though they are not always for documents. Spreadsheet applications use document windows for individual spreadsheets. The Windows file manager uses document windows to simultaneously display files on multiple disk drives. Internet e-mail applications such as Eudora use document windows for their In box, Out box, Trash, etc. The Program Manager is a good example itself: groups of application icons reside within document windows.

The hyphen in the control-menu box of a document window is much smaller than the hyphen in an application window. Document windows cannot cover the entire screen. They are limited to filling the maximum amount of screen space being used by their parent application window. Document windows can be closed by pressing CTRL+F4 or by double-clicking on the small hyphen (see the mouse arrow in Figure 7-2).

If an application uses document windows, it lists them on the menu bar under the Window menu item. You can use this list to switch to any document window within the current application window. Using this list makes it impossible to ever again "lose" a window, because even if you cannot see the window, its title will be listed under the Window menu item.

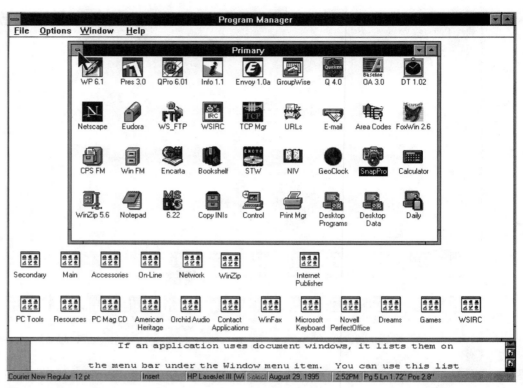

Figure 7-2

Hands On

Objective: **Activate a window.**

❑ Click **Window** on your Program Manager. Click any window on the list that you cannot see open. It will open.

> This menu only can display nine documents at once. If your application has more than nine document windows, the last item on this list will be "More Windows...," and it will list the ones you don't see on this menu.

Dialog boxes

Dialog boxes look much like application windows and document windows but they behave quite differently. Dialog boxes are activated within an application window to let you input instructions to your computer. You cannot switch between dialog boxes as you can with application or document windows. They are used one-at-a-time only—but there are exceptions, of course.

Few dialog boxes have all of the standard windows controls. Still, usually it is easy to understand how to handle them once you know the basics and learn to focus on commonality and not on the differences.

We'll give you four simple dialog box techniques that are easy to learn and that can increase productivity, yet are overlooked by legions of experienced Windows users. The first lesson is for dialog boxes that have text entry boxes (see Figure 7-3).

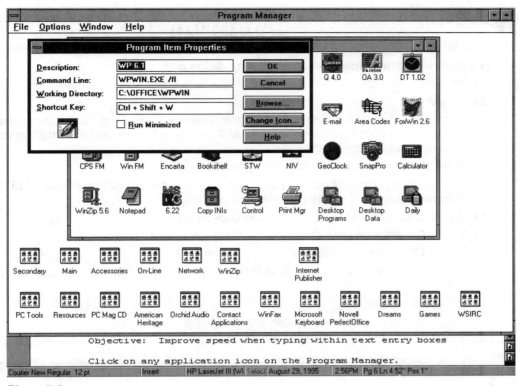

Figure 7-3

Hands On

***Objective:* Improve speed when typing within text entry boxes.**

❏ Click on any application icon on the Program Manager.

Remember the title shown under this icon.

❏ Press **ALT+ENTER**.

The highlighted text on the top line means that your cursor is on that line. Also, you're in a special, momentary state that will behave differently depending on your next keystroke. Don't waste your time using the mouse to position your cursor when you see this state, the cursor already is in the text entry box.

❏ Press **END**.

The highlight will disappear and you can edit the existing text. (Actually, any cursor movement key would have "set" the text in this box.)

❏ Press **ENTER**.

❏ Press **ALT+ENTER**.

Again, don't waste time using the mouse because the first non-cursor-movement keystroke clears the text box.

❏ Type the original title.

❏ Press **ENTER**.

The next two lessons will enable you to make dialog box selections more quickly using the keyboard instead of the mouse.

Hands On

Objective: Improve speed when using any dialog box.

❑ Press **ALT+ENTER**.

❑ Press **ALT+I**.

The letter "I" on the Change Icon button is underlined. When you see an underlined letter on a button label, you can press **ALT** plus the letter instead of interrupting your workflow by picking up the mouse.

❑ Press **ENTER** twice to return to the Program Manager.

If the dialog box does not have any text boxes, you don't need to hold down **ALT** to activate a button. Let's demonstrate that principle.

❑ Open the Accessories group and double-click on Notepad.

❑ Press **F5** to enter the date and time.

❑ Press **ALT+F4** to close Notepad.

You will be asked if you want to save the changes. Again, spare yourself picking up the mouse.

❑ Press **N** to say No.

You will exit Notepad immediately without saving.

❑ Minimize the Accessories group.

Hands On

Objective: Quickly jump to a specific, known listing.

❑ Open the Main group by pressing **ALT+W**, then press the number on the line that says Main.

❑ Use your arrow keys to highlight Control Panel.

❑ Press **ENTER**.

❑ Use your arrow keys to highlight International (see Figure 7-4).

❑ Press **ENTER**.

Notice that Country is highlighted.

❑ Press **S**.

Notice that the list jumps to South Korea.

❑ Press **S** repeatedly and check the list each time.

You will scroll through all the countries that begin with "s." Most users make changes on lists such as this one by using the mouse to click on the drop arrow at the end of the list, and then using the scroll arrows to slowly scroll through the entire list to the desired entry. They click on it, then they move their mouse pointer over and click on OK. Whew!

❑ Press **U**

The list will jump to United Kingdom.

❑ Press **U**

The list will jump to United States.

❑ Press **ENTER** to close the dialog box.

❑ Press **ALT+F4** to close the Control Panel.

Hands On

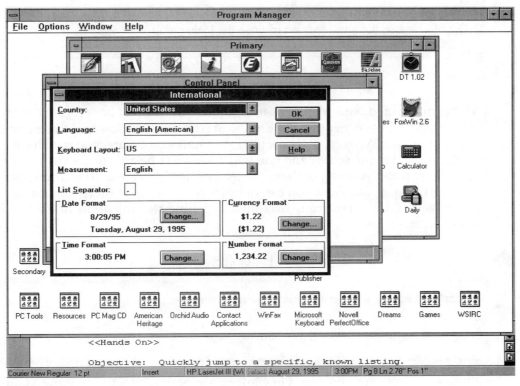

Figure 7-4

Using keystrokes is not always faster than using the mouse. When you already have the mouse in hand you may save time by continuing to use it. Still, you can go faster than the average user even with the mouse if you know the right techniques. Let's see a demonstration.

Hands On

***Objective:* Quickly jump to the general area of desired listing.**

❑ Double-click on the **Control Panel** icon.

❑ Double-click on the **International** icon.

❑ Click on the drop-arrow at the end of the **Country** list box.

Now, let's scroll down to Mexico, but instead of using the scroll arrows to slowly move through the list we'll jump quickly to the general area of Mexico on the list. We know that "M" is in the middle of the alphabet, so...

❑ Drag the scroll box to the middle of the scroll bar.

This is only a short list, but we've seen many users waste a lot of time tediously using the scroll arrows to scroll through long lists when they could have used the scroll box to quickly jump to the approximate alphabetic location. On the Internet, you're likely to see scores of long lists, so this technique may save you lots of time.

❑ Drag the scroll box to the bottom of the scroll bar.

❑ Click on **United States**.

❑ Click on **OK**.

❑ Double-click on the large hyphen to close the Control Panel.

❑ Double-click on the small hyphen to close the Main group.

Window controls

When you learned basic Windows techniques, you learned how to use the arrows in the upper-right corner of a window to maximize a window and to restore it to its previous size. When you get deeply into Internet software, you may have windows all over the screen and you will not always be able to see the maximize and restore buttons on all of them. Instead of dragging a window around to bring its buttons into view, you can double-click anywhere on its title bar to maximize it. Or, if it is already maximized, double-clicking on its title bar will restore it.

Hands On

Objective: Learn a shortcut to maximizing a window.

❑ Double-click Main again to open it.

❑ Double-click anywhere along its title bar to maximize it.

While we're here, let's go over a few important points.   Notice that the Main group covers all of your other groups. This state often happens accidentally when users inadvertently double-click on a title bar. At this point, they fear they've wiped out all of their other groups and damaged their system. Clients have called and asked us to come over and reinstall Windows because everything has disappeared. But that won't happen to you once you've completed this next lesson.

Hands On

Objective: Learn how to switch document windows.

❑ Click on **Window**.

❑ Click on any window other than the one that is checked.

❑ Click on **Window**.

❑ Click on **Main**.

None of the other groups were gone, they just were hidden by one maximized document window. Even in this state, you still have full access to every group. While we're in this state, let's make one more important observation. Notice the title bar no longer says "Program Manager." It now says "Program Manager - [Main]." That's because a document window can never fill the screen. A maximized document window can go no further than its parent application window, so it must share the title bar with its parent application window.

Look for this state when you're experimenting with new applications or when it seems that you've lost something. If you see two titles on the title bar, here's the interpretation:

⊛ The first title is the application window title.

⊛ The second title—in square brackets—is a maximized document window.

If any document windows seem to be missing, they simply are being covered by this one maximized document window. Now let's see a couple of quick ways to make all of your document windows appear.

Hands On

Objective: **Learn to use Cascade and Tile to find "lost" windows.**

❑ Click **Window**, **Tile** to Tile the document windows.

❑ Click **Window**, **Cascade** to Cascade the document windows.

❑ Press **ALT+W**, then press **T** to Tile the document windows.

❑ Press **ALT+W**, then press **C** to Cascade the document windows.

❑ Press **SHIFT+F4** to Tile the document windows.

❑ Press **SHIFT+F5** to Cascade the document windows.

Every open document window now has been neatly cascaded down from the top of the application window and all minimized document windows have been arranged at the bottom of the application window. These principles often are essential to successfully using Internet applications.

Whenever anything seems to be missing, click Window, Cascade (or press SHIFT+F5) and you'll get your bearings again.

Miscellaneous keystrokes

Here are a few keystroke tidbits that can help speed your work in Windows and sometimes bail you out when you believe you need to reboot your computer because Windows has frozen.

The **ENTER** key

On most dialog boxes pressing ENTER is the same as clicking on the highlighted button. We can't tell you how many times we've watched users who pop up a dialog box that needs a single line of text entry, then pick up the mouse to click in the box (when the cursor already is in place), then put down the mouse, then type the text, then stop, pick up the mouse, move the pointer over to a button that already is highlighted and then click. Spare yourself the agony: usually you merely need to type the line and hit ENTER!

Of course you've got to make sure that the highlighted button represents the action you want to take, but it almost always does.

There are exceptions, of course. Some text boxes allow multiple line entries. In many of these, pressing ENTER will start a new line of text. The basic principles still apply, though, because if you'll notice carefully, you'll see that there are *no* highlighted buttons on this type of dialog box. Thus, pressing ENTER can't activate a highlighted button because there isn't one.

Some multiline text boxes use another key to make new lines, such as CTRL+ENTER. Your clue will be to check whether or not any dialog box button is highlighted. If one is, then pressing ENTER *will* be the same as clicking on that highlighted button, and you'll have to find out what other key is used to create new lines in the text entry box within the dialog.

The **TAB** key

Closely related to the current subject, the TAB key can save you a lot of time. TAB moves the focus within a dialog box from item to item. It's much faster than using the mouse. We'll show you a quick example, but you'll see it's something that will be a major benefit within large dialog boxes that have more entries than we'll use in this exercise.

Hands On

Objective: **Learn to speed your work using TAB.**

❑ Open any group on the Program Manager.

❑ Press **ALT+F**.

❑ Press **ENTER** twice.

> This dialog box will let you add a new application to the Program Manager. We'll add one, then delete it. First, notice that the cursor is in the top text box.

❑ Type *solitaire*

❑ Press **TAB**.

❑ Type *sol.exe*

❑ Press **ENTER**.

That was quick, wasn't it? Your hands never left the keyboard.

Millions of users would have picked up the mouse and clicked in the first text box, typed *solitaire*, then stopped typing, picked up the mouse, moved it over the second text box and clicked, then put down the mouse and typed *sol.exe*, then stopped typing, then picked up the mouse and moved it over and clicked on OK. You're going to fill in lots of forms on the Internet and you can blaze through them if you'll type, press TAB, type again, press TAB, type again, press TAB, then press ENTER when you're done. Avoid the mouse when completing forms.

One more note. Using SHIFT+TAB will cycle backward through the available items on a dialog box in case you need to return to a previous entry.

A final quick lesson while we're here.

Objective: **Learn how to delete an application icon.**

❏ Make sure the Solitaire icon still is highlighted.

❏ Press **DELETE** to delete the icon.

❏ Press **ENTER** to confirm the deletion.

> This only deletes the icon. The application itself still occupies space on your hard disk.

The **ALT** key

We already have shown you how to activate menu items by holding down ALT and pressing the underlined letter. But ALT has a broader effect than that. Pressing ALT always activates the menu system, whether or not you press a letter while holding it down. You can tap and release either ALT key, then press any underlined menu letter.

This is a critical property of Windows to remember. Most likely, you often will tap an ALT key by mistake. Many users who did not know this principle have rebooted their systems after inadvertently pressing an ALT key. Try it yourself, using the Program Manager.

Objective: **Learn to activate the Windows menu system.**

❏ Start at the Program Manager.

❏ Press and release either **ALT** key.

❏ Type **X**.

> Your computer will beep. Notice that **File** on the menu bar is highlighted. At this point almost every key except for the underlined letters (**F,O,W,H**) and the **SPACE BAR** will cause the computer to beep. Watch for this condition; your computer does not need to be rebooted. You merely need the next step.

❏ Press **ALT** again to deactivate the menu system.

The **ALT+PRINTSCREEN** key

You quickly can copy all of the contents of any active window into your clipboard. This sometimes is a great help when you find something on the Internet that you want to transfer to your word processor. Let's do a quick demonstration, again using the Program Manager.

Hands On

Objective: **Learn to capture the image of an entire screen.**

❏ Open your Accessories group.

❏ Double-click on **Write**.

❏ Type your name.

❏ Press **ALT+F4** to exit.

❏ Press **ALT+PRINTSCREEN**.

This keystroke captures the image of the active dialog box.

❏ Press **ESC** to cancel the exit process.

❏ Press **CTRL+V** to paste the image you captured.

You may find countless uses for this as you surf the Net. It can be a wonderful tool. Of course if you don't have a small window active, then this keystroke will capture the entire screen.

❏ Press **ALT+F4** again to exit.

❏ Press **N** to confirm you don't want to save.

Switching windows

This lesson will make sure you know how to use the full power of Windows. Remember, Windows is plural. You can have a lot of them open at once, but you only can work with one at a time so you need to know how to switch between them to activate the one you want. The techniques are different for switching between document windows and application windows.

Switching document windows

You already have seen this principle, so this will be only a reminder. Remember, document windows have small hyphens in the upper-left corner and only can exist under the control of an applications window. If your application window can support multiple windows, it will have Window on the menu bar. Here's a summary of some of the methods you can use to switch document (small hyphen) windows:

- Click on any visible document window.
- Click Window, then the name of the window you want.
- Click Window, Cascade.
- Click Window, Tile.
- Press SHIFT+F5 to Cascade.
- Press SHIFT+F4 to Tile.
- Press ALT+HYPHEN, then press T to cycle to the next available document window.
- Press CTRL+F6 to cycle through available document windows.
- Press ALT+W, then press the number of the window you want.

Switching application windows

Here are the key principles to truly becoming a Windows expert. Without them, you don't have a chance of keeping up with the Internet. First, let's start several applications so you can practice using these methods.

Hands On

Objective: **Learn to switch between open Windows applications.**

❑ Use the Accessories group that is still open from the last lesson.

❑ Double-click on **Write**.

❑ Click on any blank space on the Program Manager.

❑ Double-click on **Calculator**.

❑ Click on any blank space on the Program Manager.

❑ Double-click on **Paintbrush**.

❑ Click on any blank space on the Program Manager.

❑ Double-click on **Clock**.

> You have five applications open and now we'll switch back and forth between them.

❑ Press **CTRL+ESC**.

> This opens the Task List that shows every active application (see Figure 7-5).

❑ Double-click on **Write**.

❑ Press **CTRL+ESC**.

❑ Press **DOWN ARROW** until you highlight Paintbrush.

❑ Press **ENTER** to switch to Paintbrush.

❑ Press **CTRL+ESC**.

❑ Click on **Clock**.

❑ Click on **Switch To**.

❑ Hold down either **ALT** key.

❑ Keep holding down **ALT** while pressing **TAB**.

> Use this **ALT+TAB** method until an application you want appears in the window in the middle of the screen, then release **ALT**. Pressing **ALT+TAB** once returns you to your last application; thus you can use **ALT+TAB** to jump back-and-forth between your Web browser and your word processor.

Now we'll summarize the methods you can use to switch application (large hyphen) windows. Most were covered in the exercise, but there are others you may want to test. Choose whichever method you prefer. Here's the summary:

◉ Click on any visible application window to make it active.

◉ Press CTRL+ESC, then double-click the desired application. Or, you can use your DOWN ARROW to cursor down to the desired application, then press ENTER.

◉ Use ALT+TAB to cycle through all open applications and release ALT when the desired application appears.

◉ Double-click anywhere on your Windows desktop to pop up the Task List, then double-click the desired application. This only is possible, however, if the

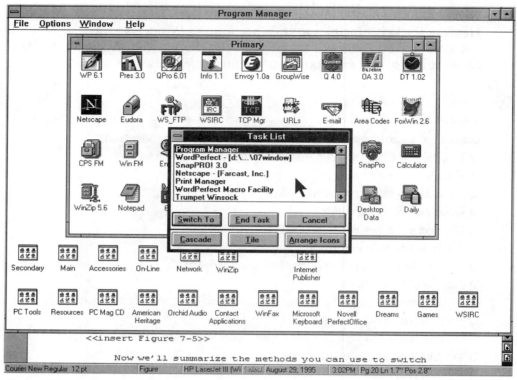

Figure 7-5

current application is not maximized and the desktop is visible behind the Program Manager.

- Press ALT+ESC to cycle between all open applications. This is not as direct as CTRL+ESC or ALT+TAB, and you may have to cycle through a lot of windows to get to the one you want.
- Press ALT+SPACE, then press W, then use DOWN ARROW to highlight the desired application and press ENTER.
- Click the large hyphen, click Switch To..., double-click the desired application.

Task manager icon (optional exercise)

If you are hooked on using the mouse, you may want to add an icon for the Task List so that you can pop it up quickly with the mouse. It's easy to add and can be a time-saver.

Hands On

Objective: Add a Task List icon to your program manager.

❑ Activate the group in which you'd like to add the Task List icon.

❑ Press **ALT+F**, press **ENTER** twice.

❑ Type *Task List*.

❑ Press **TAB**.

❑ Type *taskman.exe.*

❑ Press **ALT+I** for Change Icon.

❑ Press **ENTER** for OK.

❑ Press **TAB** to jump to the icon windows on the Change Icon dialog box.

❑ Press **RIGHT ARROW** 15 times to highlight the film director's slate.

❑ Press **ENTER** twice.

Window-switching exceptions

As you might expect, there are exceptions to the methods we've shown here for switching between windows. A popular example is Novell's top-selling networking application Groupwise.

Groupwise's application window has, as you'd expect, a large hyphen in its control-menu box. It also has Window on its menu bar. So, you would expect that each of the features you activate, such as a Mail or Calendar, would appear in document (small hyphen) windows. But here's the exception: each feature under the Groupwise application window actually is a separate application and runs in its own application (large hyphen) window. Yet, you can use Window to switch between these different Groupwise applications.

That's something that you only would expect to be able to do using application-switching techniques such as CTRL+ESC or ALT+TAB. Of course those keystrokes do work and you can use them in addition to the Window menu item. If you run Groupwise (and a lot of other networking and Internet applications as well) without understanding the difference between small hyphen windows and large hyphen windows, you may get highly frustrated.

Document window
exception (optional exercise)

If you can't do the following exercise now, keep these principles in mind, because you will encounter windows that do not behave normally. Knowing these principles will keep you from being stymied by oddly behaved windows.

Hands On

Objective: **To see an application window that you might expect to be a document window.**

❑ Start Netscape.

❑ Click **Bookmarks, View Bookmarks...**

  Note that this window has a large hyphen, even though you might have expected it to be a document window with a small hyphen. This is an exception. Let's see more.

❑ Press **CTRL+ESC**.

  We've told you that all windows with large hyphens will appear on this list. You can see that the "Netscape Bookmarks" window is not on this list. Nonetheless, when we go back to Netscape and close this window, we'll use application window commands to do so.

❑ Press **ESC** to clear the Task List from the screen.

❑ Click the large hyphen on the "Netscape Bookmarks" window.

Note that the keystroke to close it is **ALT+F4** and not **CTRL+F4**. So, even though this window was not on the Task List, it still closes with the application window command.

❑ Click close.

❑ Press **ALT+F4** to close Netscape.

Boosting your productivity

We've shown you how to quickly switch between document windows, but quick-switching methods are no match for not having to switch at all. So now we're going to help you set up your Windows for maximum productivity. A major factor in making Windows productive is to group the icons you use most frequently in a single group on the Program Manager. Once you've created this new group window, you'll keep all other group windows minimized, because you rarely will need them. Here's an example of a well-structured primary group (see Figure 7-6).

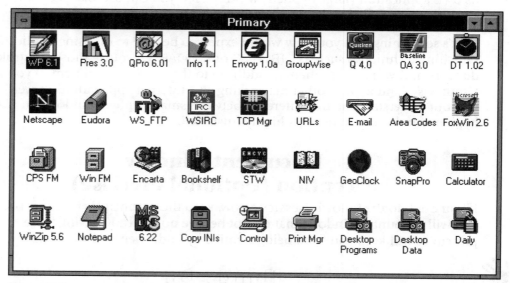

Figure 7-6

Create a primary group

Follow these steps to create your Primary group on the Program Manager. Most users find this group to be a tremendous productivity enhancement.

Hands On

Objective: **Add a primary group to your Program Manager.**
❏ Press **ALT+F** and press **ENTER**.
❏ Press **G** and press **ENTER**.
❏ Type *Primary* and press **ENTER**.
    You now have created a new group window.

The example shown here is running in Windows 3.11 with a screen resolution of 800×600. If you have a different resolution, you'll get a different number of icons on each row. For more information about screen resolutions, check out the sidebar.

You can get more icons inside each group if you'll change the icon spacing within Windows.

Hands On

Objective: **Get more icons in a group by changing icon spacing.**
❏ Open the Main group.
❏ Double-click **Control Panel**, double-click **Desktop**.
❏ Click on the arrows for **Icons Spacing** to decrease the spacing.
    The example pictured here uses 63 pixels to get 10 icons per row and 30 icons in a Cascaded window with a resolution of 800x600. Using 58 pixels with this resolution will give you 11 icons per row and 33 icons. If you use a different resolution, you'll need to experiment to find the Icon Spacing settings that will give you an extra icon on each row.
❏ Click **OK**.
❏ Double-click the large hyphen on **Control Panel**.
❏ Minimize the Main group (or double-click its small hyphen).

Windows screen resolutions

The example of a Primary group shown here uses a screen resolution of 800×600 pixels. Pixels are dots on the screen. As the number of pixels in your resolution increases, the image quality improves and you can get more information on your screen. There are, however, two trade-offs.

First, if the resolution gets too high, the text and icons will be too small to use. The ideal solution to that problem is to get one of the new 21" monitors. Because a 21" monitor alone costs more than an entire PC with a 15" monitor, few people have them. You probably won't want to go above 640×480 on a 14" monitor. Most people are happy with 800×600 on a 15" or 17" monitor. With a 17" monitor, you may even go up to 1024×768. The highest resolution in common use today, 1280×1024, makes the text too small for most users on any monitor that is smaller than 19".

The second trade-off against the joys of increasing screen resolution is a penalty in computer memory. The high resolutions require lots of memory and can render some systems inoperable. We've found that 800×600 is a good balance between resolution, readability, and memory usage.

Add your productivity icons

Now that your Primary group has been created and you've adjusted the Icon Spacing setting, it's time to add your most frequently used icons. Having the right icons in one Primary group has proven for many users to provide a dramatic increase in daily productivity. Using the Internet aggressively will have you running lots of multiple applications, so you'll want them available for speedy access. Adding icons to your Primary group won't be any harder than playing Solitaire, so let's do it.

Hands On

***Objective:* Add your best productivity-enhancing icons to your Primary group.**

❑ Open the group that contains your word processor. You only need one icon in this group, so we'll copy that one to Primary.

❑ Hold down a **CTRL** key, then drag and drop your word processor's icon to your Primary group.

❑ Minimize your word processor group.

❑ Open the group that contains your Internet icons. You may need several of these.

❑ Use the drag and drop method with the **CTRL** key to copy your frequently used icons into Primary. As a minimum you will want your primary Internet connection icon (Netscape, for example) and your e-mail icon (Eudora, for example).

Look at the example pictured earlier for ideas about which icons to include in your Primary group. Here are a few suggestions:

◉ From the Main group: MS-DOS Prompt, File Manager, Print Manager, Control Panel.

◉ From the Accessories group: Calculator, Notepad.

◉ Others: Word processor, Netscape, Eudora, Usenet reader, Network e-mail, Calendar/Scheduler, Contact Manager, Spreadsheet, Graphics Drawing Package, Database Application, File viewer, Backup program.

When all of your Primary applications are in one group window, you won't waste time hunting down the right group and locating the right icon and dragging and arranging a lot of windows. When you use ALT+TAB to return to the Program Manager, you'll be able to quickly use your cursor arrow keys to highlight a new application in your Primary group and then simply hit ENTER to start it.

You may find that you have a second tier of applications that you need regularly, but not daily. If so, create a group entitled "Secondary" and copy the icons you want into that new group. You probably will keep Secondary minimized or cascaded behind Primary.

Now let's save your new setup.

Saving your Windows setup

Click File in your Windows 3.x Program Manager, and we'll point out a glaring omission. There is no Save command to save your desktop layout. You can, however, save your latest Program Manager layout by completing this lesson.

Hands On

Objective: Learn how to save a desktop layout in Windows 3.x.

❑ Minimize every window except for your Primary group.

❑ Press **SHIFT+F5** to Cascade.

❑ Press **ALT+O** for Options.

❑ If "Save Settings on Exit" checked, press **S**.

   You do not want this checked, so if it is NOT now checked, press **ALT** to dismiss the Options menu without making any changes.

❑ Press **ALT+F** for File.

❑ Press **SHIFT+X** to save (see Figure 7-7).

   Hold down either **SHIFT** key while you press **X** or hold down either **SHIFT** key while you click **Exit**.

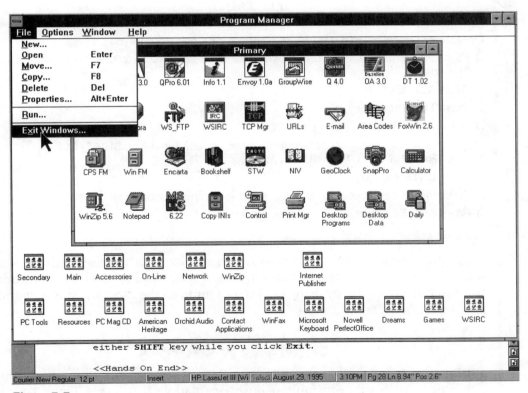

Figure 7-7

With "Save Settings on Exit" turned off, Windows 3.x preserves the setup you save. Simply Exit Windows normally, and your original desktop will appear the next time you start Windows.

 NET TIP When exiting Windows: Never turn off your computer or reboot it when Windows is running, unless it has frozen and there is no other way to recover. Windows does a lot of clean-up work when it closes down. When you turn off your computer while Windows is running, you can end up wasting a lot of hard-disk space with stray files. Even worse: It's possible for Windows to become corrupted and require reinstallation.

Special switching techniques

As you might imagine, there are many other ways to start and switch applications. The switching techniques we've shown you so far are generic and will work with all copies of Windows. Because starting and switching applications is so important when you work on the Internet, we'll show you some specialized alternatives.

Shortcut keys

Identifying your most frequently used applications and placing them in a single Primary group certainly will help you start multiple applications quickly. But you may want to go even one step further and assign a shortcut key to some applications. It's easy to do.

 ## Hands On

Objective: Learn how to designate applications shortcut keys.

❏ Highlight WordPerfect or Word (or whatever word processor you use) on your Program Manager.

❏ Press **ALT+ENTER**.

❏ Press **TAB** three times.

❏ Hold down **CTRL+ALT** and press **W**.

   You also can use any of these three other key combinations: **SHIFT+ALT**, **CTRL+SHIFT** or **CTRL+SHIFT+ALT**.

❏ Press **ENTER** to exit the dialog box.

❏ Press the keystroke you just assigned and your word processor will start.

❏ Press **ALT+F4** to exit your word processor.

These short cut keys can't be used to switch applications because they only work while you're on the Program Manager. Still, if your word processor isn't running, you can quickly start it by using ALT+TAB to jump to the Program Manager and pressing CTRL+ALT+W.

Windows resources

When you begin freely using ALT+TAB or CTRL+ESC, you will begin to run your Windows with a lot of simultaneously open applications (see Figure 7-8). If you're using Windows 3.x, you may begin to encounter system problems (such as hang-ups) that you never before have experienced.

▶ *Hands On*

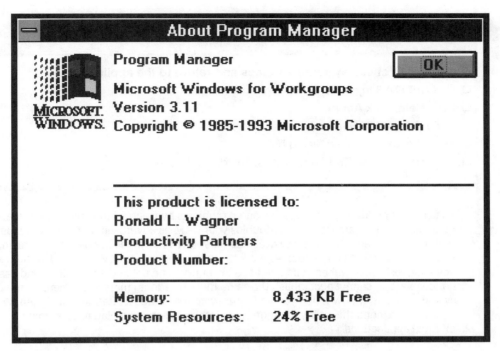

Figure 7-8

One way to keep Windows running reliably is to keep an eye on the system resources. The Hands On following this sidebar shows how you can check system resources at any time.

Anytime your system resources drops below 40 percent in Windows 3.x, you are teetering on the edge of computer oblivion. Check resources often. If they are low, try to close all unnecessary applications. Remember, you can press CTRL+ESC anytime to see a list of open applications. You can use the "End Task" button on the Task List dialog box to close any unused applications.

Check your system resources sometime immediately after you have turned on your computer and started Windows. They should be above 80 percent. If not, then you probably have a lot of fonts loaded or some out-of-date drivers. Check with the manufacturers of some of your computer's components, especially your video display card, and make sure you have the latest driver. We've seen some quirky, unreliable systems become stable simply by updating the display driver.

For example, one computer had serious problems hanging up when using WordPerfect for Windows. The owner blamed it on a recent WordPerfect upgrade. However, a check of system resources showed that the system was down to 73 percent resources at startup and that starting WordPerfect for Windows dropped the resources by 21 percent, clear down to 52 percent! Loading a couple of documents easily dropped resources to near 40 percent and made the system unstable. Installing an updated video display driver restored the system resources to 81 percent at startup. With the new driver, WordPerfect used only 15 percent, so the system was at 66 percent instead of 52 percent. The problems that WordPerfect bugs had been suspected of causing disappeared, and the troublesome system became extremely reliable.

Hands On

Objective: To check system resources and return to the application.

❑ Use **ALT+TAB** to return to the Program Manager.

❑ Click **Help**, click **About**.

    Or press **ALT+H**, then **A**.

❑ Read the last line of the dialog box.

❑ Click **OK**, or press **ENTER** to dismiss the dialog box.

NET TIP

You can just about eliminate your resource problems by using a fabulous little software utility known as "Ram Doubler." It doubles your RAM as advertised, but the big bonus is that it also increases the memory available for your Windows resources. After installing it, you may notice that your resources are lower when you first start Windows. During use, however, resources will be consumed at a lower rate. The net effect is positive and easily noticeable. You cannot accomplish the same thing by adding more RAM memory to your system. No matter how much you add, your system resource limitation will remain. We highly recommend this utility for aggressive Internet users who plan to open many multiple applications.

DAD and MOM

You can find numerous versions of small Windows applications that enhance application switching. Many are available as shareware, and others are included with major commercial software packages. The PerfectOffice suite from Novell includes the Desktop Applications Director (DAD). The Microsoft Office suite includes the Microsoft Office Manager (MOM).

Both DAD and MOM feature a small bar of icons that enable rapid launching and switching of Windows applications. You can customize the screen location, the icon-content, and the activation method of each of these pop-up bars. Once you alter them to include your most frequently used applications, you can access most of your Windows tools using these rapid-access icon bars.

Don't get too excited about using DAD, MOM, or any of the shareware application switchers until you read the accompanying sidebar on system resources. Every application saps some of your system's resources, and the icon-bar application switchers are no exception. Before you invest any effort in customizing an icon-bar to suit your needs, check its effect on your system resources.

NET TIP

If you have a suite that includes DAD or MOM but you are not using it yet, close and restart Windows, check system resources, then start DAD or MOM and recheck your resources. Expect to lose between 4 and 6 percent of your system resources. If you already are using DAD or MOM, then close and restart Windows and check system resources. Then change your system so that the icon-bar does not launch on Windows startup, then close and restart Windows again. Compare system resources now against the previous number.

If you have any system hang-ups while an application-switching icon-bar is running, disable it and run Windows for a while without it. It may have been the

Hands On

straw that was breaking your system resource camel's back. Besides, once you have configured your Program Manager with a Primary group as we outlined earlier and you begin using ALT+TAB or CTRL+ESC, you'll find that an icon-bar offers no increase in ability.

Microsoft Windows key

A new key soon will appear on PC keyboards, called the "Windows" key. It was introduced by Microsoft on their own keyboard, the Microsoft Natural Keyboard, and has the Windows logo on its face. Actually, there are two of them—much like duplicate ALT or CTRL keys.

Pressing either Windows key activates the Windows Task List. It simply reduces the CTRL+ESC keystroke combination to one keystroke and gives you two places to hit it. It will have the added benefit of increasing the awareness of the average Windows user that there is such a thing as the Task List.

Expect nearly all major keyboard manufacturers to follow suit soon. Look for the new key if you're shopping for a new PC or just for a new keyboard. The Microsoft Keyboard includes an improved version of the default Task List (see Figure 7-9) and it's an outstanding keyboard. This book was typed on one, and produced no hand cramps or other problems despite typing 105,000 words in eight weeks.

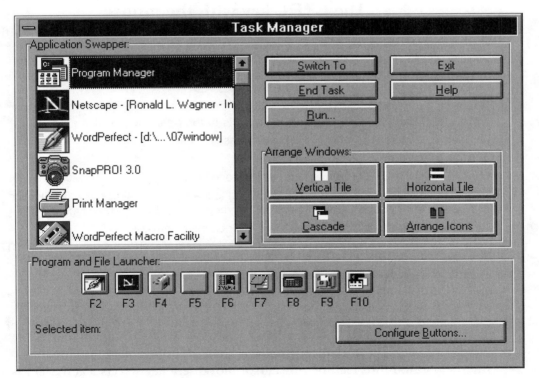

Figure 7-9

CUA keystroke summary

Here's a summary of some of the keystrokes that will help you the most when you're working on the Internet. Having every one of these techniques in your repertoire will make you a maestro of the Internet, and you'll be able to direct it to new heights of productivity.

The SHIFT key with the mouse

You also can use the SHIFT key with your mouse to quickly select multiple items on a list.

 Hands On

Objective: **Learn to select a series of items on a list.**

❏ Start the File Manager.

❏ Select any directory with a long list of filenames.

❏ Click on one file near the top of the list.

❏ Hold down **SHIFT** while you click an item near the bottom.

   All files between and including the two on which you clicked will be selected.

The CTRL key with the mouse

You can select a random assortment of files on any list using the CTRL key with your mouse.

 Hands On

Objective: **Learn to randomly select multiple items on a list.**

❏ Use the same list you used in the previous lesson.

❏ Click on any file.

❏ Hold down the **CTRL** key while you click on another item.

   Each time you click another item is added to the selection. Almost any file function you perform will be performed on this entire group of selected files (see Figure 7-10).

❏ Continue holding down **CTRL** while you click on more items.

   If you want to deselect a selected item, click on it again while holding down the **CTRL** key.

❏ Click on any item without holding down **CTRL**.

The SHIFT key with cursor movement keys

Here's one of the best Windows tricks of all. It's hard to imagine using the Internet without this feature: Any cursor movement key selects text if SHIFT is depressed. Here are a couple of examples that will greatly boost your speed.

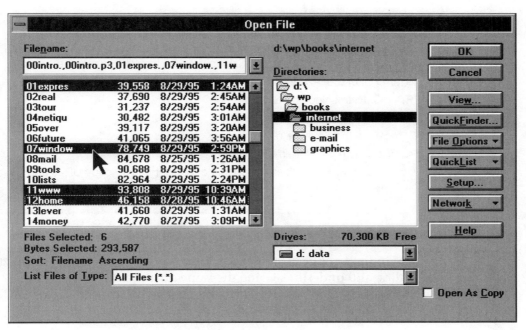

Filename: 00intro._.00intro.p3_.01expres._.07window._.11w

d:\wp\books\internet

01expres	39,558	8/29/95	1:24AM
02real	37,690	8/29/95	2:45AM
03tour	31,237	8/29/95	2:54AM
04netiqu	30,482	8/29/95	3:01AM
05over	39,117	8/29/95	3:20AM
06future	41,065	8/29/95	3:56AM
07window	78,749	8/29/95	2:59PM
08mail	84,678	8/25/95	1:26AM
09tools	90,688	8/29/95	2:31PM
10lists	82,964	8/29/95	2:24PM
11www	93,808	8/29/95	10:39AM
12home	46,158	8/28/95	10:46AM
13lever	41,660	8/29/95	1:31AM
14money	42,770	8/27/95	3:09PM

Directories:
- d:\
  - wp
    - books
      - internet
      - business
      - e-mail
      - graphics

Files Selected: 6
Bytes Selected: 293,587
Sort: Filename Ascending

Drives: 70,300 KB Free
d: data

List Files of Type: All Files (*.*)

☐ Open As Copy

OK
Cancel
View...
QuickFinder...
File Options ▾
QuickList ▾
Setup...
Network ▾
Help

Figure 7-10

Hands On

Objective: **Learn to quickly select text using keystrokes.**

❏ Start your word processor and open a saved document.

❏ Choose a document with several pages of text.

❏ Move to the bottom of the document with **CTRL+END**.

❏ Hold down **SHIFT** and press **CTRL+HOME** to move to the top of the document.

This selects all the text in any document with but two keystrokes: **CTRL+END**, **SHIFT+CTRL+HOME**. This is a time-saving, valuable trick on the Internet and an excellent way to capture entire documents. You'll use it often.

❏ Press any cursor movement key to deselect the text.

Using the SHIFT key to select text is especially important when copying URLs and addresses. Try this with your cursor in a single-line text entry window.

Hands On

Objective: **Learn to copy the contents of a text entry box.**

❏ Use your word processor and the same document as above.

❏ Click **File, Save As...**

The text in the Filename box will already be selected, so you technically don't have to use keystrokes now, but this is a demonstration for the times when the text is not selected.

❏ Press **HOME** to move to the beginning of the line.

Windows wide open—advanced basics ◀

❑ Press **SHIFT+END** to select all the text on that line.

> This is an improvement over the frustrating method of trying to drag your mouse across the entire line without missing the first or last character. Even if you use the mouse to click in the text entry box, finishing with the keystrokes may be quicker.

❑ Click at the far right of the text entry box.

❑ Press **SHIFT+HOME** to select the text.

❑ Press **CTRL+C** to copy it to your clipboard.

❑ Press **ESC** to cancel the Save As dialog box.

❑ Press **CTRL+V** to Paste the filename into the current document.

> You'll use this principle countless times on the Internet as you copy URLs and paste them to other applications or locations.

Bold, italics, and underline

Nearly every Windows application uses the same keystrokes to emphasize text with bold, italics, and underline. Using the same document you used in the previous lesson, select a few words of text and change the appearance of the text:

Hands On

Objective: **Learn the keystrokes for bold, italics, and underline.**

❑ Use the same document as above.

> Don't worry about the mess we're having you make of your document. When we're through we simply will exit without saving.

❑ Press **CTRL+B** to turn on Bold.

❑ Type some bolded text.

❑ Press **CTRL+B** to turn off Bold.

❑ Press **CTRL+I** to turn on Italics.

> Type some italicized text.

❑ Press **CTRL+I** to turn off Italics.

❑ Press **CTRL+U** to turn on Underline.

> Type some underlined text.

❑ Press **CTRL+U** to turn off Underline.

❑ Select any section of text that has none of these attributes.

❑ Press **CTRL+B** to bold the existing text.

❑ Press **CTRL+I** to italicize the existing text.

❑ Press **CTRL+U** to underline the existing text.

❑ Press any arrow key to deselect the selected text.

> All three of these font attribute keystrokes are "toggles." That means that if the associated attribute is off, the keystroke will activate it; if it's on, the keystroke will deactivate it.

❑ Press **ENTER** to start a new line.

> Using these keystrokes greatly will speed your work versus interrupting your typing to grab the mouse, find a button, click, put down the mouse, and then return your hands to the keyboard to type, then pick up the mouse to turn off the attribute, then return again to the keyboard.

Hands On

Cut, Copy, and Paste

These keystrokes will enable you to freely move text between any two Windows applications. Practice these and remember them; they are a major factor in productivity success using Windows on the Internet. They use the universal Windows clipboard to move and copy text and graphics between any two locations within Windows.

Hands On

Objective: Learn to use keystrokes for Cut, Copy, and Paste.

❑ Select any section of text in the document you have open.

❑ Press **CTRL+C** to Copy these words into the clipboard.

❑ Use **ALT+TAB** to return to your Program Manager.

❑ Start your Internet e-mail program and start a new e-mail message.

> Or, if you don't have e-mail, start the Notepad program in the Accessories group. Either way, the insertion point now will be inside a text document window.

❑ Press **CTRL+V** to Paste into this new application the words from your word processor.

> Using Paste does not affect the clipboard contents. You can repeatedly Paste the same text until you change the clipboard contents with Cut or Copy. Let's demonstrate.

❑ Press **CTRL+V** two more times to see the clipboard is preserved.

❑ Use **ALT+TAB** to return to your word processor.

❑ Select an entire paragraph of text.

❑ Press **CTRL+X** to Cut it from the document.

❑ Move your insertion point to another spot in the document.

❑ Press **CTRL+V** to Paste the paragraph to the new spot.

Using Cut, Copy, and Paste in conjunction with application switching, such as ALT+TAB, is the key to working quickly, easily, and powerfully on the Internet with Windows. For example, transferring text from your Web browser to your word processor will be a snap. Simply use your mouse to select the desired text right on the Web page, press CTRL+C to Copy it to your clipboard, press ALT+TAB to jump to your word processor, press CTRL+V to Paste the text into a document, then press ALT+TAB again to return to the Internet for more text. Of course you can reverse the process to transfer information from your word processor to an Internet application.

In the lessons that follow, we'll use most of the techniques we've presented in this chapter. Our next lesson is on Internet e-mail, featuring the Eudora for Windows mail application. Any Internet mail program can stifle your productivity by making you write down and retype lots of annoying little text strings. Or—now that you've finished this lesson—you can let in some fresh air while you tour the information superhighway by driving with your Windows wide open for maximum productivity.

Saving URLs

Here's an optional Hands On exercise that will prevent you from losing track of important information sites around the Internet. It's one of the Breathing Space tips we promised you in Chapter 5. This tip will let you "manage the beforehand."

We're going to create a new icon for your Primary group that will use the Windows Write program to save a file of important URLs along with a brief note on each. You then will be able to get to your URL list merely by double-clicking on this new icon.

 # Hands On

Objective: Create a special icon that provides instant access to important Internet URLs.

- ❑ Click **File, New, OK** to create a new program icon.
- ❑ Type *URLs* and press **TAB**.
- ❑ Type *write.exe c:\internet.wri*
- ❑ Press **TAB** and type *c:* in the "Working Directory" box.
- ❑ Click **Change Icon**.
- ❑ Type *moricons.dll* into the "File Name" text entry box and press **ENTER**.
- ❑ Press **TAB** to jump to the "Current Icon" window.
- ❑ Press **END** to jump to the file cabinet icon at the end of the listing.
- ❑ Press **ENTER** or click **OK**.
- ❑ Back at the Program Properties dialog, click **OK**.

    You now have created an icon that will instantly open a file containing valuable URLs. But the file does not yet exist, so let's create it now.

- ❑ Double-click on your new **URLs** icon to start Write.

    A dialog box will warn you that the file does not exist, but the file will pop up instantly after this exercise.

- ❑ Click **OK**.
- ❑ Click **File, Save** to save the file.
- ❑ Type *internet.wri* and press **ENTER**.

    The file now exists, so you can exit.

Anytime you discover a valuable URL on the Internet, highlight it, press CTRL+C to copy it to the clipboard, use ALT+TAB to switch to the Program Manager, double-click on URLs then use CTRL+V to paste in the URL. You then can go back to your Internet application and copy some text to paste into this document that will give you a brief note about it, or you can type a note from scratch. Keep each URL on a separate line with the descriptive paragraph immediately under it. The "Find" feature will enable you to quickly locate URLs by searching for keywords in the note that you included.

This, of course, is not the only way to save URLs. You soon will find, for example, that many of the best Internet browsers have a built-in "bookmark" feature that stores your best URLs. This bookmark list may quickly become full, or you may find URLS you want to remember that do not merit a bookmark slot.

 # Continuing Education

The Microsoft Windows newsletter

You can stay abreast of the latest developments in Windows from an online Microsoft newsletter subscription. Here are the steps to subscribe:

⊚ Send an Internet e-mail message to: *enews@microsoft.nwnet.com.*

⊚ Leave the Subject line blank.

⊚ In the body of the message, place only these words: *subscribe winnews.*

Once you've subscribed, you can discontinue your subscription at any time by using these steps:

⊚ Send an Internet e-mail message to: *enews@microsoft.nwnet.com.*

⊚ Leave the Subject line blank.

⊚ In the body of the message, place only these words: *unsubscribe winnews.*

Internet mail

INTERNET electronic mail (e-mail) is a powerful, inexpensive, and exciting new business tool. The world rapidly is becoming a global community, and e-mail is the perfect answer to communicating in this emerging global business environment. World-wide overnight package delivery and fax machines launched the global business revolution, but faxing even a short message overseas during business hours is quite costly. Internet e-mail has turbocharged the emergence of a global community by drastically reducing the cost of international communication. Few Internet accounts charge message-unit e-mail fees, thus eliminating for most users any barrier to free-flowing communication anywhere in the world.

Internet mail transforms the limitations of what will fit into a business envelope and the crudeness of choppy black-and-white text on a faxed page. E-mail today is still in a rudimentary form, but fast-moving improvements in technology will enable the Internet to complete the global communication revolution. A key lesson in this chapter will be helping you see Internet mail as more than a substitute for the standard business letter or business fax.

You won't be using Internet mail because it saves 32 cents. No, sometimes you would use e-mail even if it cost more than first-class postage or a long-distance call. But the joy is that all of its amazing abilities are essentially free—anywhere in the world, instantly!

Using some graphic screen-shots and sample messages, we'll make sure you know the basics. But Internet mail is not perfect. You'll see what happens to e-mail between here and there, why it may never get there, and how to protect your business. (A reminder: If you missed chapter 4, "Netiquette," read it now. E-mail has its own peculiar social order, and business will go more smoothly for you if you follow common netiquette rules.)

Another critical lesson will be to help you keep your Internet business address from going down with the ship if your service provider sinks. Imagine what would happen to your business if the postal service suddenly changed your business address— that can happen to you on the Internet!

E-mail addresses

Most likely you already have seen Internet e-mail addresses. Here's a typical example: *isatest@digiweb.com*

The special symbol in an Internet address (@) is called the "AT" symbol. To pronounce this e-mail address, you would say "isatest AT digiweb DOT com." And it actually represents pretty much what it sounds like. The user "isatest" is "at" the Internet location called "digiweb dot com." The part of the address before the @ is the user and the part after the @ is the user's Internet domain name.

What does the "com" represent? It's called the *first-level domain* and it identifies the broad category of the user's cyberspace domain. There are six commonly used first level domains in the U.S.:

com	commercial
edu	education
gov	government
mil	military
net	network
org	organization

Outside the U.S., other countries have their own first-level domain name. These are too numerous to list here, but some of the common ones you'll see are:

ca	Canada
de	Germany
fr	France
uk	United Kingdom

Internet addresses are used backwards, from right to left. Each step up the chain narrows down the path to the user. Let's use a longer address for another example: *jsmith@library.utulsa.edu*

Starting with the right segment, "edu," you see that this domain is an educational institution. The next step up is "utulsa" which represents the University of Tulsa. The next step indicates the library within the University of Tulsa. Finally, the user, "jsmith" AT "library.utulsa.edu" is pinpointed. Later in this chapter we'll tell you how the Internet uses these plain-language addresses, and how to get one tailored to the name of your organization.

The Eudora e-mail application

For the Hands On exercises in this chapter, we'll use the most popular Internet e-mail package today, Eudora from Qualcomm (see Figure 8-1). Qualcomm has more than four million Eudora users, and its installed base is growing rapidly.

This is not an intensive lesson on Eudora's advanced features. Eudora includes a detailed manual that will teach you additional special features of Eudora. Our purpose is to teach you Internet e-mail as generically as possible, using Eudora as the model. Check out the sidebar for information on how to get a free copy of Eudora.

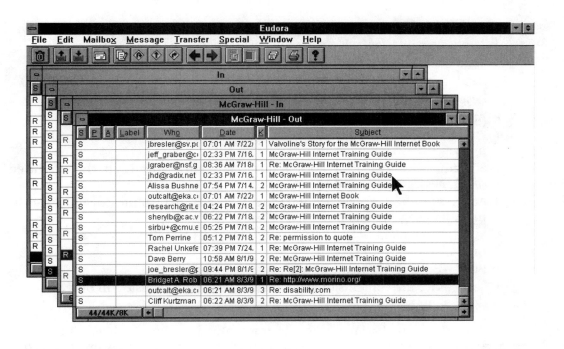

Figure 8-1

Getting your copy of the Eudora e-mail application

If you don't have Eudora—or if you'd just like to get the most up-to-date version—you can download a free copy from the Internet. Here is a URL that you can use to download Eudora: *http://www.qualcomm.com/quest*

While the free version of Eudora is good, the full commercial version is superb. We've used the full version for the examples in this book, so your screen will look slightly different if you're using the free version. Both programs, however, function basically the same, with the commercial version having some valuable enhancements.

You can purchase the commercial version of Eudora at its retail price directly from its manufacturer, Qualcomm, by calling them at 800-2-EUDORA, or by e-mailing them at *quest-rep@qualcomm.com*. If you call, however, even they will suggest that you buy Eudora at a local store because the store can offer a large price discount—Qualcomm doesn't want you to pay retail.

You can subscribe to Qualcomm's newsletter to stay abreast of the latest changes to Eudora. Send an e-mail message to *majordomo@qualcomm.com*, leave the subject line blank, and enter only the text subscribe quest_news in the body.

They also have an unmoderated newsgroup that discusses Eudora as well as general tips and ideas on using Internet e-mail. Send an e-mail message to *majordomo@qualcomm.com*, leave the subject line blank and enter only the text windows-eudora-forum in the body.

Almost all Internet e-mail applications provide the same basic services, but with different user interfaces. Here are the basic services that we'll cover:

- Send—Compose, edit, and send messages.
- Read—Check mail, open In box, and read messages.
- Response options—Reply to, forward, or redirect received messages.
- Attachments—Include computer files that "tag along" with messages.
- Housekeeping—Delete messages, create tailored mailboxes, and transfer messages between mailboxes.
- Signature files—Create a block of text that is automatically attached to the end of all messages you send.
- Address book—Create a list of frequently used e-mail addresses and assign a plain-language nickname.
- Multiple recipients—Send Carbon Copies (CC) and Blind Copies (BC) of messages.
- Print—Print the contents of any e-mail message.
- Save—Save the contents of any e-mail message for inclusion in other documents.

Eudora, of course, has all of these features, plus a wealth of others. Our recommendation for your getting started with Internet e-mail is first to master these features. Then get the commercial version—which includes a complete, printed manual—because you'll then be better prepared to know which of those added features are going to help you with your work style.

Frequently asked e-mail questions

What if my addressee's computer isn't running right now?

Internet e-mail does not pass directly between the computers of its sender and its recipient. E-mail goes through a routing process similar to that of a regular, mailed letter. Instead of being handled by a series of people, however, e-mail is handled by a series of computers across the Internet until it ends up at the local post office—technically called a *mail server*—of the recipient. The message is saved on the hard drive of that mail server. A mail server is just a computer that has been set up to handle Internet mail. Mail server computers run 24 hours a day, so they can receive mail continuously. Your computer doesn't need to be running for you to receive e-mail any more than you need to be present at your local post office when a letter for you arrives on a mail truck.

Here's where the similarity between regular mail and e-mail ends: No postal carrier delivers the message from the post office. E-mail remains at the recipient's post office—on the mail server—until it's requested.

To receive a waiting message the recipient must use mail software and activate the software's "check mail" feature. The e-mail software uses the Internet to ask the recipient's mail server if it's holding any mail for the recipient. If the mail server has any messages, it transfers them to the In box of the *client* e-mail application where the mail can be read. (If you skipped reading our glossary of terms, be sure to read it now for the definition of *client/server*, because the whole Internet is based on the process of information being transferred between clients and servers.)

All those computers—can anyone else read my messages?

Yes, they can. Internet e-mail is not secure at all. This doesn't mean that anyone *will* read your mail. Do you imagine that a lot of postal workers read postcards that travel via regular mail? And what harm would be done anyway, even if someone did read it? Well, that depends on what you're saying, doesn't it! If you need to send secure messages, be sure and read chapter 15, "Internet Security."

How often should I check my mail?

You most likely will check your Internet e-mail much more frequently than the postal carrier brings regular mail, but don't overdo it. An informal poll we took for this book revealed that many users average one to two hours a day reading and responding to Internet e-mail. Follow the guidance we gave you in chapter 5, "The over-information age" and give yourself some breathing space by making sure that you control your e-mail instead of letting your e-mail control you.

Is there a limit to the size of an e-mail message?

Currently the maximum file size allowed for Internet e-mail is 2 megabytes. If you're sending text files, that's enough space for several full-length books. Graphics, sound files, and video files, however, easily can exceed the limit. Service to small communities, however, may not permit anything close to 2 megabytes. We've seen isolated areas where e-mail messages failed to deliver attachments as small as 100 kilobytes.

If you need to give files larger than 2 megabytes to someone else, have your service providers set up an FTP site for you. You can put up files of nearly any size, then send e-mail to the recipient with the URL, directory, and filename so they can download.

Send e-mail

The first thing we'll do with your e-mail application is send a practice message to yourself that we'll use in later lessons. There are three basic phases to creating an e-mail message: composing a new message, editing it, then sending it.

Composing a new message

Here's a Hands On exercise that will run through the basics of creating an e-mail message. Eudora is going to work through a TCP/IP connection that can be established using a variety of means.

⊚ Launch Winsock and login to an Internet connection before starting Eudora.

⊚ If your Winsock logs on automatically when you issue a Send command, then you can let Eudora start Winsock for you.

⊚ If your Netscape Web browser already is connected and logged on, then Eudora will use the same connection and you need do nothing further.

Hands On

Objective: Learn to compose an e-mail message.

❏ Start the Eudora e-mail application.

❏ Click **Message, New Message** or press **CTRL+N**.

  The insertion point is flashing on the **To:** line.

❏ Type your own Internet e-mail address.

❏ Press **TAB** once to move the insertion point to **Subject:** line.

❏ Type *E-Mail Exercise 1* then press **TAB** three times to move the insertion point to the body of the message.

❏ Type a salutation, then press **ENTER** twice.

  Press **ENTER** only to end a paragraph or for blank lines, because you'll want the program to handle the word-wrapping automatically as in your word processor. (BTW: Be sure not to flame yourself!)

❏ Type a message, then press **ENTER** twice.

❏ Type a closing.

Edit a message

You easily can edit your message anytime before you send it. Use the normal Windows CUA editing commands you learned in chapter 7, "Windows Wide Open." Here's a quick summary of some of the most useful keys:

- Cut (CTRL+X), Copy (CTRL+C), and Paste (CTRL+V)
- Top of document (CTRL+HOME) and bottom of document (CTRL+END)
- Word right or word left (CTRL+RIGHT ARROW/LEFT ARROW)
- Check spelling (CTRL+6) or click Edit, Check Spelling), but only the commercial version of Eudora has this feature.

Remember that you can size a window by dragging its borders. Touch the borders in any corner with the mouse to get a diagonal mouse arrow so you can drag both horizontally and vertically with one move. Resizing the window may help you compose your message (see Figure 8-2).

Send or queue a message

Now let's spell check and then send the message you just created.

Hands On

Objective: Configure and use your spell checker and send e-mail.

❏ Click **Edit, Check Spelling** or press **CTRL+6** to check spelling.

❏ Click **Options** and check the options you want then click **OK**.

  If the spell checker has found any misspelled words, it has stopped, highlighted the word, and perhaps offered suggested corrections. You'll choose the action from the list on the right side of the dialog box. If the highlighted word is one that you expect to see repeatedly, click **Add** to add it to Eudora's dictionary. You can edit the words you've added by clicking on **Edit Dictionary**.

❑ Double-click the **hyphen** in the menu control button to close the spell checker.

❑ Click on either the **Send** or the **Queue** button.

> Depending upon which version of Eudora you're using and which screen resolution you have chosen, you may not be able to see Send or Queue. If you do not see one of these buttons on the button bar at the top of the message window, then touch the mouse to the right border of the active window and drag the border to the right to widen the message window.
>
> If you clicked on **Send**, then your message was sent instantly and you're through with this exercise. If you clicked on **Queue**, then your message still is in the Out box and you now need to execute these next steps to send it.

❑ Click **File, Send Queued Messages...** or press **CTRL+T**.

> What happens after the send command varies depending upon your Internet connection. If you established the connection before starting Eudora—or if Netscape or some other Internet application had established the connection for you— your message gets sent immediately. If you're not logged onto the Internet, then Eudora may make Winsock dial the Internet and log on. In some cases, however, you will have to use **ALT+TAB** to cycle back to the Program Manager to launch Winsock and logon, then use **ALT+TAB** again to return to Eudora and send.

❑ Close Eudora if desired, or keep it active for the next exercise.

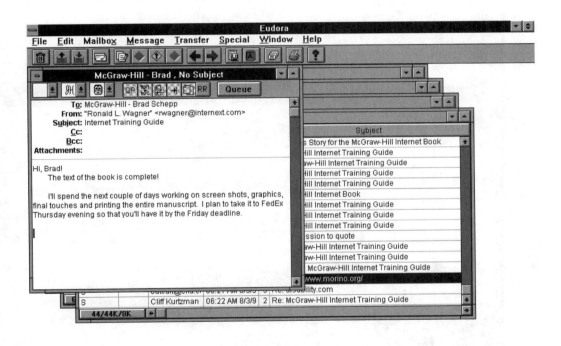

Figure 8-2

Send versus Queue

Eudora can be programmed to send your messages immediately, or to place them in a queue to be sent later. How do you decide which setting to use?

Internet mail ◀

If you have a full-time Internet connection—perhaps your company has a dedicated line—then use the Send option. If you have a SLIP/PPP account, then choose the Queue option. If you choose Send with a SLIP/PPP account, you'll force your modem to dial and log on to your service for every single message. Using the Queue option lets you write all your messages, then log on once and send them all together. The next Hands On explains how to change the option.

Hands On

Objective: Change the Send/Queue option in Eudora.
❏ Click **Special, Settings...**
❏ Scroll to the **Sending Mail** icon on the left.
❏ Check or uncheck **Immediate Send** as desired, then click **OK**.
    (See the mouse arrow in Figure 8-3.)

This e-mail message has now been launched on its journey through cyberspace. Your Internet post office knows how to forward the message to the next computer in the delivery chain, as does each computer along the chain. Eventually—usually within a few seconds—the message has found the recipient's

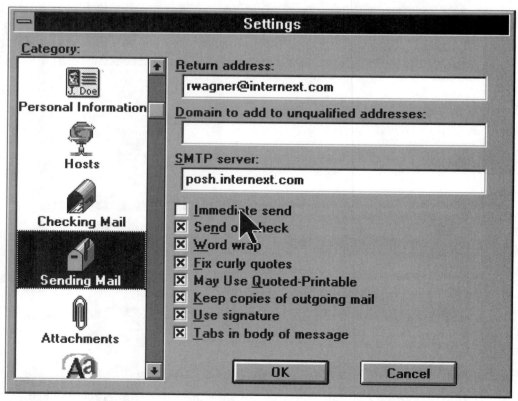

Figure 8-3

mail server and is stored on a hard drive waiting for them to check their mail. This delivery chain may baffle human logic, but it makes perfect sense to computers.

How do I lookup someone's e-mail address?

Someday you easily will be able to find almost anyone on the Internet. But that day hasn't yet come. Remember, we have compared the Internet to an early rural telephone system. If you've grown accustomed to instant directory telephone assistance and you are using a CD-ROM telephone book that can locate nearly anyone in the country, the Internet will be a disappointment.

If you've not tried any of the CD-ROM directories, we highly recommend them; they are powerful detective tools. Today, CD-ROMs are your best bet for tracking down an old friend, an old sweetheart, or a long-lost business associate. Once you look them up and call, of course, you can ask for their e-mail address and stay in touch with them for free—no matter where in the world they've moved.

But what e-mail address lookup resources are available on the Internet today? Check out some of our Internet directory references in this chapter's Continuing Education section. WHOIS lists people at large universities, government agencies, and corporations. We also will point you to AT&T's "World Wide X.500 Directory" (see Figure 8-4).

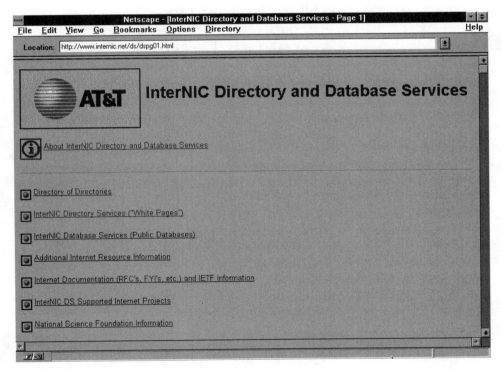

Figure 8-4

Currently, information only is available for individuals who are registered with these directories. Other Internet lookup tools are experiencing explosive growth, so look well beyond what you read in this book. For example, as this is being written, a yellow-pages directory is being built. Right now it's small, but by the time you read this—well, who knows? And there will be others.

What about people who are searching for your e-mail address? Help your clients, customers, associates, friends, and family find you by registering yourself in as many directory services as you can find. It will take a bit of work, but if you begin with the resources we listed under Continuing Education, you'll dramatically increase your chances of being found. Since you're joining us here in cyberspace, you might as well let us all know how to find you!

Read messages

Before you actually can read an e-mail message, you must get it from your mail server by checking your mail. After you've received an e-mail message, you can read it and then perform a wide variety of follow-up actions. In this section we'll cover receiving, reading, and basic reply actions.

Receive, open, and read messages

After starting Eudora, you'll need to activate the Check Mail function. If you have a dedicated line or if your system is set to perform automatic dialing and logon, then you're ready to check mail immediately. If not, then establish your Internet connection before proceeding with the exercise.

Hands On

Objective: **Learn to check mail in Eudora.**

❑ Start Eudora.

❑ Click on **File, Check Mail** or press **CTRL+M**

Dedicated-line accounts check mail immediately. Auto-logon accounts first will dial your Internet provider, connect to your mail server, then check mail. In either case, your message will be placed in the In box.

❑ Click **Mailbox, In or press CTRL+I** to open the In box.

❑ Double-click on *E-Mail Exercise 1* to open a message window.

You can scroll through the message with your mouse or with **Page Up** and **Page Down**. Don't use the cursor arrow keys, though, because they will jump you to the next message on the list—or, because you don't have any more messages, the cursor arrow keys will return you to the In box.

❑ Double-click the menu control box (small-hyphen) to close the message window.

What happens between here and there?

Your e-mail messages do not traverse the Internet in a straight line or even as a single unit. Messages are broken up into digital units called packets. Your mail server (digital post office) then performs some very fast magic on the packets that will carry the pieces of your e-mail.

Your mail server begins by checking its own directory of Internet addresses to see if it knows how to get your message to the destination address. If you've e-mailed before to this addressee, your mail server knows the address and the message begins its journey. If not, then your mail server hasn't a clue about how to locate the addressee and must go for help.

When a mail server does not know an addressee's location, it can contact the InterNIC domain name registry in Reston, Virginia and use the directory there. The InterNIC is the central location for all domain names, so they can translate your addressee's e-mail host address into computer-coded numbers. Your mail server can store that number for future reference so it won't need to waste resources going back to the InterNIC if you send to the same addressee again.

Once the plain-language address you typed has been converted into a computer-coded address that the Internet understands, your e-mail's packets are ready to start their journey.

The Transmission Control Protocol/Internet Protocol (TCP/IP) that the Internet uses to handle traffic always checks for the quickest route for each packet. It is theoretically possible for each packet in your message to take a completely different route to its destination. In practice this never happens, but it's the reason the Internet could survive even a nuclear war. The Internet hardly would miss a beat even if an entire major city instantly vanished.

Response options

Most of your e-mail will elicit a response from you. That's why the Internet is so busy—everyone is responding to everyone else in a cascade of e-mail. Still, quick and easy responses are part of the value of Internet e-mail, so let's learn the options. We'll cover replying, forwarding, redirecting, and requesting a return receipt.

 NET TIP Remember that you can resize windows. Messages often will look poorly formatted when you read them, but normal appearance will be restored by making the window slightly wider. Of course you always can maximize the window for a full-screen view.

What is all this junk at the top of my messages?

The top of your e-mail contains several lines of text before the actual message. These extra lines are called a *header*, and they include the return path, identity of the sender, date of the message, and its subject. But there's more.

Near the upper-left corner of the message window, you'll see a BLAH, BLAH, BLAH button. Click on it to see more than you ever need to know about your message. All the extra text you see now—it's called "cruft"—traces the path the message followed to reach you and can help sort out (with the aid of an expert) any problems you might have with a message that is undeliverable. Fortunately, Eudora filters the cruft for you automatically, so you can now click on BLAH, BLAH, BLAH again and keep it that way.

Reply to a message

Eudora simplifies the task of replying to a current e-mail message by automatically addressing the new message to the sender and entering your address and the subject, using the original subject as a pattern (see Figure 8-5).

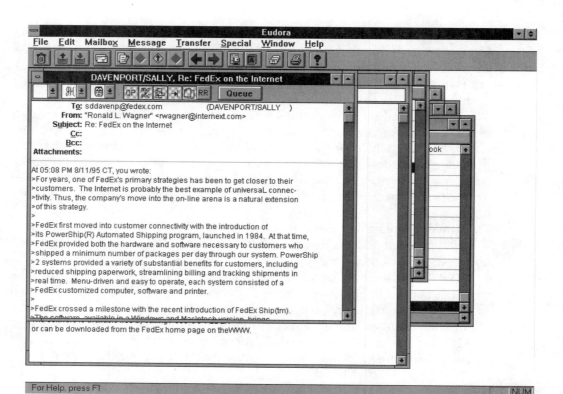

Figure 8-5

Hands On

Objective: Learn to reply to an e-mail message.

❑ Click **Message, Reply** or press **CTRL+R** to open a reply window.

> You also can click on the 180° reverse-arrow icon immediately under the menu word "Message."

> The original message has been copied into this window and an angle-bracket (**>**) has been placed at the beginning of each line. You probably will need to use your mouse to stretch the box slightly wider (to the right) if the lines don't wrap correctly and you may want to stretch the window taller as well.

❑ Review the **To:**, **From:** and **Subject:** lines.

❑ Use your mouse to select any text you want to cut away then press **DELETE** or **CTRL+X** to delete it.

> Don't return the entire contents of the original message to your sender; this is extremely annoying unless it was no more than a couple of lines. Instead, leave just enough to provide a lead-in to your reply.

❑ Separate parts of the reduced message by topic (see Figure 8-6).

❑ Type your responses to each topic in turn (see Figure 8-7).

❑ Click **Send** or **Queue**.

> If you clicked **Queue**, you now will need to click **File, Send Queued Messages** or press **CTRL+T** to transmit.

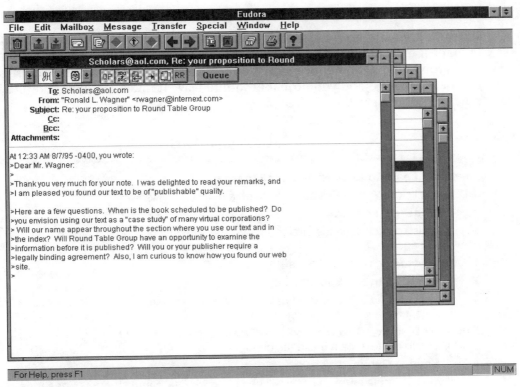

Figure 8-6

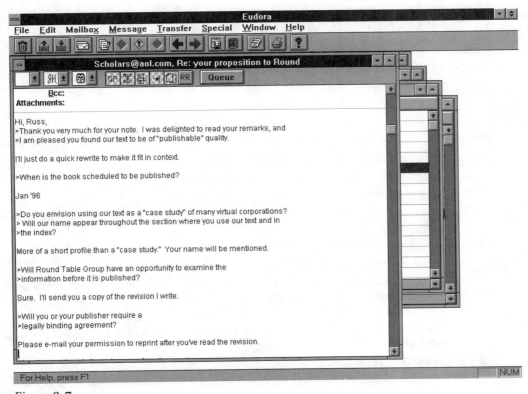

Figure 8-7

Forward a message

Instead of replying to a message, you may want to forward it to another recipient. Perhaps if the message did not pertain to your department, for example, you could forward it to someone who could handle it. The entire original message will be transferred and you probably should leave it intact, perhaps adding a note of your own to the new recipient.

Hands On

Objective: **Learn to forward an e-mail message.**

❑ Double-click on *E-Mail Exercise 1* to open a message window.

❑ Click **Message, Forward**.

>   You also can click on the straight-arrow icon immediately under the menu word "Message."

❑ Type the new recipient's address.

❑ Review the **From:** and **Subject:** lines.

>   Your name has been inserted as the sender; the forwarded message will appear to the recipient to have come from you.

❑ Press **TAB** until you reach the body of the message if you want to make any changes or additions to the text, then make the changes.

❑ Click **Send** or **Queue**.

>   If you clicked **Queue**, you now will need to click **File, Send Queued Messages** or press **CTRL+T** to transmit.

Redirect a message

Redirecting a message is quite similar to forwarding, except that the new recipient will see both the name of the original sender as well as your name. The process, however, basically is the same as with forwarding.

Hands On

Objective: **Learn to redirect an e-mail message.**

❑ Double-click on *E-Mail Exercise 1* to open a message window.

❑ Click **Message, Redirect**.

>   You also can click on the 90° right-turn-arrow icon immediately under the menu word "Message."

❑ Type the new recipient's address.

❑ Review the **From:** and **Subject:** lines.

>   The original sender has been inserted as the new sender, and your name has been added after that, preceded by "(by way of...)" so the new recipient will know the path the message has taken.

>   Press **TAB** until you reach the body of the message if you want to make any changes or additions to the text.

❑ Click **Send** or **Queue**.

>   If you clicked **Queue**, you now will need to click **File, Send Queued Messages** or press **CTRL+T** to transmit.

Request a return receipt

The outgoing message window has a button that you can use to request a return receipt for messages you send. This is not yet a reliable system, because many mail servers lack automatic response capability and will not respond with a return receipt. Simply click on the RR button to activate this option.

Attachments

Any computer file can be sent along with an e-mail message as an "attachment." Attachments ride along across the Internet with e-mail messages and enable you to send word processing documents, spreadsheets, programs, configuration files, full-color drawings, photographs, charts and graphs, sound clips, and video. The recipient gets the e-mail message in his or her normal In box, and the attachment file or files are transferred into a "download" directory.

Attachments are easy to include and greatly expand the value of e-mail for your business. Attachments even are useful for personal e-mail—for example, you could attach a scanned, digitized photo to e-mail to a friend or family member.

Multipurpose Internet Mail Extensions (MIME)

The primary format for sending attachments is the rapidly growing protocol called Multipurpose Internet Mail Extensions (MIME). MIME attachments deliver across the Internet to the destination computer exact duplicates of original files on the originating computer. Thus if you MIME a WordPerfect file to a business associate, the file will contain every graphic image, table, and formatting command. If the recipient has the same version of WordPerfect, they'll see the file exactly as you created it. Eudora easily handles MIME attachments. Let's check your attachment setting, learn to send an attachment, then learn to open an attachment you've received.

Setting attachment options

Before proceeding with the lessons, let's make sure that your copy of Eudora is set to the most useful attachment options. Another objective of this exercise will be to create a special "download" directory so you always will know where to find your downloaded attachment files without searching all over your hard drive (or, worse, your entire office network!) to find them.

Hands On

Objective: **Set Eudora's attachment options.**

❑ Use **ALT+TAB** to cycle back to the Program Manager.

❑ Open the **Main** group and double-click **File Manager**.

❑ Use the drive icons on the toolbar to select a drive for the download directory.

❑ Click on the root folder of the selected drive.

    For example, click on the folder **C:** at the top of the list.

❑ Click **File, Create Directory...**

❑ Type *download* and click **OK**.

❑ Double-click the menu control box (large-hyphen) to close the File Manager.

❑ Use **ALT+TAB** to return to Eudora.

❑ Click **Special, Settings...**

❑ Scroll to and click on the **Attachments** category.

❑ Click **Encoding Method, MIME**.

❑ Click the two check boxes as desired.

❑ Click the large bar under **Attachment Directory**.

    (See the mouse arrow in Figure 8-8.)

❑ Select the drive that includes your download directory.

    If you're on a network and you created your download somewhere other than on your local hard drive, click on **Network...** to select the network drive that includes your download directory.

❑ Browse through the directories and highlight your download directory.

❑ Click **Use Directory**, then click **OK**.

You can pretty much forget about the BinHex option, because that is most compatible with old Macintosh mailers and early versions of Eudora. The Uuencode option also is of little use to you because it's intended for older PCs and Unix systems. MIME should be all you need today.

Now that your attachment settings are correct, we'll help you send yourself an attachment and then we'll download and open the attached file (see Figure 8-9).

Hands On

Objective: **Learn how to include a MIME attachment with e-mail.**

❑ Start a new message to yourself by clicking **Message, New Message** or by pressing **CTRL+N**.

❑ Type your own address on the **To:** line and press **TAB**.

❑ Type *E-Mail Exercise 2* and press **TAB** to get to the message body.

❑ Click **Message, Attach File** or press **CTRL+H**.

❑ Double-click on the **c:** folder to go to your root directory.

❑ Click on **autoexec.bat**, then click on **OK**.

    The complete path and filename will be entered automatically for you on the **Attachments** line. You can repeat the last three steps and include multiple files with a single e-mail message.

❑ Type in the body of the message *Practice e-mail with attachment*.

❑ Click **Send** or **Queue**.

    If you clicked **Queue**, you now will need to click **File, Send Queued Messages** or press **CTRL+T** to transmit.

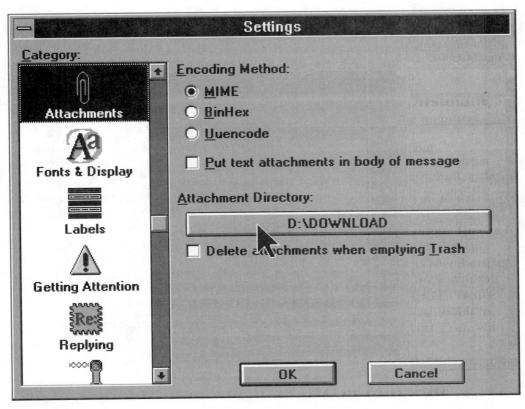

Figure 8-8

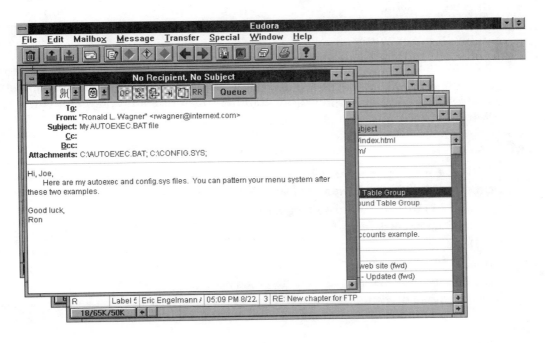

Figure 8-9

Transmission times

Transmitting a normal e-mail message does not place a major burden on Internet bandwidth. The transmission time is almost insignificant and no one has to wait and watch the file download anyway, because mail is delivered to mailboxes even while the user isn't logged onto his or her mail server.

Attachments, however, bring the possibility of significant transmission time because you can include nearly any computer file. Still, even moderate-size graphics images won't encounter a noticeable delay in transmission. Nonetheless, quite a lot of Internet bandwidth is being squandered these days by people attaching huge graphics images to e-mail just to show a picture to a friend.

Finally—regardless of Internet bandwidth issues—before you attach a large file, you may want to verify that your recipient has enough free hard disk capacity to store files you plan to send as e-mail attachments.

Receiving an attachment

Your mail server now should have received the attachment practice document and we can retrieve it. Use the same steps outlined earlier because attachments do not require any special efforts on the part of the recipient. Retrieve it now.

The e-mail message itself will be in your normal In box and the attachment will be in the download directory you specified. The body of the message will contain the text, "Attachment Converted: DOWNLOAD PATH\FILENAME." Another clue that a message includes an attachment is a document symbol in the "A" column in the In box window.

So now let's look at the copy of your autoexec file. We'll use the generic Windows Notepad, but IRL (netspeak for "in real life"), you probably would use your word processor, spreadsheet application, graphics software, sound player, or video player.

Hands On

Objective: **Verify the download of an attachment file.**

❑ Use **ALT+TAB** to return to the Program Manager.

❑ Open the **Accessories** group.

❑ Double-click on **Notepad**.

❑ Click **File, Open**.

❑ Select the drive that includes your download directory.

> If you're on a network and you created your download somewhere other than on your local hard drive, click on **Network...** to select the network drive that includes your download directory.

❑ Browse through the directories and highlight your download directory.

❑ Highlight **autoexec.bat** and click **OK**.

> Attachments always create complete copies of all original files, so this is an exact copy of your autoexec.bat file; the original is untouched, and remains unaffected by the copy.

❑ Double-click the menu control box (large hyphen) to close Notepad.

❑ Use **ALT+TAB** to return to Eudora.

Housekeeping features

We have completed the coverage of the basic e-mail features. We now would like to give you some bonuses that will make your life easier. We won't cover everything—there's a wealth of Eudora features that can help you if you have specialized needs. What we'll include next, however, are "advanced basics" that nearly everyone can use.

Delete messages

You soon will have a plethora of messages stored in your Eudora mailboxes. The list of messages in your In box and Out box quickly can grow to unmanageable lengths. Fortunately, deleting messages from *any* mailbox is easy.

As a safeguard, Eudora does not actually delete your messages when you use the normal delete function. Instead, they are transferred into a separate mailbox called "Trash." When a message is deleted from the Trash mailbox, then it truly is gone, but you must take specific action to delete messages from Trash.

 ## Hands On

Objective: Learn to delete messages.

❑ Click **Mailbox, In** to open your In box.

> Or click on the In box icon immediately under the menu item "Edit." (It's the one with the red arrow pointing down.)

❑ Highlight **E-Mail Exercise 1**.

❑ Click on **Message, Delete** or press **CTRL+D**.

> Or click on the Trashcan icon immediately under the menu word "File."

❑ Click **Mailbox, Out** to open your Out box.

> Or click on the Out box icon immediately under the menu item "Edit." (It's the one with the blue arrow pointing up.)

❑ Highlight **E-Mail Exercise 1**.

❑ Press **CTRL+D**.

❑ Click on **Mailbox, Trash** to open your Trash mail box.

These messages may or may not be deleted when you exit, depending on the option you've set. Let's set Eudora to automatically delete the messages in Trash upon exiting.

❑ Click **Special, Settings...**

❑ Scroll through the list and click on **Miscellaneous**.

❑ Check **Empty Trash when exiting** and click **OK**.

You can manually delete a message from Trash right now, and it will be gone immediately rather than waiting to exit. If you'd like to practice this, highlight a message in Trash and click **Message, Delete** or press **CTRL+D**.

Create tailored mailboxes

Eudora includes only the three basic mailboxes: In, Out, and Trash. Most likely you soon will need additional mailboxes, so we'll explain the basic concepts and show you how to create more mailboxes. Also, you can use either one of two different methods so we'll show you both of those.

When you create a new mailbox, you'll have the option to place it directly under the Top Level, or to make it a folder. We'll cover more on folders in the next section, so for now, let's create a new, Top Level mailbox.

Hands On

Objective: **Create a new Top Level mailbox.**

❑ Click **Mailbox, New...**

❑ Type *Test*, then click **OK**.

❑ Click **Mailbox, Test** to open the new mailbox.

❑ Click **Mailbox, New...**

❑ Type *Company Messages*.

Note the reminder: Creating a mailbox in the Top Level.

❑ Check **Make it a folder**, then click **OK**.

❑ Type *Company Messages - In*.

Note the reminder: Creating a mailbox in folder "Company Messages."

❑ Click **OK**.

The first time you create a folder, Eudora immediately asks you to create a mailbox under it. If you want more mailboxes under the new folder, you'll have to create them manually. Let's do that next.

❑ Click **Mailbox, Company Messages, New...**

❑ Type *Company Messages - Out*, then click **OK**.

Transfer messages between mailboxes

After you've created new mailboxes, you'll want to move messages into them. Let's transfer one of our test messages into the Test mailbox.

Hands On

Objective: **Learn to transfer messages between mailboxes.**

❏ Click **Mailbox, Out** to open the Out mailbox.

❏ Click on **E-Mail Exercise 2**.

❏ Click **Transfer, Test** to transfer this message into the Test mailbox.

Folders

Eudora also has a special mailbox dialog box in which you can create, delete, and manage your hierarchical folders and mailboxes.

Hands On

Objective: **Learn to manage mailboxes and folders.**

❏ Click on **Window, Mailboxes** to open the Mailboxes dialog.

❏ Click on **Test**, then click on **Remove** and then confirm.

   You'll be warned that the mailbox "has stuff in it," but you can delete it anyway. You also can use this dialog to create new mailboxes and folders. Let's make one more mailbox.

❏ Double-click on the folder **Company Messages** to see its mailboxes.

   You also could use the drop-list to switch the folder.

❏ Click on **New**.

❏ Type *Company Messages - Archives*, then click **OK**.

   There is no save or close button on this dialog box, so you'll have to use basic Windows principles to exit.

❏ Double-click the menu control box (small hyphen) to exit.

❏ Click **Window, Cascade** to see all of your open mailboxes.

   If you are feeling cluttered by too many open mailboxes, you can close or minimize any of them.

❏ Click the **Minimize** button on Trash.

   This probably is the best state for your Trash mailbox. You rarely will need to see what's in it, especially if you've set Eudora to empty the Trash upon exiting.

❏ Double-click the menu control box (small hyphen) on **Company Messages - Archives** to close it.

Signature files

One of the biggest time-saving features in most e-mail applications is the automatic signature file. Eudora lets you have two different signature files. All you have to do is write a message and Eudora will add a default closing for you.

We'll show you how to set up Eudora to use a signature file automatically on every message you send, how to create both your primary and your alternate signature files, and how to select the alternate signature when you want it (see Figure 8-10).

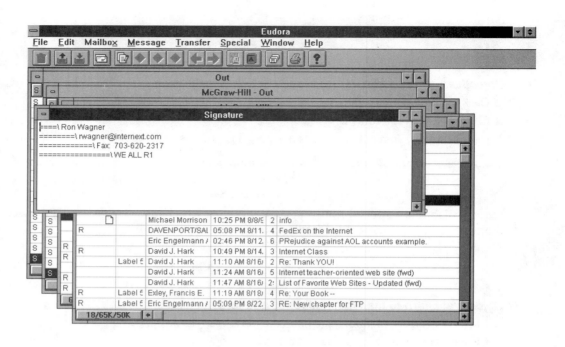

Figure 8-10

Hands On

Objective: **Learn to create and use signature files.**

❏ Click **Special, Settings...**

❏ Scroll to and click on **Sending Mail**.

❏ Check **Use signature**, then click **OK**.

❏ Click **Window, Signature**.

❏ Create your signature block.

> Common netiquette is to keep your signature block to about four lines, perhaps five if you truly need the space. Scrolling through some of the obnoxiously long signature blocks that you're going to encounter surely will inspire you to keep yours short.

> The example shows one of the authors' signatures; note that no phone numbers are included, only e-mail addresses. A good practice is to have phone numbers in only one of your signature blocks, and then decide which one will be your default.

❏ Double-click the menu control box to close the signature window.

❏ Click **Yes** to save the changes.

❏ Click **Window, Alternate Signature**.

❏ Create your alternate signature block.

> This one can include telephone numbers for those cases in which they're appropriate. Consider carefully before including your phone numbers in your primary signature file—after all, with e-mail, anyone who gets a message from you has sufficient contact information without getting your phone numbers.

Hands On

❏ Change to your other signature file by clicking on the second drop list on the message window's icon bar.

❏ Click on **Signature**.

> You can cancel the use of a signature file for any one message by clicking on the second drop list and clicking on **None**.

❏ Double-click the menu control box to close the signature window.

❏ Click **Yes** to save the changes.

Address book

Eudora calls its address book "Nicknames." You'll want to start your own list of e-mail addresses right away so you'll have a place to store important addresses, and to speed your handling of daily e-mail duties. We'll guide you through creating one nickname and then show you a quick method for using them.

Create a nickname

We'll create a sample nickname that can be deleted later. At least you'll see the pattern to use to create your own later.

Hands On

Objective: Learn to create a nickname.

❏ Click **Window, Nicknames** or press **CTRL+L**.

❏ Click **New**.

❏ Type *Bloggs - Joe*, check **Put on the recipient list**.

> Eudora automatically will alphabetize your list, so you probably will want to type the last name first, but you *cannot* use commas. We use a hyphen between first and last names.

> Nicknames that you put on the "recipient list" will show up on Eudora's main menus for quick access. Note that this nickname is going into the "Main Nicknames" file and that you can create and maintain several different nickname files.

❏ Click **OK**.

❏ Type *test@digiweb.com*

❏ Click in the **Notes** box and type *Practice Nickname*

❏ Double-click the menu control box to close the window.

❏ Click **Yes** to save the changes.

NET TIP

The Address(es) list under nicknames permits up to 64K of text. That's enough room for more than 2,000 addresses. If you don't want to manage so many names in this little window, you could maintain them in a database until you're ready to send, have the database output a list into your word processor in plain ASCII, use the Windows clipboard to Copy the list, go to Eudora, delete the current list, and then Paste the new list into the Address(es) window.

Using the address book

You now have saved your first nickname. Names on the recipient list will pop up on the menu items New Message To, Reply To, Forward To, and for Redirect To. Even if you don't put a nickname on the recipient list, you still can access the name quickly by pressing CTRL+L. Let's use the nickname list to quickly create an e-mail message to Joe Bloggs.

Hands On

Objective: Learn to use the nickname list and to delete nicknames.

❏ Click **Message, New Message To, Bloggs - Joe**.

> That's it! You now are set to complete and send the message. Note, however, that you can see only the nickname "Bloggs - Joe" on the **To:** line instead of the actual e-mail address. We now will show you how to get the actual address on the **To:** line instead of the nickname.

❏ Cancel this message by double-clicking the menu control box.

❏ Press **CTRL+L** for the nickname list.

❏ Click on **Bloggs - Joe**, then hold down **SHIFT** while clicking **To:**.

> Note that you now see the actual address. Let's finish this exercise by removing Joe Bloggs from your nickname list.

❏ Cancel this message by double-clicking the menu control box.

❏ Press **CTRL+L** for the nickname list.

❏ Click on **Joe Bloggs**, then click on **Remove**.

❏ Double-click the menu control box and click **Yes** to save changes.

Multiple recipients

Any e-mail message you send with Eudora can have multiple recipients. They simply will be listed in a string on the To: line in the message window. Just separate them with commas, and keep adding as many as you need. If you choose to use the nickname list to enter multiple To: entries (or for multiple carbon copies or for multiple blind copies), you simply hold down CTRL to highlight multiple nicknames before clicking on To:. When you use this method for multiple addresses, Eudora automatically inserts the commas.

Carbon copies

You may send a carbon copy of any e-mail message by entering the recipient's address on the CC: line. If you use the nickname list, highlight the nickname and then click on CC: instead of To:. Carbon copies are copies of your message that are sent to additional recipients who are not prime recipients of your message.

Blind copies

This function is similar to the carbon copy function except that the prime recipient will not know that additional copies were sent. If you use the nickname list, highlight the nickname and then click on BCC: instead of To:.

Print messages

You easily can print any e-mail message with Eudora. Eudora also gives you
several print preview functions (see Figure 8-11). Let's run through the print
options now.

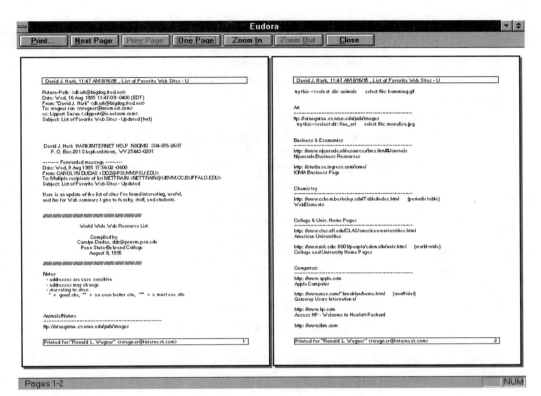

Figure 8-11

Hands On

***Objective:* Learn to use Print and Print Preview.**

❑ Click **Mailbox, In** and highlight **E-Mail Exercise 1**.

❑ Click **File, Print Preview**.

> Your e-mail message is formatted with a header that includes basic information about
> the sender and a footer that includes information about you. If the message is long,
> you can use the **Two Page** option to see two pages at once and you can use the **Next
> Page** and **Prev Page** options to browse through multiple pages. You also can use
> **Zoom In** and **Zoom Out** and if you click on **Print...** the message would be printed
> now, but let's wait.

❑ Click **Close** to close Print Preview.

> Make sure you have a printer online and available before completing the remaining
> steps, or just read them instead.

❑ Click **File, Print** or press **CTRL+P** to see the Print dialog box.

❑ Select any desired special options, then click **OK** to print.

Save messages

Messages can be saved to a disk file so that they're readily available for editing in one of your word processing directories. The messages are formatted in basic ASCII, but you still have a couple of save options.

Hands On

Objective: Learn to save an e-mail message.

❏ Use the message window that was opened in the last exercise.

❏ Click **File, Save As...**

❏ Select a word processing directory.

Note that Eudora has used portions of the message's Subject line to create a suggested file name. Before the next step, note the two check box options in the lower-left corner of this dialog box (see the mouse arrow in Figure 8-12).

Include headers

The saved e-mail message will not include the headers unless you specifically check this box. If you want the header information to be saved with the message, then check the Include Headers box.

Guess paragraphs

If you leave the Guess Paragraphs box unchecked, then Eudora will save the message with a carriage return at the end of each line. This can make editing difficult in your word processor, because each line of the message will be treated

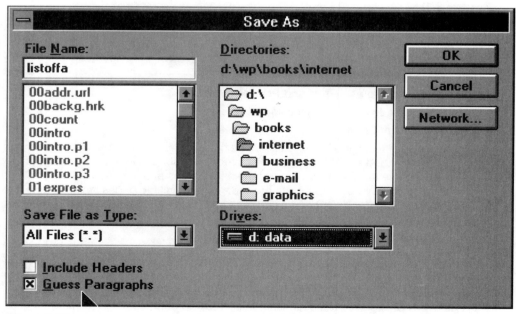

Figure 8-12

as a separate paragraph—automatic line wrapping will not work. If you check this box, Eudora will attempt to save the message so that paragraphs will wrap normally in your word processor.

A quick transfer method

You don't need to save an e-mail message to transfer it to your word processor. Remember the Copy and Paste exercise in chapter 7, "Windows wide open," that told you how to transfer information in Windows using the clipboard. The next exercise assumes that your word processor is running. If not, start it now, then return to Eudora.

Hands On

Objective: **Reinforce the use of the Windows clipboard.**

❏ Use your mouse to select some text in the message window that you want transferred to your word processor.

❏ Press **CTRL+C** to copy the selected text to the clipboard.

❏ Use **ALT+TAB** to cycle to your word processor.

   You could repeat these steps with other blocks of text within the same message, or with text in other messages.

❏ Press **CTRL+V** to paste the clipboard contents at the insertion point.

❏ Press **ALT+TAB** once to return to Eudora.

Domain Naming System (DNS)

If your e-mail address uses the name of your Internet service provider, then your e-mail success depends on that provider's continued success in business. If the provider goes out of business, your clients, customers, associates, and friends may have difficulty e-mailing you.

Your Internet address can be permanent if you set up an independent domain name for your organization that can travel with you from provider to provider. If your provider goes out of business or you find a better deal elsewhere, you can transfer your personal e-mail address. Getting your own domain name registered takes several weeks and your Internet provider may charge you for the service— typically between $50–$100—but it's a wise business investment.

Why your own domain name is important to your e-mail

Nearly all major companies have their own domain name registered. For example, Novell uses "novell.com" and Microsoft uses "microsoft.com." Today, a tailored domain name is practically expected if your business's Internet presence is to be taken seriously—so you need one for the good of your business image.

But we'll tell you a bit about how e-mail addresses work, so you'll understand why your own domain name can move with you.

NET TIP

You can quickly put your organization on a par with the big guns at Microsoft and IBM by contacting Digiweb. They'll register your domain name and in about three weeks you'll be able to receive e-mail at *yourname@yourdomain.com*. Their service also includes a Web site at *www.yourdomain.com*. You no longer will have to settle for being a subdirectory underneath someone else's domain name. Check out the Digiweb home page at *www.digiweb.com*, e-mail them at *sales@digiweb.com*, call them at 301- 977-6000 or fax them at 301-977-5400. They charge only $25 to establish your domain name and $20 per month to maintain your Web site, FTP site, e-mail routing, and much more. It's the best deal we've encountered so far.

The Internet actually exchanges messages using cryptic, numbered addresses that consist of four numbers separated by periods. They're called "dotted-quads" because they look like this: 198.137.240.100, a "quad" of numbers separated by dots.

Humans wouldn't enjoy remembering dotted-quad addresses, so the Internet ties these numbers to plain-language addresses and stores them as matched sets. For example, the dotted-quad in the last paragraph represents "whitehouse.gov;" much easier to remember and much more informative, isn't it? When you use a plain-language address, the Internet converts it to its associated dotted-quad and then uses the dotted-quad address, but then computers are comfortable calling the President of the United States "president@198.137.240.100."

The good news for you is that any dotted-quad can be assigned to any domain name, and that's the secret to having a long-lived e-mail address, because the dotted-quad points to a specific mail-handling system—such as your current Internet service provider. If you switch Internet service providers, you can get your domain name reassigned to the dotted-quad of your new system, and your plain-language e-mail address won't change. Only the Internet look-up table will change and no one sees that anyway, so your company can have the same e-mail addresses forever even if you get a different dotted-quad.

That completes our lesson on Internet e-mail. In the next chapter we'll show you how to use some Internet user tools: FTP, IRC, and Gopher. The Gopher lesson will be brief, because usage of the Gopher tool is waning rapidly, but we'll give you enough to handle Gopher the few times that you encounter it. FTP still is common, and may remain a useful Internet tool for a long while. IRC seems to be evolving into the videoconferencing we introduced you to in Phase 1. So, let's move on to chapter 9 and to some more Internet tools.

Continuing Education

Online e-mail guide
http://www.nova.edu/Inter-Links/email/email.html

This Web page is just for Internet e-mail help. You can learn about e-mail addresses, how to find people on the Internet, and how to send e-mail across different networks other than the Internet. It includes a listing of college e-mail addresses and a section on electronic mailing lists. It also can help you find a number of Internet e-mail programs other than Eudora, including Berkeley Mail, Elm and Pine.

▶ *Hands On*

InterNIC Whois search

http://rs.internic.net/cgi-bin/whois

This takes you to the Web interface for the InterNIC's searchable Whois database. Enter a company name in the text box and press ENTER. You'll get a list of domain names for all companies whose names contain the word or words you entered.

InterNIC directory and database services

http://www.internic.net/ds/dspg01.html

Your primary use of this site most likely will be its "InterNIC Directory Services" (white pages). It's one of the most comprehensive e-mail address locations that you'll find. This page also features the "InterNIC Database Services" (public databases) and an area entitled "Additional Internet Resource Information."

Directory of directories

http://www.internic.net/ds/dspg01.html

The InterNIC Directory of Directories is an index of references that will link you to resources, products and services all over the Internet. The links on this page include descriptions of available Internet resources. The Directory of Directories is compiled by the InterNIC Directory and Database Services (e-mail at: *admin@ds.internic.net*). This work is in conjunction with the National Science Foundation (NSF). Neither of the parties assumes any responsibility for the accuracy of the directory listings.

World Wide Yellow Pages

http://www.yellow.com

Here's an easy to remember URL that may find its way onto millions of browser bookmark lists (see Figure 8-13). You can use this page to search for a wide range of businesses with a Web presence. It's incomplete today, but is expanding rapidly. World Wide Yellow Pages is a commercial, for-profit venture, and is a trademark of Home Pages, Inc.

Four11 directory services

http://www.four11.com

Here's a Web page with links to several good directory services. Be sure to check out the link to the new "Four11 Internet Mail Directory." This is a commercial service of the SLED Corporation, but they provide free basic listings for all Internet users as well as free searches. They get money to buy their Cokes and Twinkies by offering premium services for a fee. Check them out. They do a nice job because they hope you'll sign up for premium services so they can keep the pantry full of goodies.

Domain Name System (DNS)

http://rs.internic.net/rs-internic.html

This is the Registration Services home page for the InterNIC, the organization that handles all Domain Name System (DNS) registrations. This page has hypertext links to a wealth of InterNIC services and can help you better

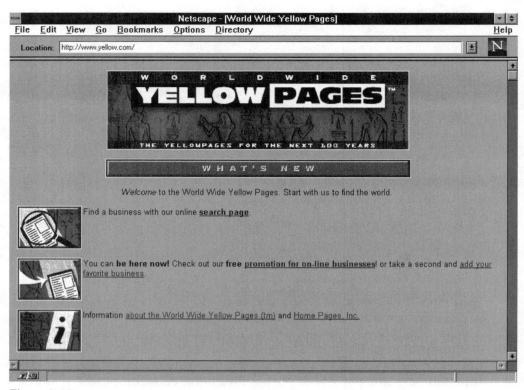

Figure 8-13

understand the Internet DNS. Of course your Internet service provider also will be helpful in setting up your tailored domain name.

Signature file ideas

http://falcon.cc.ukan.edu/~aaronh/documents/collectn.htm

You'll read a lot of witty aphorisms in e-mail and newsgroup signature block. You also will read a lot of ridiculous junk. Whichever you want to include in your signature file, you probably can find something "good" if you check out this site and its many one-liners. Enjoy yourself, but remember the generally-accepted "4-line-limit" on signature files.

Basic Internet research tools

OKAY, we've covered the most commonly used Internet tool: e-mail. Now we're going to help you learn to use some other valuable Internet tools. Knowing how to use Internet research tools is an absolute must, because more information is added to the Internet each day than you could comfortably read in the rest of your life. Fortunately, most of the information that is on the Internet is, literally, none of your business. So, we're going to show you how to use some tools that will locate the information that *is* your business.

Yet, many people may never need the tools to which we dedicate most of this chapter: FTP (File Transfer Protocol) and IRC (Internet Relay Chat). Here's why:

◉ If you use FTP, it most likely will be within a Web page that will have the FTP function built-in. In Netscape, you barely will notice that you've found an FTP page; and when you've completed your FTP download, you'll back right out and return to normal Web functions (more on this later).

◉ IRC is a live-action tool that is useful today only if you want to communicate with someone in real-time by exchanging typed text messages. Increasingly, however, the IRC will be used for telephone and videoconferencing. Today, Internet videoconferencing still has severe limitations, but those limitations soon will vanish.

HYPERJUMP

Download
Copying files *onto* your computer *from* a remote computer.
Upload
Copying files *from* your computer *onto* a remote computer.

Despite their limited usage, we would be remiss if we ignored FTP and IRC. Because FTP also can be used to upload files, you may need it to collaborate on joint projects, as did the authors of this book (see appendix C, "How we did it"). Or you may need FTP to update the files in your own organization's Web site if you maintain your Web site on an outside server.

IRC software is evolving rapidly. As this book is being written, IRC packages are improving their videoconferencing capabilities. Few organizations today have the hardware necessary for videoconferencing, and the Internet barely can handle video capacity demands anyway; but both of those factors are changing rapidly. Turnkey videoconferencing packages may become common in 1996.

We'll conclude this chapter with a brief overview of some tools of which you may have heard, but on which we only briefly will touch: Gopher, Archie, Veronica, and Telnet. As we mentioned earlier, these are the Internet's equivalent of vinyl records—still useful, but only if you're content with "oldies but goodies." Just as quickly as compact discs replaced vinyl records, the latest happenings on the Internet are moving to the Web.

Entering Internet commands

As you use the Internet, you'll be typing a lot of Uniform Resource Locator (URL) strings. Almost all of them today are written with lowercase letters. A few, however, contain mixed-case letters, and the case of each letter is critical in filenames and directory names. Protocol and host names are case-insensitive.

Remember that much of the underlying structure of the Internet is based on the UNIX computer operating system. You may notice that UNIX filenames look much like familiar DOS filenames. That's because DOS was patterned after UNIX; but there are two important and readily identifiable differences between them.

The first difference is that UNIX uses the normal slash to separate directory levels and filenames, while DOS uses a backslash (\). The second difference is that filenames in UNIX are case-sensitive. When writing down any URL string, be sure to copy every letter exactly, then be sure you enter it in the computer exactly as written. Of course, if you completed the "Windows wide open" lesson, you'll use the Windows Copy and Paste commands to eliminate the risks and wasted time associated with writing down URLs and retyping them.

FTP (File Transfer Protocol)

The backbone of file downloading on the Internet is the File Transfer Protocol (FTP). Using FTP gives you access to an incredibly vast world of computer files—definitely more than any one person ever could use. But FTP is a two-way street, so you also can use it to upload files; i.e., you can contribute to the Internet's growth!

While FTP technically is a two-way street, few Internet users today transfer files both ways. Among the new wave of users in the late 1990s, most people only download files via FTP. Most of the uploading is done by computer professionals. Downloading is done by mainstream users who are seeking information.

HYPERJUMP

Anonymous FTP

Using FTP at a remote site that has left its system open and that does not require a secret login ID. In other words, the remote site lets you remain anonymous, although common netiquette calls for using your real e-mail address as a password if you're prompted for it.

If you directly use FTP, you most likely will use it to implement an *anonymous FTP*. If the target system does not permit anonymous FTP, you will need a login ID or an account (and perhaps a password) to gain access to any of the system's files. With anonymous FTP, your login ID is "anonymous" and your password, if required, is your e-mail address. The password in an anonymous FTP is not truly a password, because any e-mail address will work, and the host system will not know if a user enters a bogus address. You are, of course, asked to use your correct e-mail address. There are advantages to this, because the host system has a record of who has received its files, and therefore has the ability to contact you if the host computer's administrators later discover a software bug or a computer virus in the files you downloaded.

Practice FTP netiquette

FTP can consume large amounts of Internet bandwidth and contribute to slowing down the system for everyone. If you locate and plan to download a very large file, consider the time of day. Try to avoid downloading large files during the peak of business days—from about noon on the East Coast until about 1:00 p.m. on the West Coast. Late at night or over weekends the Internet is less busy. Practicing good netiquette can benefit you, too, because during peak times, Internet traffic delays may cause a "time out" that will force you to begin the entire transfer process again... and again... and again.

Netscape FTP summary

The acronym FTP (pronounced *effteepee*) has come to be used both as a noun (referring to the File Transfer Protocol) and as a verb (referring to the act of using FTP). Using the term as a verb, someone might say "I'll go see if I can FTP some information about using FOIA." As a verb describing human activity, the days of FTP are waning. You likely will do little direct FTPing on the Internet.

As a verb describing computer activity, however, FTP will remain for many years a staple of cyberspace. Increasingly, the way you'll use FTP will be through a hypertext page on the World Wide Web, so most of your FTP downloads automatically will use Netscape's built-in FTP capabilities. Many Web pages include FTP jumps that will transfer requested files to your computer. Sometimes the jump will lead you to a Web page that still is under construction, and you'll be thrown directly into actual FTP mode because they have not fully blended all of their information into their Web site.

Keep an eye on the Location: box at the top of your Netscape screen. If you encounter a page that looks like the FTP pages you've seen in these exercises and you see "ftp://" at the beginning of the text string instead of "http://," you'll know you've jumped out of the Web hypertext document. Use the FTP techniques you've learned here to download the information you want.

If you find yourself at an FTP location, don't worry; you haven't "lost" the Web and there are five easy ways to return:
- Click the right mouse button, then click Back;
- Click the Back command button or click View History to get back to your last hypertext Web location;

- Click View History and choose your last location;
- Click on the drop arrow at the end of the Location: text entry box.
- Press ALT+RIGHT ARROW

If the software package you got from your Internet service provider included a stand-alone FTP application, you may never use it. But if you need to perform extensive FTP transfers, including file uploading, we recommend that you get a stand-alone FTP application. A couple of references given later in this chapter will help you download a copy of a popular FTP application called WS_FTP. After two exercises using Netscape for FTP, we'll give you an optional lesson using WS_FTP. WS_FTP also includes many features that are missing from Netscape's built-in FTP. WS_FTP will be especially useful if you want to transfer large numbers of files, or if you experience connection difficulties while attempting to FTP with Netscape.

FTP Exercise 1

Using FTP, you can download any type of computer file. The system doesn't care what the file contains. You can download graphics images, programs, operating systems, spreadsheets, word processing documents, or database files. For your first exercise on using the Internet FTP, we'll have you download something fun, then we'll do a business-related download for a follow-up exercise. So, now let's download a beautiful, full-color image from The Exploratorium in San Francisco (see Figure 9-1).

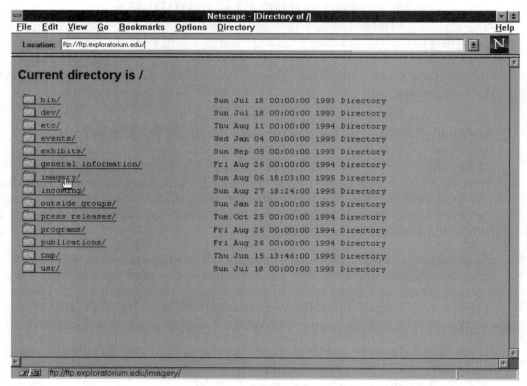

Figure 9-1

Hands On

Objective: Use Netscape to FTP a graphic image.

- Start Netscape.
- Double-click in the **Location:** window.
- Type *ftp://ftp.exploratorium.edu* and press **ENTER**.
- Click on the folder **imagery/**

  Note the file titled *Prism.jpg* and its file size of 20K bytes. Because this is one of the smallest files in this directory, we'll use it for this lesson.

- Click on *Prism.jpg* to download the image (see Figure 9-2).
  Depending on your modem, your Internet connection type and the time of day, downloading this file could take from a few seconds to several minutes. If you have the time to download more images, you can return to the previous directory for more.

- To save the image, click the right mouse button on it, click **Save this image as...**, click **OK** to accept the default filename.
- Click the right mouse button, then click **Back**.
- Click on the filename or the icon of any file to download it.
- Click the right mouse button, then click **Back**.
- Return to the main FTP directory by clicking the right mouse again and then clicking **Back**, or by scrolling to the top of the list and clicking **Up** to the higher level directory.

  We have returned you to the root directory. You now can either explore other directories or move on to the next lesson, in which we'll download a text file. The Exploratorium is generous in granting reprint rights for the art you find here—they ask that the original copyright remain visible and that you credit them specifically, as we've done in this book.

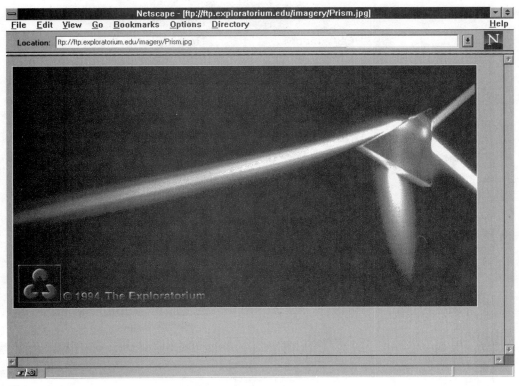

Figure 9-2

Common FTP filenames

Many files that you'll encounter when using FTP are UNIX files that cannot be used by your standard IBM PC-compatible machine running Microsoft Windows or DOS. Of course you also will encounter many files that you *can* use, so we've included this table to help you know which is which.

To save you the agony of finding out the hard way which files you can and cannot use, we'll give you this quick list of file extensions that will help you decipher the file types on FTP directories. Table 9-1 lists common Internet FTP file extensions, their typical usage, and a description of what you can expect them to contain.

TABLE 9-1. Typical FTP file extensions

Extension	File Usage	File description
.avi	Windows	Compressed video files
.bmp	DOS/Windows	Bit-mapped graphics files
.c	ASCII/Text	Source code for C-programming code
.com	DOS/Windows	Command files (programs)
.exe	DOS/Windows/ VAX/VMS	Executable files (programs)
.gif	DOS/Windows	Graphics Interchange Format (compressed graphic images)
.gz	UNIX	Compressed files that must be expanded by the UNIX GNU gzip utility to be of use
.h	DOS/Windows	Header files for C-programming code
.hqx	Macintosh	Compressed files that must be expanded by the Macintosh uncompression program to be of use
.htm	DOS/Windows	Hypertext Markup Language files
.html	UNIX	Hypertext Markup Language files
.jpg	DOS/Windows	Compressed graphic images
.mov	Windows/Macintosh	Compressed video files
.mpeg	UNIX	Compressed video files
.mpg	All	Compressed video files
.ps	DOS/Windows	PostScript files that are only usable with a PostScript viewer or PostScript printer
.sgm	DOS/Windows	Standard Generalized Markup Language files
.sgml	UNIX	Standard Generalized Markup Language files
.tif	DOS/Windows	Tagged Image File (graphic images)

| .txt | DOS/Windows | Text files that can be opened by most word processors, the DOS Edit program, or the Windows Notepad |
| .zip | DOS/Windows | Compressed files that must be expanded with the pkunzip program to be of use |

Netscape also indicates general file type by use of icons that appear as folders in front of FTP filenames (see Figure 9-3):
- Icons that appear as file folders are directories
- Icons that appear as blank pages represent text
- Icons that appear as pages decorated with colored images represent image files.

The current version of the most popular stand-alone FTP application, WS_FTP, does not display graphic file-type icons. Netscape thus is more user-friendly for FTP downloading, especially because it does not require any additional software juggling.

Current directory is /imagery

Up to higher level directory

	.cache	2 Kb	Mon Aug 29 23:39:00 1994	
	.cache+	7 Kb	Tue Aug 29 16:56:00 1995	
	00Whats here	764 bytes	Fri Feb 25 00:00:00 1994	
	A.M. Lightning.jpg	35 Kb	Sun Apr 03 00:00:00 1994	Image format
	Bells.jpg	64 Kb	Sun Apr 03 00:00:00 1994	Image format
	Bernoulli ball.jpg	55 Kb	Sun Apr 03 00:00:00 1994	Image format
	Bubble Film.jpg	20 Kb	Sun Apr 03 00:00:00 1994	Image format
	Catenary arch.jpg	86 Kb	Sun Apr 03 00:00:00 1994	Image format
	Color mixing.jpg	44 Kb	Sun Apr 03 00:00:00 1994	Image format
	Colored shadows.jpg	51 Kb	Sun Apr 03 00:00:00 1994	Image format
	Distorted room.jpg	47 Kb	Sun Apr 03 00:00:00 1994	Image format
	Duck Into Kaleidos...	84 Kb	Sun Apr 03 00:00:00 1994	Image format

Figure 9-3

NET TIP If you use a lot of zip files, (either for download or upload) you'll appreciate "WinZip" compression software. You can FTP it from *ftp.cc.utexas.edu/microlib/win/archiver* and get the file *winzipXX.exe* (where *XX* represents the version number). It's a self-extracting and self-installing file, so the first time you run WinZip, it sets itself up on your system, and automatically becomes a part of the menu system on your Windows File Manager. After that, you'll find zipping and unzipping to be a breeze. Be sure and register if you find that you'll use the software.

FTP Exercise 2

Now that that beautiful image has given you an enjoyable introduction to FTP, let's perform a more typical, business-oriented FTP download. For the next exercise, we'll assume that our organization needs some government information that is covered by the Freedom of Information Act (FOIA). We'd like to submit a request, but we don't know what forms we need, or where to send them when we have completed them.

The Electronic Frontier Foundation (EFF) maintains an FTP site from which you can download a vast array of files. The EFF was founded to ensure that constitutional principles are protected as the electronic communications revolution emerges. Naturally, you would expect the EFF to have information on the FOIA. We'll visit their FTP site and see if we can discover how to file a request under the FOIA.

Hands On

***Objective:* Reinforce the first FTP lesson by using a different server.**

❑ Netscape still should be running from the last exercise.

❑ If the text in the **Location:** box is highlighted, you can begin typing immediately. If not, then double-click in the **Location:** box to highlight the current entry.

❑ Type *ftp://ftp.eff.org* and press **ENTER**.

  Read the introduction and you'll notice two important items. First, notice that they ask you to get README for information on their FTP server. README files are common and can be a time-saver if anything at all goes wrong, but we'll skip this README for now.

  Second, notice that they suggest you use their Web site if you have a Web browser (see Figure 9-4). They make the comparison clear by saying "same files, better site"; check it out at *http://www.eff.org/pub*. Of course you have a Web browser, and normally would use that at this point—but we're learning how to FTP now, so let's remain here.

❑ Scroll past the text until you see the directory listing.

  Click once on a document icon to download and display that document. Click once on a folder icon to open that folder and display its contents.

❑ Click on **00-INDEX.ftp** to open the EFF basic index file.

  Checking the index file in any directory can save time by giving you a quick list of what's in the directory. The first paragraph of the index text tells us that pub/ is the directory in which we can expect to find their public access archives. So now we need to go back to the full directory listing and switch to pub/.

❑ Click your right mouse button anywhere on the page and click **Back**.

  Or, if you have the Toolbar displayed, click its **Back** button.

❑ Scroll down to click on **pub/**.

  Read the notice at the top of this page for an explanation of the general subjects. We're in luck this time because the first directory listed, "Activism," contains FOIA information.

❑ Scroll down to the Activism folder.

  We'll skip the document **00-INDEX.pub** because we already have a pretty good idea we'll find what we need in Activism. Also, note the document **00-index.html**. We won't use that now, either, but this is twice that the EFF FTP site has dropped hints to use the Web.

❑ Click on **Activism** to open the folder, then scroll to **FOIA**.

❑ We'll skip the document **00-INDEX.Activism** this time.

❑ Click on **FOIA** to open the folder.

❑ Click on **00-INDEX.FOIA** to open the document.

  Scroll through this document and you'll read that the documents *foia.guide* and *foia.kit* are the ones we need.

❑ Click your right mouse button anywhere on the page and click **Back**.

❑ Click on *foia.kit* to open the document.

The first paragraph makes it clear that we've got the right document, so now we'll save it to our hard drive so we use it in our word processor. Make sure the full document is downloaded before you save it. Watch the byte count on the status bar at the bottom of the screen and wait until it says: "Document: Done."

❑ Click **File, Save As...** or press **CTRL+S**

❑ The filename already has been entered for us.

❑ Select a different directory, if desired, and click **OK**.

Remember the name (foia.kit) and the directory in which you saved it.

❑ Click your right mouse button anywhere on the page and click **Back**.

Because the *foia.guide* document is large (227K) and *foia.kit* seems to have everything we need, let's not download that one now. Now let's go see the file we've downloaded.

❑ If your word processor is already running, use **ALT+TAB** to cycle to it.

If your word processor is not running, use **ALT+TAB** to cycle to the Program Manager and start your word processor.

❑ Open the *foia.kit* file.

If you've ever wanted to make a FOIA request, here's the opportunity, but you're on your own now.

❑ Press **CTRL+F4** to close the *foia.kit* file in your word processor.

❑ Use **ALT+TAB** to cycle back to Netscape.

You now are ready to look for more documents at the EFF FTP site, or to use the **Location:** text box to enter another FTP site.

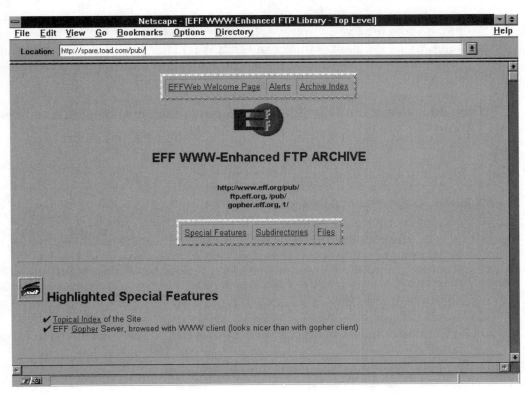

Figure 9-4

We now will move on to the WS_FTP application, a dedicated FTP client software package with which you can use FTP to upload files to other computers on the Internet.

Stand-alone FTP application

In this optional FTP lesson, we're going to run through a quick overview of using the stand-alone FTP software application for Windows called WS_FTP. You may skip this lesson for now, but this is where we'll show you how to upload files using FTP. Our practice download will be to acquire the latest version of some software for using the Internet Relay Chat (used in the next lesson), so you may want to run through these steps just to get some updated IRC software.

How to Get WS_FTP

ftp://ftp.cica.indiana.edu

If you need more FTP power than Netscape gives you, you'll want to download and use WS_FTP, a Windows FTP client software application. At the time we wrote this, WS_FTP had more detailed FTP options and functions than Netscape, but Netscape constantly improves, so check the FTP capabilities in the latest version.

Once you're connected to the URL listed above, change directories to *pub/pc/win3/winsock* and download the file *ws_ftpXX.zip* (where *XX* represents the two-digit number corresponding to the version of WS-FTP). You'll have to use pkunzip to uncompress the required files.

WS_FTP can be used with the same Winsock connection that you use with Netscape. For example, if you were using Netscape and wanted to use FTP to upload some files, you can leave Netscape connected. Simply use ALT+TAB to change to the Program Manager and start WS_FTP. When you're finished with your FTP activity, close WS_FTP and use ALT+TAB to return to Netscape.

If you don't have a copy of WS_FTP, check out the accompanying sidebar titled "How to Get WS_FTP."

Hands On

Objective: **Learn to configure and use WS_FTP.**

❏ Establish your Internet connection.

Your WinSock application may be setup to dial-in automatically when you start WS-FTP. Or, you may already be using Netscape. You also may have a current Internet connection via your local area network. If any of these cases is true, go directly to the next step. Otherwise, start your WinSock application, login and then minimize WinSock once you're connected.

❏ Start WS_FTP.

You probably see the dialog box titled, "Session Profile." (See Figure 9-5.) If not, then click **Connect** to open it. We're going to create a new FTP profile, then save it.

❏ Click in the **Host Name** text box and type *ftp.internext.com*.

❏ Press **TAB** to jump to **Host Type**.

❏ Use the drop list to select **UNIX** (standard).

Unless you know for certain the operating system of the host computer, use this list to enter **automatic detect**, so that WS_FTP will determine the system type for you.

❏ Press **TAB** to jump to **User ID** and type *anonymous*.

❏ Press **TAB** to jump to **Password** and enter your e-mail address.

❏ Press **TAB** twice to jump to **Initial Directories, Remote Host**.

You almost always will skip the **Account** entry unless you do, indeed, have an account number. In that case, you also would use an actual User ID and Password.

❏ Type */pub*.

This entry will set the initial directory that will open when you connect with the host computer. /pub is commonly used for public directories at FTP sites. Many URL references will give you the entire directory string so you can enter it here instead of having to navigate through directories after you connect. If you don't know which directory you want, then set this entry to the root directory by entering a forward slash (/).

❏ Press **TAB** to jump to **Local PC** and type a directory on your hard drive.

In the lessons on mail, we walked you through creating a default download directory. You can enter that directory now.

If you intend to perform FTP uploads, we suggest that you also create a default upload directory. Once your hard drive has an upload directory, you can use your file manager to copy all the files to be uploaded into this one directory and then you can enter that directory here in WS_FTP. This will spare you the wasted time of having to navigate all over your hard drive to find files while you're online. And better yet, it may prevent you from overlooking a file while you've got WS_FTP connected. After the upload is complete, you can use your file manager to clear your default upload directory in preparation for your next transfer.

❏ Click in the **Profile Name** text entry box and type *Internext*.

❏ Click **Anonymous Login** and click **Auto Save Config**.

❏ Click **Save**.

This saves the information you just entered into a profile that you can use again. Saving profiles will be a tremendous time-saver if you routinely make a lot of FTP connections. You need only once to take the time to specify and save all the defaults for each of your regular FTP sites.

❏ Click **OK** to connect to the Internext FTP site.

❏ Click the **Binary** button at the bottom of the screen.

This will put you in the binary transfer mode, which will permit you to transfer any type of file. You now are ready for file transfers in either direction. The WS_FTP program will have no idea of the file type or its usage; it simply transfers between the host computer and your computer exact copies of the file or files you select. Your local PC's drive is represented in the window on the left, Local System. It will show whatever directory you specified in the Session Profile dialog box. The host computer's drive is represented in the window on the right, Remote System (see mouse arrow in Figure 9-6).

The letters in the Local System window that are enclosed in square brackets ([-a-] or [-c-]) represent your local drive letters. The double dots (..) at the top of the list represents the parent of the current directory. Double-click on the (..) to go up to

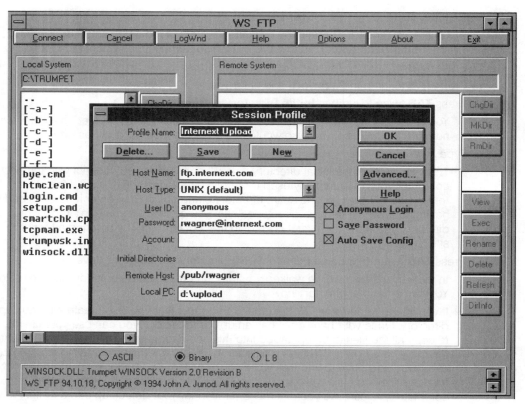

Figure 9-5

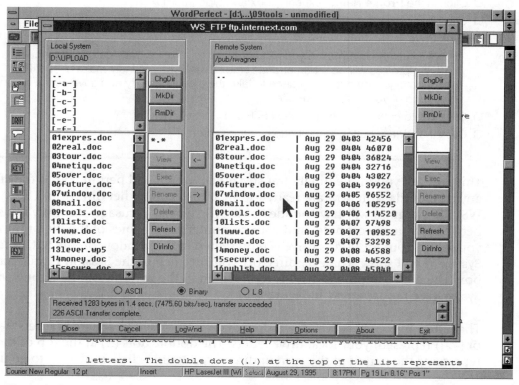

Figure 9-6

► *Hands On*

the next higher directory level. Then double-click on your download directory to switch down to it.

Instead of navigating through your directory structure by clicking, you can jump directly to any directory by clicking on the ChgDir button and typing the exact path name. You could use the MkDir button to make a new directory on your local drive. For example, if you don't yet have an upload directory, you could click MkDir, type \upload and click OK. You can use the RmDir button to remove a directory from your local drive. You also will see the same buttons on the right, but generally a host computer will not have given you the rights to use MkDir or RmDir. We now will continue the lesson so you can download files from this site.

Hands On

Objective: Complete the WS_FTP lesson.

❑ Scroll through the directory list within **Remote System**.

❑ Double-click the directory **mcgraw-hill**.

❑ Click on the file **welcome**.

❑ Click the **Left Arrow** button that's between the directory windows.

> This will initiate the download transfer from the remote system to your local system. When completed, you will have a file from the authors of this book that will tell you about the other files in this directory. You can read it later and see if you want to return to this directory for any of the other files we have placed here for you.
>
> If you had wanted to upload a file instead of downloading, you would have highlighted a file in the **Local System** window and clicked the **Right Arrow** button between the directory windows. Let's switch now to another remote system.

❑ Click the **Close** button to close the remote directory.

> As soon as you do this, that same button changes names. It now is the **Connect** button.

❑ Click the **Connect** button to get the **Session Profile** dialog box.

❑ Click the drop list **Profile Name**, then scroll to **OAK Archives**.

> If SunSite UNC is not on the list, then create it by using as a pattern the steps we did earlier. The host name information is in the Continuing Education section at the end of this chapter.

❑ Click **OK** to connect to OAK.

❑ Double-click on **/pub** in the **Remote System** window.

❑ Double-click on **/irc**.

❑ Double-click on **/clients**.

❑ Double-click on **/windows**.

> This is the listing of Windows IRC client software applications. You have several from which to choose.

❑ Click on **wsircv20.zip** to highlight the WSIRC file.

❑ Click the **Left Arrow** button between the directory windows.

> This will download the compressed application file to the download directory on your local system. You'll have to uncompress it later using pkunzip, then we'll use this application in the next exercise.

❑ Click **Exit** to exit WS_FTP and disconnect.

You're on your own now. There are millions of files around the world that are available via anonymous FTP. We haven't even attempted to list them here. You can find in your local computer store or in the computer book section of any major bookstore plenty of other books that feature extensive lists of FTP file sites.

Internet Relay Chat (IRC)

Internet Relay Chat (IRC) users convene on "channels" to "chat" in groups or privately. Think of IRC as a virtual gathering place, usually focused on specific topics of conversation. Currently, all IRC chats are conducted using typed text messages. As you read this, the Internet has hundreds, perhaps thousands, of ongoing IRC chats.

Though many IRC participants are college students, the IRC is available to any Internet user and is increasingly used for "conference calls" by businesspeople. The IRC has been used for serious projects that simply could not have been completed using any other communication tool. Your organization could conduct a formal meeting via the IRC that would give each participation an instant written record of the proceedings. Of course, the meeting will proceed smoothly only if each participant is a fairly accurate and speedy typist.

Depending on the IRC software you choose to use, you can simultaneously connect to multiple IRC channels. Usually the freeware versions that you download via Internet FTP will let you establish between two to five simultaneous channels. Commercial versions, and registered shareware versions, permit one user to connect to as many as 255 chat channels simultaneously.

The IRC was designed as a replacement for an earlier UNIX system known as a "talk" program, but has advanced far beyond its predecessor. The original talk program connected only two users at a time while the IRC is a multi-user chat system. The IRC originally was written by Jarkko Oikarinen (e-mail address: *jto@tolsun.oulu.fi*) in 1988. Since appearing in Finland, the IRC has been used in more than 60 countries, but English is the primary language of the IRC.

The IRC at work

The Internet Relay Chat (IRC) gained international fame during the 1991 Persian Gulf War when updates from around the world came across news wires and most IRC users who were online at the time gathered on a single chat channel to read those reports. IRC had similar uses during the coup against Boris Yeltsin in September 1993 when IRC users from Moscow gave live reports about the unstable situation as events unfolded.

An IRC chat has advantages over telephone conference calls because long-distance fees are not charged for connect time, even when the chat conference is global in scope. An IRC chat can be logged and saved to disk so that it automatically provides a written transcript of the discussion. An IRC chat, of course, has the disadvantage of requiring everyone to type or to send previously typed material—voice communication is just beginning to be used.

Internet Phone: talk for free over the Internet

The move from half-duplex Internet phone service to full-duplex Internet phone service occurred, with the release of Internet Phone 3.0, as this book was being written. Full-duplex enables users on either end to speak simultaneously, creating a natural conversation. Half-duplex is comparable to using a speaker phone with which each user takes turns listening and speaking. Both half-duplex and full-duplex versions are fully compatible with each other.

To support full duplex capabilities, you will need in your PC a full-duplex sound card capable of recording and playing back at the same time or two standard sound cards. The system is voice-activated to minimize bandwidth usage.

For more information, check out the Internet Phone Web site at *http://www.vocaltec.com*. They offer a free demo copy of the Internet Phone software that's limited to 60 seconds of speech. All features work normally for the short test time, but to eliminate the 60-second limit, you'll need to register the software and enter a special code. The full version of the software sells for less than one hundred U.S. dollars. After you're registered, you can FTP version updates for free.

Normal IRC conversations are not secure at all. Anything you type usually travels across multiple Internet servers and your messages easily can be intercepted and read. It is possible, however, to set up a private channel using a Direct Client-to-Client protocol (DCC), which provides a secure form of communication because messages are not sent through the IRC network. DCC conversations also allow much more efficient Internet bandwidth usage, because messages do not need to be broadcast all over the world just to reach one individual.

How the IRC works

In typical network parlance, the IRC consists of clients and servers. When you use the IRC, you use client software (see Figure 9-7). IRC servers are located all over the world, waiting for you and other users to connect to them. When you connect to an IRC server, your client software will display a status window that lists messages from the server to you. For example, the server will confirm that you are connected and, most likely, will welcome you and tell you how to contact the server's administrator.

Everyone on the IRC uses a nickname. When you "join" a channel, everyone on that channel gets a message that you (masquerading as your nickname) have joined. You also will see a list of the nicknames of everyone logged on with you. Similarly, when anyone leaves, you'll see a message that that nickname has left and the nickname will disappear from the list.

You'll create your own default nickname with the setup function of your IRC software, but be prepared to change it on the fly because IRC servers do not permit duplicate nicknames. Unlike e-mail addresses, you cannot "own" a nickname. Prior usage gives you no claim to a nickname. You may use a nickname once and then find it rejected the next time you connect with the server because someone already connected is using that nickname. You cannot

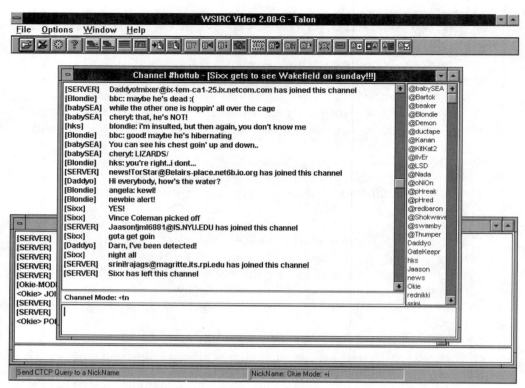

Figure 9-7

demand your previously-used name for that session, although the next time you connect, it may be available again.

The client software has a "List" function that can list all the currently opened channels. This may produce such a huge list that you won't even want to see it come across your screen. Fortunately, you can limit the channels that will be displayed by your list command. For example, you could filter out all channels that have fewer than five users connected.

IRC application software that has DCC capability also gives you the ability to transfer files between users. But you first must notify the individual with whom you want to transfer files and establish a DCC with that individual.

Keep up with IRC changes

The IRC constantly evolves, so read the Message Of The Day (MOTD) to stay abreast of updates and new procedures—the MOTD should display automatically every time you use IRC. The bottom line is this book cannot be your final word on the IRC. It's a fast-moving target.

The CU-SeeMe Project

CU-SeeMe is a free videoconferencing program that is available to anyone using the Internet with a Macintosh or with Windows. With CU-SeeMe, you can video conference with another site located anywhere in the world, or by use of a reflector, up to eight sites can link into a single CU-SeeMe conference.

Unfortunately, security precautions have forced many organizations to block access to advanced Internet services such as telephone and videoconferencing. The same protocols that make this technology possible also open the door to hackers. Nonetheless, you still can use these services on a computer that's isolated from the rest of the network.

To send video, you will need a video capture board that supports Microsoft Video For Windows and a video camera to plug into the video capture board. Be sure to check the Web site before buying hardware—standards are changing rapidly and they have a list of boards that support CU-SeeMe as well as one that do not.

To learn more about CU-SeeMe, check out the Web site at *http://cu-seeme.cornell.edu/*. It's the site of the CU-SeeMe Development Team of the Advanced Technologies and Planning group of the Network Resources division of Cornell Information Technologies. As of the summer of 1995, the software carried this disclaimer, "WARNING: Although being improved with each version, CU-SeeMe is not a mature production software—USE AT YOUR OWN RISK."

Some popular IRC applications, such as the WSIRC applications that we use here, have evolved to include videoconferencing and audio. Still, the IRC may be used for many years in text-mode by individuals and within organizations that lack videoconferencing equipment. Also, because the IRC requires no special equipment, it may continue to bring us the latest-breaking news on world events that might otherwise be difficult to disseminate.

You also will want to check out the Continuing Education section at the end of this chapter for sites at which you can download the latest copies of Windows IRC software applications.

The zip file (*wsircv20.zip*) that you downloaded earlier in this chapter using the WS_FTP program provides IRC software that enables two users to videoconference. Audio is supported only in half-duplex mode, which means speaker phone-style—one party speaks the other party listens. It provides multiple DCC Video windows simultaneously, although it is practical to have only one at a time unless you use a high-speed Internet connection. It's an excellent, user-friendly application, but several of its functions only work in the registered version.

Registering WSIRC

You may register WSIRC online using CompuServe's Shareware Registration facility, which will prompt you for a credit card payment. Register WSIRC Classic using *WSIRC.ZIP* as the filename, or by ID: 2442 or US $39.95. Register WSIRC Video using *WSIRCV.ZIP* as the filename, or by ID: 6349 for US $59.95.

Students may register WSIRC Classic by check for US $24.95 after first sending e-mail from a *.edu* account to qualify.

You also may register by snail mail by sending a check for the correct amount for the version you are registering, along with your e-mail address, to the program's author:

Caesar M. Samsi

P.O. Box 9966

Arlington, VA 22219 USA

The IRC Hands On lesson will be a bit different from the others. We cannot possibly write any IRC lesson steps that you could follow precisely from beginning to end. Instead, we will show you how to set up your software, connect to a server, and join a channel. After you've joined, you're on your own. We will conclude the lesson by showing you how to disconnect from the server and exit the WSIRC application.

Hands On

Objective: Learn to join an IRC channel.

❏ Make sure you have an established TCP/IP Internet connection.

If you already are connected to the Internet via your Netscape browser, simply use **ALT+TAB** to locate the WSIRC icon.

❏ Double-click on the **WSIRC** icon.

If you have just downloaded this software and this is the first time you have run it, WSIRC automatically will take you to the "Server Options Setup" dialog box. If this box does not appear, then click on the third icon, **Server Options Setup**.

❏ Click on the **IRC Server** drop-list and select a nearby server.

❏ Click on the **NickName** text entry box and type a nickname.

Nicknames currently are limited to 9 characters.

❏ Click on the **UserName** text entry box and type your username.

❏ Click on the **Email** text entry box and type your e-mail address.

❏ Click **OK** to acknowledge the "Note!" dialog box.

❏ Click **OK** to connect to the server you selected.

The server will process your entry attempt and notify you if the nickname you are using already is in use. If so, to enter an alternate, you type */NICK nickname* and press **ENTER**. Once you're connected, the **Server Messages** window will display the Message of The Day (MOTD). If you don't see the MOTD, type */MOTD* and press **ENTER**.

This window will remain open during your IRC session. Note that this is a Windows "document window." Remember the lessons in Chapter 7 about moving, sizing, minimizing and restoring windows in case you want to rearrange your desktop.

❏ Click on the tenth icon, **List Channels**.

❏ Type *-min 10* and click **OK**.

This will list, in a scroll window on the right side of the **Server Messages** window, all open IRC channels that have a minimum of 10 active participants. The number of active participants is listed after the name of each channel. Scroll through the list to see if the name of any of the channels intrigues you.

❏ Double-click on the channel name you choose to join.

If you prefer to enter a channel directly, you can click on the ninth icon, **Join a Channel**, type *#hottub* and click **OK**. Note that all IRC channel names begin with the pound sign (#).

You now are in a document window in which you will participate in the chat channel. Everyone on the channel just got a message that said you have joined. The upper box contains messages. The right side of the window lists all active participants, including you. Note that your insertion point is flashing in the small text entry box at the bottom of the channel window.

Okay, now you're on your own! Hottub always should have some members. Good luck and have fun.

NET TIP You don't really have to count over a number of icons to find the right one. Although the WSIRC buttons don't have drop-tags, there is a way to find out what they do: Position the mouse over a button—but don't click now—and read the status bar at the bottom of the screen.

The current participants are listed on the right side of the chat window. They're in alphabetical order in two groups: The first group lists members with the "at" symbol (@) in front of their nicknames and the second group lists members without the "at" symbol. You'll be in the second group, without an @ symbol. Members with the @ symbol are channel "operators" who have special rights. This is not a big deal. Operator rights are about as prestigious and difficult to obtain as owning the rights to the air in your lungs right now. Neither one will do you much good if you keep it to yourself.

Some frequently used IRC commands

Here's a list of a few of the essential IRC commands. Note that they all begin with the forward slash command (/). Once your insertion point is in the text entry box at the bottom of the chat channel window, you can type any of these commands and then press ENTER to send it. You transmit commands exactly as you would transmit a message to another user, but the software sees the / symbol and intercepts the text as an IRC command. We've organized the IRC commands into two categories: Generic commands that are available to everyone and operator commands.

Generic IRC commands

/CHANNELLOG *<filename>*—turns on a channel log file using the specified filename

/CHANNELLOG—without a filename, this stops the current log

/CLEAR—clears the current screen

/HELP—gets help from your connected server

/IGNORE *<nickname>*—ignores messages from the specified nickname in case another user is annoying you

/JOIN—joins a channel (available via menu and a button)

/MSG *<nickname>*—sends a message directly to the specified nickname instead of to the entire channel

/PLAY *<filename>*—plays the specified filename to the channel so that you can write a script ahead of time and then transmit it during the session without having to type it in real-time

/WHOIS *<nickname>*—reports information on the specified active nickname, such as the person's e-mail address and location

/WHOWAS *<nickname>*—reports information on the specified nickname if the person just left the channel

Operator IRC commands

/BAN *<nickname>*—bans the specified nickname from the channel

/CKICK—channel kick, kicks all users off the channel

/CDKICK—channel kick and ban, kicks all users off the channel and bans them

/KICK *<nickname>*—kicks the specified nickname off the channel

/OP *<nickname>*—grants operator status to the specified nickname

/TOPIC *<text>*—sets the topic of the active channel to the string specified in *<text>*

/UNBAN *<nickname>*—unbans the specified nickname from the channel

There are many more IRC commands. You can access them using the WSIRC Help command, then click on the Search button and scroll to Commands. The registered version contains an even more extensive list of commands.

The first user to "join" a channel automatically becomes an operator. Operators have the right to kick users off the channel, to ban users from the channel, to reinstate users to the channel, and to designate other users as operators. If you're feeling a touch inferior and naked out there without an @ symbol, hold on. We'll soon get you an @ symbol.

After you join a channel, read the messages for a while to sample the flavor of the chat before typing your own message. Here's a short description of some of the things you'll see as you watch the action.

- **[LOCAL]**—Commands by your local client application.
- **[SERVER]**—Message from the server, such as "*nickname* has joined this channel" and "*nickname* has left this channel."
- **[Nickname]**—The nickname of a user followed by the message that user just entered.

When you're through with this session, let's try one more lesson in which you'll create your own channel and get one of those prestigious @ symbols).

Hands On

Objective: **Create your own channel and close your IRC session.**

❏ Click on the ninth icon, **Join a Channel**.

If you're using this book in a class, you all can join the same channel and practice using the IRC. Agree on a channel name and the first one to join becomes the operator.

❏ Type *#yourname* and click **OK**. (Remember, nine letters maximum.)

Now you finally have your own personal @ symbol! If you're in a class, as other members join you can grant them operator rights. If you're doing this exercise alone, you can wait and see if anyone out there joins you.

The more intriguing the channel name, the more likely strangers will jump in to see what's going on in your channel. In addition to the channel name, you can designate a topic for your channel (see Figure 9-8). An intriguing topic title may lure visitors. In the next step, we'll set a channel topic.

❑ Type */TOPIC Looney Tunes* and press **ENTER**.

You now will see this topic in the title bar of your chat channel window. Depending on their software, other Internet users will be able to see this topic when they browse a list of open channels.

❑ To grant operator rights to other students, type */OP nickname* and press **ENTER**.

Go ahead and use the channel in your class. Be sure and try some of the IRC commands we listed in the previous sidebar. Try a "whois" and then pick someone in the class to "kick" off the channel. Let them right back on, of course!

❑ To leave the channel, double-click the **hyphen** in the menu control box.

As each user leaves, the remaining users will see a "leave" notice. When the last user leaves, the channel is closed.

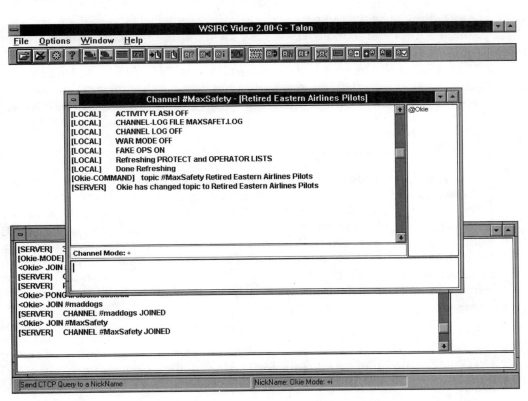

Figure 9-8

Uses for Internet Relay Chat

Because you instantly can establish your own IRC channel and become its operator, consider some ways you could use this capability:

- Business conference call
- Formal meeting, with recorded minutes

- Family reunion, or joint planning session for an in-person family reunion
- Class reunion planning session
- Keep up with students away at college, especially if the family has more than one student attending different schools
- Creative brain-storming session
- International customer technical support or trouble-shooting on your product, especially if several users in different countries are involved
- Coordinating overseas business travel plans that otherwise might require numerous, lengthy international telephone calls
- Collaborating on a book, article or report.

All you need to do is to e-mail the participants in advance and schedule an IRC meeting. Be sure you specify the channel name and include the # sign. The first to "join" that channel automatically becomes an operator. As others join, they can be granted operator rights, if necessary.

With millions of users, there always is a chance that some unknown person will join you after seeing the name of your channel when they do a "list" command. As operator, though, you have the rights to ban that user from the list.

DCC Video works best with an Intel Smart Video Recorder Pro video capture board and the included Video for Windows driver, although you can use any capture board that supports Intel's Indeo video compression format. Intel's board provides on-board hardware-based compression for higher throughput than other boards out today, but check current specifications. DCC Video naturally includes simultaneous audio transmission.

DCC Video on a standard modem line only produces about 1 frame every 2 seconds. An ISDN dial-up PPP connection provides up to 5 frames per second (fps), and a T1 line will produce up to 30 fps. Audio is sent at 1,300 bits per second (bps) and should be acceptable even over modem lines. Audio is half-duplex due to limitations in Windows 3.1 wave device driver specifications, but this will change as future releases add video compression that will increase video throughput up to an estimated 5 frames per second even on standard modem lines and up to an estimated 15 frames per second on ISDN lines. Users with T1 lines can expect full video performance.

Other companion products to WSIRC 2.0 Video will follow. WSIRC 2.0 Video Pro will provide videoconferencing via IRC servers or private multi-cast servers. This will require high bandwidth connections, which soon will not be a problem. A WSIRC 2.0 Video Phone with answering machine software should be available by the time you read this. This version will allow users that have dedicated connections to have a video phone available to record video calls whenever they aren't available personally.

So, in the very near future, you can expect to be able to hold video conferences inexpensively with anyone in the world and even be able to leave video messages to someone who is away from their computer. The Internet has a golden future, but it also had a glorious past. Let's come down out of the clouds of full-color, live-action videoconferencing and close this chapter with a quick overview of the other side of the Internet: the Oldies But Goodies.

Ancient history

Yes, the Oldies But Goodies—those "vinyl records" of the Internet: Gopher, Archie, Veronica, and Telnet. Please don't take offense if you love one of these tools and you feel that we're insulting your preferences. We're not. We both are children of the 1960s and some of our favorite music is on vinyl and we'll keep them forever, too. So we understand if you love your Internet Oldies.

But the point of this book is to teach the Internet of today and of the near future, so these tools will get only a light coverage. So, if you sold your vinyl records and your turntable at a yard sale when compact discs overran the music industry, then you don't live in the past and you can skip the rest of this section and jump straight to the Continuing Education section.

Gopher

Gopher is used to locate Internet resources on topics in which you are interested. The Web performs even more powerful searches and most of the new information on the Internet is going on the Web. Thus, because more information is added to the Web in a single day than you might read in a lifetime, do you need Gopher to find even more?

Still, the Web is in its infancy and may not yet have what you're looking for. If you want to try Gopher, here's a short exercise that will get you connected. We'll guide you through a couple of directories to give you the feel of it, but you'll see that when you're using Netscape, Gopher feels very much like the Web (see Figure 9-9).

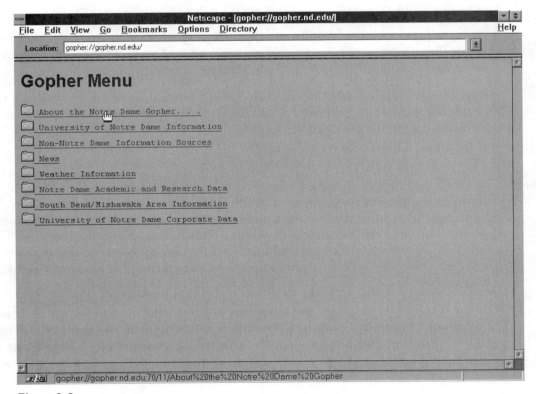

Figure 9-9

Hands On

Objective: Browse a Gopher directory.

❏ Establish an Internet PPP connection.

❏ Start Netscape.

❏ Double-click in the **Location:** text entry box.

❏ Type *gopher://gopher.nd.edu* and press **ENTER**.

This URL will take you to the Worldwide Directory Services at Notre Dame University.

❏ Click on the folder **About the Notre Dame Gopher...**

❏ Click on the file **Gopher FAQ (Usenet)**.

You can read all about the Internet Gopher in this Frequently Asked Questions document. If you'd like to save it on disk for future reference, click **File, Save As...**, select a directory (use the **Network...** button to change your network connection if desired), change the filename if desired, then click **OK**.

❏ Click the right mouse button, then click **Back**.

❏ Click on the file **About Gopher**.

The last time we checked, this document said, "As we are moving to integrate Gopher and World Wide Web space at Notre Dame, you may want to strongly consider using Netscape as your Internet browser of choice. This will enable you to see things in Gopherspace as well as easily view other information sources as well."

❏ Click the right mouse button, then click **Back**.

❏ Click the right mouse button again, then click **Back**.

You now are back to the first Notre Dame Gopher screen and we'll stop this lesson here.

See, as we said, you don't really need Gopher. If you'd like to see more, click on any of the other folders that interest you and browse around for awhile. When you've seen enough, you can exit Netscape by clicking File, Exit.

You can get a stand-alone Gopher software application—several are available for Windows—but we don't recommend that you use one. Netscape is easy to use and you will be using it regularly anyway.

Veronica

Most public Gopher sites have a built-in menu selection that opens Veronica. Veronica is a program—developed at the University of Nevada—that maintains a database of Gopher menus. Veronica frees users from hit-and-miss browsing all over Gopherspace because it provides a unified location of Gopher resources. Veronica will help you locate Gopher resources based upon a keyword search either on Gopher menu titles or on the actual text of Gopher documents.

By the way, even though the name Veronica sounds cute because Veronica was Archie's girlfriend in the old comic strip series, it actually is an acronym of "Very Easy Rodent-Oriented Net-wide Index to Computerized Archives." The rodent, of course, is Gopher, so Veronica isn't related to Archie at all!

Archie

Archie—an Internet service that can be used to locate *archives* that contain files you want to download via FTP—once was a mainstay of Internet work. The Web, however, has nearly eliminated the need for Archie. Archie's biggest problem now is a factor that once gave Archie its power: it only searches for filenames. If you know the name of a file you want, Archie can find it quickly. But if you are researching a broad topic and have no idea of the filenames of the documents you might need, then Archie won't help.

In case you think you're missing something because we didn't teach you Archie, here's a Web substitute: "Archie-Like Indexing for the Web (ALIWEB) at *http://www.nexor.co.uk/public/aliweb/aliweb.html*. This site searches other Web sites the same way you would use Archie to find FTP files (see Figure 9-10). It's got a simple-index search, multiple index keyword search and form-based searching.

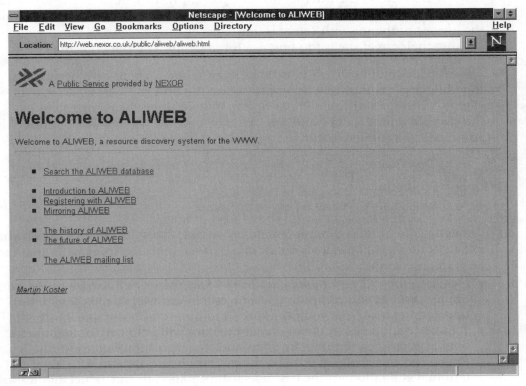

Figure 9-10

If you plan to use Archie regularly, you'll benefit from subscribing to the Archie mailing list. To subscribe, send an e-mail message to *Archie-people-request@bunyip.com*, after entering the phrase, *subscribe (your e-mail address) Archie-people* in the body of the message. But you don't have to wait to receive news about Archie on the Internet—just check out the newsgroup *comp.archives.admin.*

Telnet

Telnet is an Internet tool that enables you to tap the resources of remote computers. Telnet turns your PC into a terminal for a remote (host) computer so that your PC functions much as it would if you were on-site—even if the host computer is in another hemisphere! After you're connected, the remote computer will treat you pretty much as it would if you were local—but with limited rights. This means that it will expect you to enter a login ID and a password.

Because the remote computer's administrators have made their resources available to outsiders, they also will have made a login and password available to outsiders. If you don't know what to use, try to login with *guest, visitor, newuser* or the name of the site. Try using the same words as passwords if the host doesn't automatically supply you with one. Or, the system may accept a blank password entry.

Measured by the standards that have been set by the Web, Telnet is primitive. Telnet works best at the hands of people who love computers. If you have become hooked on the Internet because you enjoy the colorful, easy-to-use look of the Web, you won't like Telnet at all. Still, despite all of its rough edges, one of the biggest problems with Telnet is that users encounter a lot of failed logins because their target site is too busy—a lot of people use Telnet regularly.

Telnet is difficult to teach. You need to learn Telnet on your own because its functionality is completely dependent upon the host computer. Each site is slightly different and you will not find many user-friendly or consistent interfaces at any of them—and you won't be needing your mouse because Telnet requires typed command entries.

NET TIP Using Telnet demands patience. Do not expect rapid response times because a busy system can be very sluggish. Remember, this is someone else's computer—it may have cost them millions of dollars and be the backbone of their organization—so as a guest, you probably have the lowest priority on the system.

Telnet may be primitive, but it remains powerful. Many Telnet sites permit you to use all of the host computer's programs. Here's a short listing of URLs that can help you use Telnet:

⦿ Hytelnet (*http://library.usask.ca/hytelnet*)—This site has a database of electronic library catalogs and computing resources that are available via Telnet. It is updated frequently, so you can expect it to have a fairly complete listing of Telnet site addresses. A menu-driven interface will help you locate bulletin board systems, community free-nets and remote computing resources. Telnet to *wdn.com* to see one of our favorite bulletin-board systems. Use ANSI terminal emulation for the best screen appearance, if your Telnet application supports it.

HYPERJUMP

Free-net

A local computer internet (small "i" version) that may be funded by a community, a school, a government, a library, or a non-profit organization. Users are not charged for connect time, and the system is oriented toward helping people with local issues. We profiled Cleveland's free-net in chapter 1. Their Telnet address is *freenet-in-a.cwru.edu.*

- Melvyl (*melvyl.ucop.edu*; terminal emulation *VT100*; login is not required, but enter *CAT* to access the catalog file)—Here's a link to the online library card catalog for the University of California library system, which has more than 11 million resources on file.

Once you're logged on via Telnet, one of your first reactions may be to wonder how to get logged off. Whenever you've had enough, look for an Exit or Quit menu option. If you can't find any menu item that will log you off, type *bye* or *quit* at a prompt and press ENTER.

 # Continuing Education

Internet tools summary

http://www.rpi.edu/Internet/Guides/decemj/internet-tools.html

This Web page present a hypertext reference work that relates to tools available on the Internet for network information retrieval (NIR) and Computer-Mediated Communication (CMC). It is neither a strict categorization nor an exhaustive list, but more of a reference catalog. It includes aids on using finger, FTP, Gopher, Telnet, e-mail, Usenet newsgroups, and the Web.

North Carolina FTP SunSite

ftp://sunsite.unc.edu

This is Sun's anonymous FTP server at the University of North Carolina. It archives most of the Sun related Usenet news groups there as well as distributing Sun related announcements. When you connect, scroll down to the *pub/* folder and scroll through the topics it offers because, as they tell you, it will "take you to the good stuff." You can e-mail to *info@sunsite.unc.edu* to receive information about how to use the different services SunSite offers.

Oakland FTP site

ftp://oak.oakland.edu/

This is the Oak Software Repository FTP site at Oakland University in Rochester, Michigan. This is an extremely popular site, typically having hundreds of users connected. It can service a maximum of 400 simultaneous users, but you still may be denied access because it is at capacity. It now has on-site file searching available. You'll find a lot of files here, requiring three directories: *pub*, *pub2*, and *pub3*. You also will find much more good stuff in the SimTel directory. That's where the SimTel mirror site is, and where you can find all of the EMS files. (EMS is Eric Engelmann's company.) Oak also can be reached on the Web at *http://www.acs.oakland.edu/oak.html*.

Magellan, McKinley's Internet Directory

http://mckinley.netcom.com/

The McKinley Internet Directory (MID) was the first Internet "yellow pages" to employ a rating system. It has an online directory of reviewed, described, and rated Internet sites (Web, Gopher, FTP, mailing lists, and newsgroups) that provides rapid, targeted access to the best resources on the Internet before you access the site.

More than 30 percent of MID resources originate internationally. Each profile includes the resource's producer, audience field, language origin, and cost of access, if any. Each MID site is reviewed and rated using "The McKinley Star Rating System," which analyzes depth and freshness of content, resource organization and site user-friendliness. Ratings are performed by The McKinley Editorial Advisory Board, whose members are renowned authorities in their fields.

CARL Telnet site

pac.carl.org

This is the Colorado Alliance of Research Libraries (CARL), and it is an online library resource for a whole group of libraries. Even though "Colorado" is in the title, CARL's resources span the continent. You'll find a public access catalog of services, encyclopedias, and databases for libraries across the U.S. Login is *PAC* and terminal emulation is *VT100*; choose option 4 ("Other Library Systems") then choose whichever region in the U.S. you want to search.

FTP site for IRC client software

ftp://oak.oakland.edu/pub/irc/clients/

To acquire your IRC software via FTP, you can use this Oakland University site in Rochester, Michigan. You'll find IRC for a wide variety of operating systems, but most likely you'll use the *msdos/* or the *windows/* directories found under the URL listed above. Several good versions are listed here. Be sure to check back regularly for updated versions. With the coming transition to videoconferencing and full audio capability, you'll find lots of changes in IRC software.

Web site for IRC client software

http://www.kei.com/irc.html

This site has hypertext links to IRC software for a variety of systems: MS-DOS, Windows, OS/2, Macintosh, VMS, UNIX, and X11. Be sure and check this site often, as updates in the field are coming at a fast clip (see Figure 9-11).

IRC servers

http://www.word.net/~pirovich

This site has a complete listing of available IRC servers. From time to time you also will find a list of IRC servers posted to the alt.irc newsgroup. To get you started, here's a short list of available IRC servers in the U.S.:

> *irc.ais.net*
> *irc.caltech.edu*
> *irc.colorado.edu*
> *irc.digex.net*
> *irc.escape.com*
> *irc.funet.fi*
> *irc.uiuc.edu*
> *irc-2.mit.edu*
> *irc.virginia.edu*

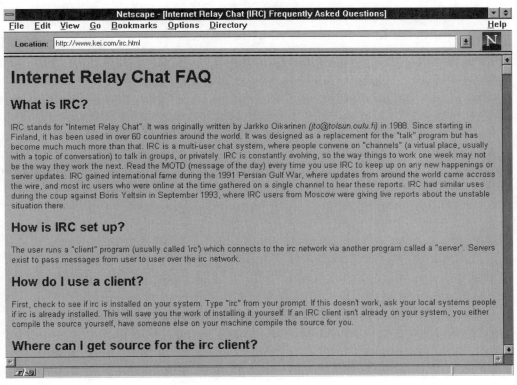

Figure 9-11

Internet Phone

http://www.vocaltec.com

This is the site we profiled in an earlier sidebar. If you're interested in Internet telephone service—especially in setting up conference calls—be sure and check this site regularly.

CU-SeeMe Internet video

http://cu-seeme.cornell.edu

This site is maintained by a department of Cornell University in Ithaca, New York. Here you'll be able to stay abreast of the rapidly changing field of Internet videoconferencing, download free versions of the latest software, and track which hardware is compatible with the system.

Newsgroups and mailing lists

THIS CHAPTER is dedicated to showing you how to use the Internet as a source of up-to-the-second news. We'll cover two basic Internet functions:

- Mailing lists—Electronic services that can broadcast automated e-mail newsletters on targeted topics. The Internet has thousands of mailing lists to which you can subscribe. A mailing list usually is operated by software called a "list server," and you can create your own mailing list.

- Newsgroups—Electronic "community bulletin boards" that serve as "info central" for targeted topics. Messages are "posted" in the open and anyone who looks at the newsgroup will see all the messages that have been posted by all of the group's users.

Both services offer options to subscribe or unsubscribe. Mailing list subscriptions use a formal process that usually requires recipients to send e-mail to a list server, but subscribers can be entered manually. Once you've subscribed to a mailing list, you usually will continue to receive electronic mailings until you formally unsubscribe.

HYPERJUMP

List server

A computer program that serves automatic mailing lists to clients (subscribers), usually without human intervention by the list's authors. List server software accepts "subscribe" and "unsubscribe" orders from list recipients and sends e-mail to the current subscriber list.

Subscribing and unsubscribing to newsgroups, on the other hand, uses an internal process that is handled by your own software. All Internet newsgroups are available on a smorgasbord basis. When you subscribe to one, your newsreader automatically checks that group for new messages when you start it.

Newsgroups are not mailed directly to you—you go to them. But because there are so many thousands of them, newsreader software enables you to select—from the master list of all the groups it finds on your news server—only the groups you choose to see. This process is called subscribing, although your system maintains full access even to the newsgroups to which you are not subscribed. At any time that you decide to see an additional group, you can subscribe and instantly see the group's postings. Similarly, if you unsubscribe to a group, your software merely stops displaying the postings; yet the group remains available for resubscription.

Mailing list overview

The Internet has countless mailing lists and their numbers continue to grow. We believe, however, that the rapid growth of the World Wide Web (see the next chapter) is going to curtail interest in mailing lists. In fact, many mailing lists now include a Web address and offer the same information either way.

There is, however, one important difference between mailing lists and Web sites. Mailing lists offer bidirectional information flow—they involve input and feedback from subscribers. This isn't easy to do with traditional Web pages, but a new generation of products called "hypermail" enables a mailing list to become a Web page.

Mailing lists were most useful before the Web became popular, when the Internet was comprised almost entirely of text-based messages. Further, searching for information on specific topics—before the Web made it easy—was not a task for busy, mainstream users whose business lives do not revolve around computers. Thus, mailing lists gave users a powerful information tool that automatically would send them targeted information without the use of arcane, primitive research tools.

Soon we may see mailing lists used only to send short messages to clients, customers, or members to alert them that a Web site now contains an important information update. Users then will know to jump to Netscape with a couple of mouse clicks and read the latest news. Once they're at the Web site, they'll be able to print the updated document, including charts, sound clips, video clips, graphs, photos, tables, spreadsheets, forms, and artistically formatted text. And the updated text may contain links to other news items that are related to the main article. Mailing list newsletters, in contrast, generally only include plain, unformatted text, though people increasingly are including MIME attachments.

Tell me more about list servers

We know people who run mailing lists using a regular e-mail account and Eudora. Usually these lists are small, but some unbelievably diligent people have manually run lists with hundreds of subscribers. If repetitive, menial tasks are not your forte, then you'll want an automated list server. One of the most popular list servers available today is called "listserv"; another is called "majordomo."

The Internet distributes thousands of discussion groups, digests, electronic journals, and newsletters via e-mail by allowing users to place themselves on electronic mailing lists. Listserv is a program that maintains a database of mailing list subscribers. Listserv automatically distributes an e-mail message from one subscriber of a list to all other subscribers on that list.

Hands On

When you subscribe to a list, your name and e-mail address are automatically added to the list. New users automatically receive an e-mail welcome letter that will include background on what the list provides. You then will receive all e-mail sent by that list server to its subscribers. You may simply read the e-mail you receive, or you may become an active participant in the list. If you respond, your message can go either to all of the list's subscribers or to an individual subscriber. You can have your name removed from the list by sending an "unsubscribe" message. You also can get a listing of the e-mail addresses of all subscribers.

If you'd like to set up your own listserv software, check out the listing in the Continuing Education section at the end of this chapter. This is not for mainstream users, because it will require some technical expertise and patience.

Mailing lists now, in contrast to the Web, deliver only plain-text messages. Some mailing lists offer a choice between a plain-text version and a Hypertext Markup Language (HTML) version, but it's a trick. If you subscribe to a mailing list's HTML version, you will have to read it using Netscape. Nonetheless, there are advantages to subscribing to an HTML version of a newsletter, as you'll read later. HTML is the programming language that creates Web pages, but it actually is plain-text that is interpreted by your Netscape Web Browser to produce special effects. In other words, the mailing becomes a vehicle that delivers a hypertext document to you, instead of accessing it through the Web.

 NET TIP One of the most annoying things about mailing lists is that the method to unsubscribe is *different* from the method for posting messages. Newbies who want to unsubscribe to a list frequently send instead a message to all group members—this is a good way to fill up your mail box with flames! SAVE the unsubscribe instructions when you subscribe. If you forget to do this, you always can subscribe again and then unsubscribe with the instructions sent with the new subscription notice.

It's up to you, of course. Subscribing to a mailing list has the advantage of doing the work for you, because a mailing list subscription gets you the essential information without having to remember to check a Web site. On the other hand, if you take the time to check a Web site for information updates, you may be rewarded with additional hypertext links to related items you might miss with an e-mailed list. A compromise is to subscribe to an HTML version and see the special effects, although you won't be able to use the hypertext jumps unless you connect Netscape to the Internet.

Whichever method you choose, mailing lists are ubiquitous and will not soon disappear. We'll now profile one for you and run a Hands On exercise that will get you a subscription.

Your own electronic newsletter

Internet newsletters can transform your company's ability to inform. You don't have to print them, fold them, stamp them, or mail them—and they're up-to-the-second fresh. The best part, though, is what you *won't* have to do to create a newsletter. You don't have to write and edit a lengthy tome, because you can give your subscribers scads of information from around the world using but a few short pages of linked hypertext. Your document may be no more than one short paragraph describing each link you include.

You easily can create a simple hypertext newsletter using WordPerfect for Windows or Microsoft Word for Windows, because both include free add-on HTML Internet publishing functions. You'll begin by browsing the Web looking for URLs that will interest your clients, customers, or members. When you find one with Netscape, click the right mouse button on the link, then click Copy this Link Location to put the underlying URL in the Windows clipboard. Use ALT+TAB to switch back to your word processor. Then create a hypertext link and, when prompted for the link's URL, press CTRL+V to Paste it in.

If you only need to inform a short list of prime clients and customers, you can run your newsletter with Eudora. Once you've saved your newsletter document, you can switch from your word processor to Eudora. In Eudora, click on Window, Nicknames and then New to create a mailing list. Give the subscriber list a nickname, then enter the e-mail addresses of subscribers in the Address(es): text entry box.

When you're ready to send out an issue, simply e-mail the saved document to your subscriber nickname. Of course, Eudora won't let your subscribers add and remove themselves from your list like the listserv program will, and it won't let subscribers send their own messages to other subscribers. But sending your organization's newsletter to a short subscriber list is not a problem in Eudora—you can save up to 64K of text within one nickname, enough for more than 2,000 subscribers.

Your subscribers will open Netscape, click on File, Open File, and then enter the name of the file you sent them. They'll get all the benefits of hypertext formatting and—if they're connected to the Internet—they will be able to click on the links you gave them. They may greatly appreciate you for giving them a wealth of information without their having to search for any of it.

The Scout Report

The Scout Report is a weekly publication offered by the InterNIC to the Internet community as a fast, convenient way to stay informed about network activities. It merges, in one place, selected new and newly discovered Internet resources. The Scout Report includes a wide range of topics that emphasize resources that will interest the InterNIC's primary audience: the research and education community. Each Scout Report resource is evaluated within a day of its inclusion for content value and accessibility.

Autoresponders

Occasionally you'll see an organization offer an e-mail address that you can use to get information on the organization or its products or services. This is not the same as subscribing to a mailing list because it's just a one-time deal and the information comes to you upon demand—the demand of sending the e-mail request. Such systems are called "autoresponders." Autoresponders are no more complicated than simple e-mail accounts that respond automatically to all e-mail they receive by sending a previously saved message.

Remember that any e-mail message can include attachments such as word processing documents, spreadsheets, programs, configuration files, full-color drawings, photographs, charts and graphs, sound clips, and video. You may be able to dazzle your clients, customers, or prospects by including your pricing schedule in a spreadsheet, or a color map to your location.

Some organizations maintain several autoresponders to handle requests for different types of information. For example, if your organization were a training company, it might have two autoresponders. One could respond to the e-mail name *schedules@yourfirm.com* by sending a schedule of classes to anyone who e-mails to that address. Another account could respond to the e-mail name *courses@yourfirm.com* by sending a synopsis of courses that you offer.

For awhile, it seemed that autoresponders would be a major marketing factor, but the Web now gives your clients and customers such complete and instant access to your information that you may not need an autoresponder. If, however, a lot of your clients and customers don't have up-to-date computers and only have Internet e-mail, then autoresponders can give you a way to respond to their information needs. Ask your Internet service provider to set up an autoresponder account. Not all of them can handle it, so you may have to shop around.

For more information on autoresponders, contact your Internet service provider. Many now have autoresponder capability and can set up accounts for your organization. Expect to pay about $10 per month for each account.

The Scout Report is available in three formats: mailing lists that can send you either a plain-text or an HTML version and an online Web version. The online Web version of the Report includes links to all listed resources. The report is released every weekend.

If you subscribe to the HTML version, your organization could post it on local Web servers. This would give instant access to local users without requiring multiple Internet connections nor be hindered by weekday afternoon Internet traffic bottlenecks. The Scout Report includes full rights to repost and re-distribute the report, provided that the Scout Report's copyright statements are left intact.

If you haven't yet subscribed, let's do it now in a short Hands On exercise that will serve as a model for subscribing to other Internet mailing lists. Once you've subscribed, you can send comments and contributions to the Scout Report to Susan Calcari at *scout@internic.net*.

Subscribing to the Scout Report

To receive either the plain-text or the HTML e-mail version of the Scout Report each Friday, join the Scout Report mailing list using the next exercise.

Hands On

Objective: Learn to subscribe to a mailing list.

❏ Start your Eudora mail application.

❏ Click **Message, New Message**.

❏ Type *majordomo@dsmail.internic.net* (see Figure 10-1).

❏ Press **TAB** until the insertion point is in the message body.

❏ Type one of the following for your message:

　　subscribe scout-report (plain-text version)

　　subscribe scout-report-html (HTML version)

　　unsubscribe scout-report (to later cancel your subscription)

❏ Click on either the **Send** or the **Queue** button.

　　If you clicked on **Send**, then your message was sent instantly and you're through with this exercise. If you clicked on **Queue**, then your message still is in the Out box, and you now need to execute the next step to send it; otherwise skip the next step.

❏ Click **File, Send Queued Messages...** or press **CTRL+T**.

　　What happens after the **Send** command varies depending upon your Internet connection. If you established the connection before starting Eudora—or if Netscape or some other Internet application had established the connection for you—your message gets sent immediately. If you're not logged onto the Internet, then Eudora may make WinSock dial the Internet and log on. In some cases, however, you will have to use **ALT+TAB** to cycle back to the Program Manager to launch WinSock and logon, then use **ALT+TAB** again to return to Eudora and send.

❏ Click **File, Exit** to close Eudora.

To access the online Web version of The Scout Report, check out the Continuing Education section at the end of this chapter.

Now we're ready to move on to newsgroups. These Internet news sources don't deliver news to you—you have to go to them. We'll cover an overview of Usenet

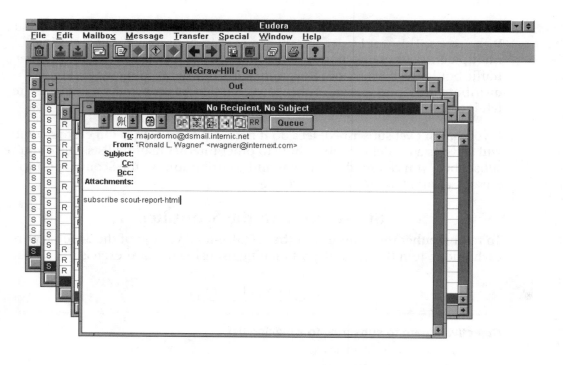

Figure 10-1

newsgroups, give you an outline of a popular and important one, and then run a Hands On exercise that will guide you through subscribing, unsubscribing, reading, and posting to newsgroups.

Usenet newsgroup overview

Newsgroups on the Internet are experiencing an unprecedented explosion in growth. All newsgroups collectively are called the Usenet. New newsgroups are appearing on the Usenet rapidly and existing groups are garnering new members faster than ever. One drawback to the newsgroup phenomenon, however, is that the wealth of information they offer can seem to be more of a burden than a blessing. With more than 15,000 public newsgroups, you can't even read the subject lines for each day's new messages. And if you ever skipped a day's reading, you'd never catch up.

Finding specific information within the Usenet newsgroups can make the proverbial "finding a needle in a haystack" look easy. At least if you were looking for a needle, you could use a powerful magnet and extract the needle. Fortunately, we've got computerized magnets (the next topic in this chapter).

Generically, we'll call these computerized magnets *infomagnets* because they can extract valuable needles from all the "hay" that chokes most of the Usenet. There are two types:

● You can subscribe to a tailored news service that will send you articles after it finds the ones you want.

● You can write a program that scans the Usenet and pulls in the articles you specify.

We'll cover both methods. Let's begin by looking at one popular, tailored news service as an example.

How many newsgroups are there? How many can you stand?

How many Usenet newsgroups are on the Internet? No one knows for sure. As we did research for this book, we got a wild variation in numbers. The highest trustworthy number that we found was 15,000 public newsgroups. But only a few months earlier, we had heard 11,000. Today? Well, there's no way to tell. And that's just the public newsgroups—it literally would be impossible to count the private newsgroups because they can't be seen by outsiders.

It's not likely that your Internet service makes all newsgroups available. For example, one Internet service provider we use currently offers 5,450 newsgroups. Another service provider may offer more or fewer newsgroups. Check with your Internet service provider (ISP) to find out how many newsgroups are available to your basic account, and ask if you will get more by paying a premium above your basic fee.

Your ISP must pay a fee to provide some newsgroups so they may need to cover their increased costs by charging you a premium to receive these newsgroups. For example, the ClariNet news services charges your ISP one dollar a month for each Internet account. This is a bargain, but in the highly competitive world of Internet services, some providers cut costs by cutting out such premium services because few customers ask any more than "How much per month?" when shopping for services.

So, if newsgroups are important to your work, be sure and ask about newsgroups when you shop for an ISP. You will need a service that can use a "Network News Transfer Protocol" (NNTP) server. If your organization is large, it may have an internal NNTP server—so check with your system administrator to discover if you can use your internal system to read newsgroups.

ClariNet news services

Our first infomagnet coverage is about the ClariNet e.News, an electronic newspaper that delivers professional news and information directly to your computer. It sends live news (including technology-related wire stories), timely computer industry news, syndicated columns and features, financial information, stock quotes and more.

You can receive, upon request, a free sample of selected articles that are posted to the Usenet newsgroup *biz.clarinet.sample*. If you want more information, contact ClariNet for a targeted sample of the news topics you want to track (see Figure 10-2). If that isn't enough, they will give you a free, two-week trial of the e.News with no obligation.

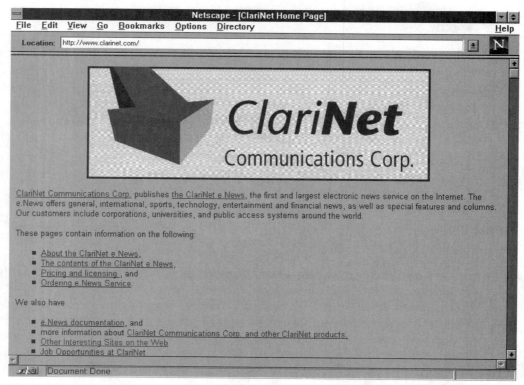

Figure 10-2

With the e.News, you can put the Internet to work for you to receive the news that directly impacts your life and your business. This is one answer to the Over-Information Age that can increase your "breathing space," as we discussed in chapter 5. e.News combines the in-depth coverage of print media with the speed of broadcast media to give you the best of both worlds. Many U.S. media limit their international coverage for reasons of space and time, but e.News doesn't suffer from either of those limitations.

How e.News works

Many on-line services store the news on a computer at their site, but the e.News sends selected articles directly to you. When you want to read the news, it's available instantly because you won't have to wait while it's transferred via a modem—and you'll never again pay per-minute connect charges while you scan headlines trying to find news you need. Instead, everyone in your organization can read targeted e.News, anytime, for a fixed monthly fee—there are no per-user charges.

The e.News is delivered as a Usenet-style newsfeed. So, any standard Usenet reading capabilities will work and if your organization doesn't receive Usenet-style news, ClariNet will help you get connected for free, including free software. Hard disk space may become an issue, however, because a full e.News feed collects daily approximately four megabytes of data. Of course a carefully targeted feed will consume disk space at a slower rate. Let's look at the targeted e.News topics from which you can select.

Techwire

Specific categories for stories on science and technology and the industries around them: computers, electronics, health issues, space, aerospace, telecommunications, defense, biotechnology, research, education, AIDS, and more. It also includes a daily price report of computer industry stocks.

Business News

This service delivers business and financial stories on all topics: economic indicators, corporate news, regular stock market reports, legal issues affecting business, government information, commodity reports, and a great deal more. The e.News Business News option features the North American, European, and Asian Business Reports of Reuters, the world's most respected international business information source.

Newsbytes

Here's a daily computer industry magazine that brings you timely information well before weekly print media reaches your desk. Newsbytes stories are gathered from 11 bureaus around the world. Within the computer industry, Newsbytes covers trends, legal issues, reviews of new products, and corporate news. It also specifically addresses news on products that work with Apple, Unix, and IBM computers and telecommunications products.

Syndicated Features

This service delivers top syndicated columns and features, such as etiquette from Miss Manners and movie reviews and cultural commentary from Joe Bob Briggs.

The Annals of Improbable Research

The e.News isn't entirely serious or stuffy. You can receive this journal of scientific funnies that includes "Bizarro," an off-beat look at the world and "Views of the World," which presents a series of daily editorial cartoons from newspapers around the globe.

Matrix News

This source delivers a newsletter about cross-networking that covers the connections between all the computer networks worldwide that exchange electronic mail. Naturally that includes the Internet, but also covers UUCP-Net, BITNET, FidoNet, and conferencing systems such as the Well and CompuServe.

Global and National News

This is a major news source that includes global and national news, sports, and features from the wire services of Reuters and The Associated Press (AP). It covers U.S. and international news events, as well as regular coverage of sports (with detailed statistics).

As you'd expect from any newspaper, this service includes many standing features including editorials, columns on politics, entertainment, and consumer products, reviews of books, movies, and videos, a daily almanac, and a daily news summary.

And it also provides something you can't get in a regular print newspaper: Every two hours the e.News releases updated summaries of current events.

Local News

Right now this only delivers coverage of the San Francisco Bay Area, featuring reports from the Bay City News Service. Local news soon will be available for regions outside the Bay Area.

NewsClip™ news filtering language

Here's the second type of infomagnet. As we mentioned earlier, this type enables you to filter your own information from newsgroups. ClariNet has developed a programming language that includes a high level of filtering control over Usenet newsgroup information, and it automatically sends you the filtered information. Earlier filtering programs only gave users control over the newsgroups they received and offered a "kill" feature that eliminated unwanted articles. For example, systems less sophisticated than NewsClip will let you kill articles that are posted by a user who consistently posts nothing but annoying trash. NewsClip, by contrast, puts at your disposal all the tools of a powerful programming language. NewsClip goes well beyond creating a kill file by giving you the ability to make positive selection choices as well as negative elimination choices.

Your only news-filtering limitations will be self-imposed and determined by how much time you decided to invest in writing the program. If you have a large organization, your organization almost certainly will enjoy a productivity payoff if someone invests in the programming time to write a targeted filtering system to get the news that you and your coworkers need.

NewsClip programs are compiled, so they not only filter newsgroups exactly the way you specify, but they work quickly. Your compiled NewsClip programs will accept, reject, or weight articles based on programming expressions that describe what you want to receive and what you don't want to see at all.

How you can use NewsClip

Compiled NewsClip programs can work interactively with you as you read articles in real time, usually with no noticeable delay. As you browse through your chosen newsgroups, you will see only the articles that you've specified.

The program can be run in the background while you perform other tasks or it can be run after business hours to filter your chosen newsgroups. To do this, you'll need a newsreader that maintains a "newsrc" (news subscription) file that contains a list of the newsgroups to which you subscribe. In unattended mode, your filter program will read your newsrc file, scan all unread articles and mark as already read any articles that fit your elimination criteria. Thus, you never will see those articles. Let's close the NewsClip coverage with a list of usage examples:

- Screen out messages posted by a particular user, a group of users, or even all users from a designated site. You even can screen out follow-up messages posted to articles by the users you've specified.

- Receive messages that contain specified keywords or that exclude specified keywords. For example, if you were a die hard fan of the game of dominoes, you might select all articles that include the word "domino" but that exclude the word "pizza."

- You'll see thousands of follow-up articles that copy the entire original message—perhaps duplicating thousands of words you already have read— and then close with "I agree!" You never will waste time on this kind of poor netiquette if you say to eliminate articles in which the amount of copied text greatly exceeds the amount of new text.

- Filter out all articles except for originals (so that your default is to not see any follow-up articles), and then have the program include follow-ups to articles as you specify.

- Specify priority handling of follow-ups to articles you have posted—or to articles posted by anyone within your organization as well as follow-ups to those articles.

- Make sure you get all the articles posted on any newsgroup by a known competitor. You can include either articles posted by anyone within an entire organization or posted by specific individuals within an organization.

- Ban the spam by filtering out cross-posted articles. For example, if an article is cross-posted 10 times, you can just about bet it's spam and your program will ignore it. Unfortunately, ClariNet filtering requires that the user be able to construct the filter and compile it with their own C programming-language compiler—not something mainstream users are likely to do.

The Netscape newsgroup reader

If Netscape is not already the top newsgroup reader on the Internet, it soon will be. Its newsgroup reader offers easy access—it's built into your Web browser—

and a wealth of efficient and productive features. Those two factors practically eliminate—for mainstream users—any reasons to use other newsreaders.

One of the best features of the Netscape newsgroup reader is that it makes the Usenet appear almost like the Web (see Figure 10-3). You'll barely notice the difference. Before Netscape, stand-alone newsgroup readers had a completely different look and feel and few presented the articles in any sort of user-friendly format. Now, however, Netscape brings the familiarity of hypertext links to the Usenet and greatly simplifies article tracking.

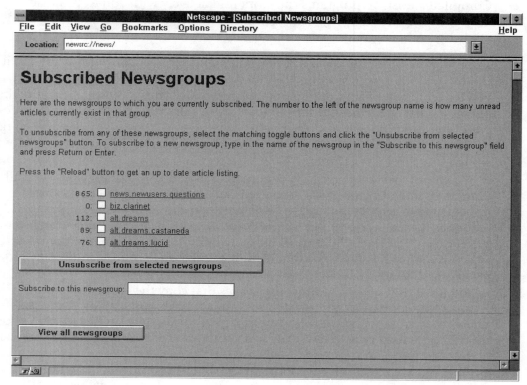

Figure 10-3

Other Newsgroup readers

WinVN is one of the most common stand-alone Internet newsgroup readers. With Netscape as your browser, however, you may prefer the simplicity of using its built-in newsgroup reader, but one of the wonders of the Internet is that it provides something for everyone. The latest version of WinVN is available via anonymous FTP from: *ftp.ksc.nasa.gov*. The last time we checked WinVN files could be found in the directory */pub/winun/win3* (see Figure 10-4).

WinVN runs under Windows 3.x, Windows/NT, Windows/NT-AXP and Windows 95. The same site also offers complete sources and documentation. A new minor version is released about every month or two. The user's guide is not always updated with the software, so after downloading a new version, check back to keep tabs on the status of the documentation.

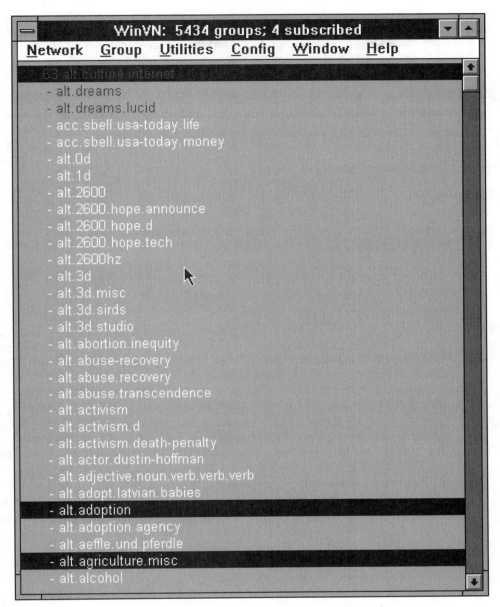

Figure 10-4

WinVN is programmed with government, university and corporate users in mind and is intended to be used interactively online. This programming orientation hurts the lower-speed SLIP/PPP user because WinVN doesn't have the offline reading capabilities found in news readers that are designed to store articles locally and quickly disconnect to save access or telephone charges. It is, however, one of the fastest Windows-based news readers around, and it can handle groups with extremely large article counts. The penalties for its lack of offline features are waning as fewer and fewer users are billed by the hour for Internet access time.

If you really want to be unique in your office, here's the FTP site of yet another Newsgroup reader, WinTrump. Start with the URL *ftp://ftp.trumpet .com.au* and then go to the directory *pub/wintrump* to find WinTrump's files.

Read Usenet newsgroups

Let's get started with the Hands On exercises and use Netscape to check out some Usenet newsgroups.

Hands On

Objective: **Learn to find and read Usenet newsgroup articles.**

❑ Start Netscape.

❑ Click **Directory, Go to Newsgroups** or click the **Newsgroups** button.

This will open the "Subscribed Newsgroups" screen—unless you subscribe to more than one NNTP news server, in which case it lists the various new servers you can use. Groups to which you already are subscribed show up on a list of hypertext. Each line also tells you how many unread articles are in each group.

❑ Click **View all newsgroups**.

If this is the first time that this Netscape browser has been connected to newsgroups, you'll get a dialog box telling you that Netscape must download a current copy of the Usenet newsgroups listing. This may take several minutes.

❑ Click **OK** to copy the newsgroups listing.

Well, now you've done it. This is the Usenet—more newsgroups than you possibly can read. We can't know for certain which ones are showing on your list, but there are some that we can rely on, so we'll use one of those. Check the sidebar for a listing of the most popular newsgroup categories.

❑ Click on **alt.***.

Listings that end with an asterisk indicate that you are seeing a hierarchical header that leads to other topics beneath that level. Clicking on a topic will expand the listing to increasingly specific topic levels. Watch the lower-right corner of the screen because the red bar will indicate how much of the list has been downloaded—some topics, such as this one, have a lot of subtopics and require some patience.

❑ Scroll down to **alt.quotations** and click on it.

You can scroll down this list by using your mouse on the scroll bars or by using the **UP ARROW** or **DOWN ARROW** keys—it's just a document and behaves as would a document in your word processor. You can use **CTRL+HOME** to go to the top, **CTRL+END** to go to the bottom, and you can use the **PG UP** and **PG DN** keys.

Finally, be patient while the alt.quotations newsgroup is loading—watch the byte count on the bottom line until you see the full list of all of the articles within the *alt.quotations* newsgroup (see Figure 10-5), then let's pause here and resume the lesson after we've identified some of the buttons you see.

News reader buttons

The Netscape browser presents two different sets of buttons when you're inside an individual newsgroup. One set is displayed when you're viewing the listing of the group itself (see Figure 10-6). A different set of buttons appears when you're viewing a specific article.

Note that both sets of buttons appear both at the top and at the bottom of each document screen. You can jump quickly to the buttons by pressing CTRL+HOME or CTRL+END. Here are two tables that explain the buttons you see in either case.

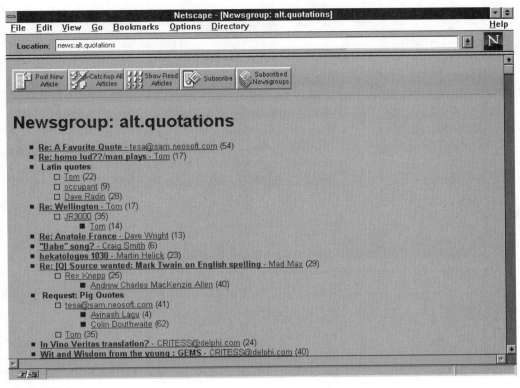

Figure 10-5

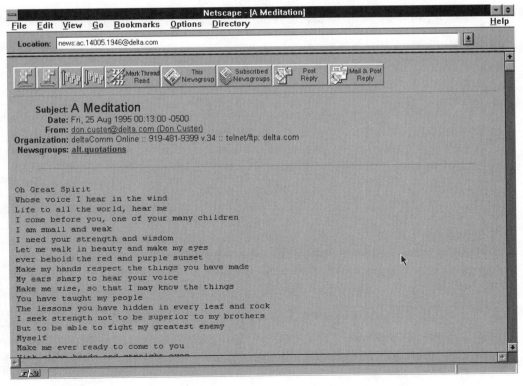

Figure 10-6

TABLE 10-1. Buttons within a newsgroup

Button	Function
Post New Article	Opens a dialog box that enables you to create an original article to post (more on this later).
Catchup	Treats all articles as if you had read each one—thus, catching up—and hides the read articles.
Show Read Articles	Redisplays articles that you already have read.
Hide Read Articles	If you've previously used the "Show Read Articles" button, this will hide articles that you already have read.
Subscribe	Adds the current newsgroup to your subscription list.
Subscribed Newsgroups	Jumps to your subscription list.

TABLE 10-2. Buttons within a specific article

Button	Function
Back Arrow	Jumps to previous article in this thread (grayed-out if you're reading the thread's first article).
Forward Arrow	Jumps to next article in this thread (grayed-out if you're reading the thread's last article).
Up Arrow	Jumps to previous thread (grayed-out if you're reading the first article in the newsgroup).
Down Arrow	Jumps to next thread (grayed-out if you're reading the last article in the newsgroup).
Mark Thread Read	Marks the entire thread as being read regardless of which article you're reading.
This Newsgroup	Jumps back to the full listing of all articles in the current newsgroup.
Subscribed Newsgroups	Jumps you to your list of subscribed newsgroups.
Post Reply	Opens a dialog box that lets you reply to the currently displayed article—the default Subject line for the article will be entered for you as "Re: *Title of original article.*"
Mail & Post Reply	Opens a dialog box that enables you to reply to the currently displayed article and send e-mail to its author—the default Subject line for both the article and the e-mail will be entered for you as "Re: *Title of original article.*"

Popular Usenet newsgroups

No one has any idea how many newsgroups are on the Internet at any given time. The numbers you'll read vary across a wide range. Further complicating the newsgroup counting game is that a lot of newsgroups that show up on your list are empty. During a trial run, while randomly browsing newsgroups to which we've never subscribed, about one newsgroup in three was empty. Still, there are thousands of active newsgroups. Here's a list of some of the major categories:

TABLE 10-3. Usenet newsgroup categories

Category	Topics
alt	Alternative topics, many of which are just plain fun, so be ready for anything you can imagine, a lot that you never have and don't take anything you read here seriously.
bionet	Professional biologists.
biz	Business discussions, advertisements and postings of new products and services.
clari	ClariNet news services (requires a premium fee, though it may already be a part of your basic package).
comp	Computer-related topics.
k12	Kindergarten through 12th-grade teachers.
misc	Miscellaneous topics, but none as far out as alt.
news	The Usenet is so big it actually has its own group for news about itself.
rec	Recreational topics; you won't believe what some people consider to be recreation—here's something for everyone.
relcom	The former Soviet Union
sci	Science topics.
soc	Social topics with an international flavor as well as covering religions.
talk	Not enough talk radio stations for you? At least you can get through to this one.

Some of these categories have thousands of subtopics. This is just a gentle orientation. The real thing is practically brutal. Read chapter 5, The over-information age, before you get too deeply into newsgroups.

Each original article is listed against the left margin. Indented paragraphs under an article are related articles that are replies to the original. If someone replies to a reply, that article will be shown indented yet another level, etc. This hierarchical listing system creates a *thread*—sort of a focused, ongoing conversation. Threads help you easily track a focused conversation as if you were eavesdropping on it.

Let's get back into the Hands On exercise now and finish browsing through the Usenet.

Hands On

Objective: Complete the newsgroup reading exercise.

❏ Click on the blue text of any article title that interests you.

The number in parentheses after each title is the number of lines of text in the article.

❏ Click the right mouse button and click **Back** to go back one level.

Notice that the article now appears in red instead of blue, exactly as with Web hypertext links.

❏ Click on any other articles that interest you.

Creating follow-ups to Usenet newsgroup articles

We'll stop the exercise here and give you a chance to read as many articles as you'd like. When you're through, please stop while you're inside an article so that you will be set up to complete this exercise.

Start your own Usenet newsgroup

news.announce.newgroups

Can't find a newsgroup for your favorite topic? Are you kidding? Well, if not, this newsgroup is for you! It contains posts of announcements of either the creation of new newsgroups or the consideration of proposed newsgroups. Newsgroups are created after a successful "call for votes" (CFV), which begins with a posting to this newsgroup. Also, calls for discussions, vote results, and creation notices of all hierarchies should be posted to here as well. Post submissions for a CFV to announce newgroups@uunet.uu.net. Follow-ups will be redirected to *news.groups*.

Post only *after* reading about the process by checking out these sources:

- "How to Create a New Usenet Newsgroup," found in *news.admin.misc*, *news.announce.newgroups*, *news.announce.newusers*, *news.answers*, or in *news.groups*.
- "Usenet Newsgroup Creation Companion," found in *news.announce.newusers*, *news.answers*, or *news.groups*.
- "So You Want to Create an Alt Newsgroup?" found in *alt.config*, *alt.answers*, or *news.answers*.

What if "they" reject me, but I don't want to give up?

There is a service that will bring you newsgroups that were deemed "unnecessary" or "of too little use to store on corporate news servers." How many? Well, for $5 per month you can get 13,000 "rejects." For details, e-mail to *ccaputo@alt.net*. Perhaps this service will bring you alternatives for creating your own newsgroup if the normal channels don't work.

You still will need to keep your main news service, but you can add this one—Netscape automatically handles multiple news servers if you use them.

Often, reading an article will bring to mind some snappy reply that you feel you must share with the world. No one knows for sure exactly why this happens, but that natural human urge to get in the last word seems to be a fact of life and certainly is the foundation for the Usenet. There are two ways to reply:

- Post a follow-up article in the same newsgroup so that everyone in the world can see it—provided that everyone in world browses through this newsgroup.
- Mail a reply directly to the author of the article you're reading and keep it between the two of you. This is a good choice either when you have a narrowly focused reply that would not interest general readers in the group, or when you prefer to keep the reply private—well, as private as e-mail can be, anyway.

The next exercise will complete the Hands On phase of newsgroups by showing you both of the ways that you can reply to a newsgroup article. You should have an article on-screen from the last exercise.

Nine keys to newsgroup netiquette

When you use the newsgroups on the Usenet, you're jumping into a global realm that can reach anyone in the world. They are powerful communication tools that deserve a lot of respect, courtesy, discretion, and common sense. These nine keys will help you improve our global cyberspace community.

1. Get the FAQs

Almost every newsgroup has a FAQ (Frequently Asked Questions) file. Look for it or ask for it. Most questions you'll ask as a newbie to a group already will have been asked repeatedly. The established users of the newsgroup are sick of browsing through posts that ask the same old questions. Get the FAQ and *read* the FAQ before you ask the group a "dumb newbie" question.

2. Lurk around first

Newsgroups can get quite personal and develop a timbre of their own. Each is slightly different. Until you've sampled that timbre, you don't know what might be considered offensive, rude, or stupid. The proper term for sampling a newsgroup is "lurking." You know the kind of people who don't lurk: the same ones who butt into your verbal conversations. If you post to a newsgroup where you've never lurked, don't be surprised if you quickly are flamed.

3. Remember the global community

Lurking will help you abide by this principle. Newsgroups likely will have members from all over the world. Keep this in mind when you post. For example, if you live in the United States, don't refer to your country as "America." Having done consulting and training work all over the world, we've seen how that reference is considered arrogant by people in the other Americas. Also, ethnic and regional jokes will at best fall flat, could be misunderstood, and easily might offend thousands of your fellow Interneters.

4. Forgive and forget

If you read something annoying, offensive, misplaced, misguided, or just plain stupid, probably your best course of action is to forget it and move on. The Internet already has speed problems that are exacerbated by electronic tennis matches of flames and counter-flames. Every group seems to have one or two real idiots who seem to have never heard of netiquette and you'll come to know them quickly, so don't worry about the occasional accidental offender. Save your flames for the really bad guys. Or, consider e-mailing a chronic repeater's ISP—you may get his account canceled, which flaming will never do.

5. Follow the threads

Most interesting newsgroup posts evoke replies. Most up-to-date software links these posts together into "threads" that follow the same theme. Read the entire thread before posting a reply yourself. Several others may already have said the same thing. No one will appreciate reading your belated opinion. Reading the whole thread is somewhat of a corollary to the last key—

forgive and forget. If a post really has you steamed, you can count on it annoying others as well, and they probably already have done plenty of flaming for you.

6. Short and sweet

Remember an ancient adage on writing that says, "I'm sorry this is so long... I didn't have time to make it short." You've got two ways to keep your posts short. First, keep them short. This truly does take longer than simply spewing forth every word on a topic that comes to mind. But the time you spend will be multiplied many times over by happy newsgroup members who in appreciation actually may read your post and actually may respond. Second, don't make them long. This, too, can take more time than making them short. You soon will get sick of wading through replies in newsgroups in which the respondent copied the entire text from the original post, which you just read. (These people often tack on only the brilliant reply, "I agree.") People can follow threads, you need not copy any more of a post than a brief contextual reminder. Sure, it takes time to delete chunks of a post that don't need to be repeated, but the time you spend will be rewarded.

7. Put it where it belongs

Stick to the subject. Usually you can tell by the title, but make sure you're in the right place by lurking and reading the FAQs file. Post only when you're certain you're writing to the right audience. Posting to the wrong newsgroup wastes a lot of resources. If you accidentally post to the wrong group, just forget about it. If you see an accidental post, ignore it. One of the most annoying events in newsgroups often begins when someone accidentally posts to the wrong group, then six people post to say how stupid this person is, then the person posts again to say to ignore the first post, which draws several more flames about brain size and family lineage, to which the original poster apologizes, then the apology draws a string of posts commenting on what a stupid waste of resources this whole event has been. Twenty messages can cascade out of a single errant post. Post correctly and remember to forgive and forget when others slip—hopefully, they'll do the same for you.

8. Remember that you're invisible

No one can see you smile on the Internet. No one can hear you chuckle, either. If you joke, don't assume that everyone understands you're joking. Remember the global community. Jokes or twisted humor on newsgroups rarely come across as funny. If you must make a crack about something, at least use one of the emoticons we've listed in chapter 4, "Netiquette," so that everyone will know that you *meant* it to be a joke. They still may not get the joke, but perhaps they won't get riled.

9. Use e-mail when appropriate

Newsgroups are an excellent place to get answers to tricky or obscure questions. If you've read the FAQs file, lurked in the background for a while, and followed all the threads, but still have a question—that's the time to post. But if the answer is not going to be of general use to the group, ask for replies by e-mail and make sure your e-mail address is included in your signature file at the end of your post. (It's supposed to be in the header, but a backup is a good idea.) Conversely, if you want to send a personal reply to a posted question, then use e-mail and spare everyone in the group the clutter of unnecessary messages.

 ## Hands On

___

***Objective:* Learn how to reply to newsgroup articles.**

❏ Click on **Post Reply** (see Figure 10-7).

❏ Press **TAB** until the insertion point is in the large text box.

❏ Click **Quote Document** if you want to include the original text.

> This is optional, but it is a good idea that will help other readers follow the thread. Please, however, **do not** keep the entire text of the article in here. Generally, you can cut out most of it, leaving enough that your reply will make sense to other readers. Often, you can break up the article into chunks and insert immediately after each piece a reply that is tailored to that section of the original. Be sure to remove the original poster's signature file—we've all read enough of those without seeing them repeated.

> If you need help on how to edit text in Windows, please be sure and complete the lessons in chapter 7, Windows Wide Open.

❏ Type your reply.

❏ Click **Send** to actually post the article to this newsgroup or click **Cancel, OK** to return to the reader.

___

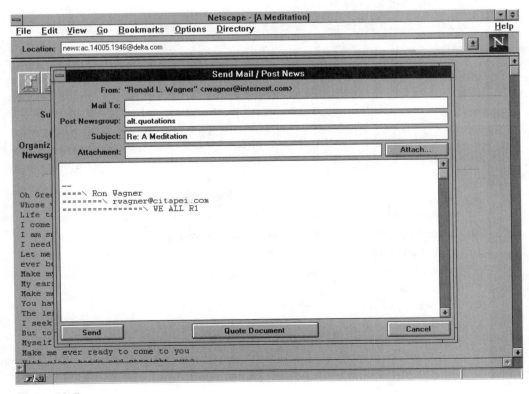

Figure 10-7

Netscape e-mail signature file

You can designate a signature file for your Netscape e-mail, but it's done differently than in Eudora. In Netscape, you create a separate text file using the Windows Notepad, save it in your Netscape directory, then tell Netscape to use that file.

Use Notepad to create and save your signature file, then follow these steps to designate it as your default signature in Netscape so that it automatically will appear at the end of all e-mail and article postings that you send with Netscape.

Hands On

Objective: **Designate a Netscape signature file.**

❑ Start Netscape.

❑ Click **Options, Preferences...**

❑ Click the **Mail and News** tab.

❑ Click in the **Signature File:** text entry box.

   Type the full directory path and filename of your saved signature file, or click on **Browse** to help you locate the file. After you've found the file, highlight it and click **OK**.

❑ Click **OK**.

❑ Click **Options, Save Options**.

   The next time you use Netscape to send e-mail or to post an article, your signature file automatically will be loaded in the message-entry window.

❑ Click **File, Exit** to close Netscape.

Posting original Usenet newsgroup articles

Sometimes you'll have an original idea for a newsgroup. Or perhaps you may have a question that you believe someone in the group might be able to answer. In either case, you'll want to create and post an original article for the newsgroup. It's basically the same as posting a follow-up, with one major exception that we'll mention twice: The subject line will be blank unless you fill it in manually!

Hands On

Objective: **Learn how to post an original newsgroup article.**

❑ Click on **Post New Article**.

❑ Press **TAB** twice to jump to **Subject**.

❑ Type *your own subject*.

❑ Press **TAB** until the insertion point is in the message body.

❑ Type your article.

   This editing window is rudimentary. **TAB** will not indent paragraphs, but instead jumps you to the **Send** button. If you miss that fact after pressing **TAB** and hit **ENTER,** you just posted a half-baked article! Be careful!

Better yet, use **ALT+TAB** to jump to your word processor, write the article there using the spell checker and thesaurus, use the Windows Copy command, use **ALT+TAB** to return to Netscape and use **CTRL+V**.

❏ Click **Send** to actually post the article to this newsgroup or click **Cancel, OK** to return to the reader.

❏ Click **File, Exit** to close Netscape.

You're about to see another advantage to using Netscape as your newsgroup reader: When you're reading a newsgroup, you remain no more than a few seconds away from the World Wide Web. All you have to do is to double-click in the Location: text entry box and enter a Web URL or click on one of your bookmarks. But now we're starting to get ahead of ourselves, so that must be a clue to move on to the next chapter. In it we'll show you the most important Internet function of all: the World Wide Web!

Continuing Education

Usenet FAQs

http://www.cis.ohio-state.edu/hypertext/faq/usenet/FAQ-List.html

This Web site contains a list of all USENET FAQs found in the newsgroup *news.answers*. This FAQs listing is alphabetized by topic as much as possible. Many of the FAQs in this list are presented in the same format as they appear in the newsgroup, while others have been enhanced and split into additional documents. A few of the documents are provided in hypertext and there is a limited search capability. We couldn't run a full-text search when we checked out this site, but search capability was available for the newsgroup names, archive names, subjects, and keywords are searched.

Farcast

http://www.farcast.com

Farcast is an agent-based personal news and information service (see Figure 10-8). Farcast lets you browse and search its collection of news, press releases, reference material, and stock quotes. The service is available interactively 24 hours a day, or you can contract with Farcast to automatically send you news articles from a wide range of topics. You also can create your own information robots (they call them "Droids"; must be *Star Wars* fans) that search more than 5,000 articles daily to retrieve news that interests you. Farcast uses your regular e-mail account, so you probably are ready to begin using it today without any special software or equipment. The last time we checked, Farcast offered its complete service for a flat-rate price of $22.95 a month, but they also offered a free ten-day trial subscription.

Online weekly

http://www.cybertours.com/yccs/online.htm

"Online" is a weekly column that currently appears in print in the *York County Coast Star* newspaper in Kennebunk, Maine, but you can receive a free e-mail

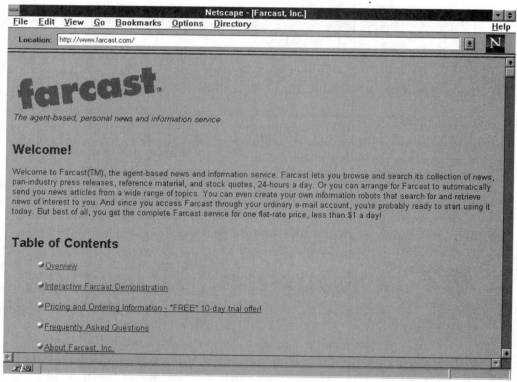

Figure 10-8

version of "Online" approximately every week by forwarding a request to *skelley@cybertours.com*. "Online" covers a broad spectrum of online topics, including services, Internetica, how-to, reviews of shareware and books and BBS topics. The "Online" Web site features the current column plus months of archived information. Resources that are mentioned in columns are hypertext-linked whenever possible to related Internet resources.

List server (listserv) information
http://www.nova.edu/Inter-Links/listserv.html

Here's a Web page dedicated to listserv topics. In addition to defining listserv, it presents some of the infrequently used listserv commands, and helps you search a listserv archive. It's most valuable section for your research is the "Directory of Scholarly E-conferences" that lets you browse by category its 1,790 e-conferences under 62 topics. You also can search the directory by keyword. Put this URL on your bookmark, and you'll always be able to jump to a listserv user guide with a mouse click.

Government, business, and general news
http://www.clarinet.com/Samples/nb-other.html

This is a summary of computer and technology news from ClariNet Communications Corporation, publishers of the ClariNet e.News electronic newspaper. The e.News was the first and currently is the largest Internet newspaper. This site offers a sample of some of the live news that the e.News

Hands On

offers to its subscribers. You can call ClariNet toll-free at 1-800-USE-NETS or e-mail them at *sales@clari.net* and ask for an application.

NewsClip news filtering language

http://www.clarinet.com/newsclip.html

Here's the Web site of the ClariNet NewsClip programming language we profiled earlier in this chapter. This site has extensive information on the language, including detailed programming examples—programmers will get the most benefit from reading the programming examples. Also, this site will keep you up-to-date on the latest changes to the language and to the services that ClariNet provides. NewsClip is a product of Looking Glass Software Limited. It's marketed by ClariNet Communications Corporation, it is free to most ClariNet e.News subscribers, and it can be downloaded from this Web site.

The Scout Report

http://rs.internic.net/scout_report-index.html

Here's the mailing list profiled earlier in the chapter. If you'd like to subscribe to either the plain-text or the HTML versions, run through the Hands On exercises that follow the writeup of The Scout Report.

The Red Rock Eater news service (RRE)

http://communication.ucsd.edu/pagre/rre.html

The information on the Red Rock Eater news service (RRE) mailing list comprises a diverse cross-section of technical, political, and privacy-related topics. Its target audience is anyone interested in electronic communications, but it includes an eclectic mix of philosophy, politics, Internet culture, and technology theory. This is one of the Internet's most respected sources of news and information about the social and political aspects of computing and networking. Established in 1993, RRE provides five to ten messages weekly of useful materials filtered from a wide range of different sources—no clutter, no flaming, no endless discussions, no subscription fees. To subscribe to RRE as a mailing list, send e-mail to *rre-request@weber.ucsd.edu*, type *subscribe <firstname lastname>* as the subject. No message is required. For more information about RRE, send e-mail to *rre-request@weber.ucsd.edu*, and type *help* as the subject. No message is required.

The World Wide Web

WHILE THE WORLD Wide Web (the Web) is vast and it may seem complicated, the Web's underlying principles are surprisingly simple. The task of implementing those simple principles across a dizzying array of incompatible computer systems has not been simple at all; we give a gold star to the people who invented and created the Web. Still, the principles are simple.

The Web is nothing more than computer documents. That basically is it. Using Netscape to browse the Web involves nothing that's any more complicated than loading documents into your word processor. As you most likely are aware, your Windows word processor can display embedded graphic images and play embedded sound files. So can Netscape. Netscape just can't edit the files it loads. So, you can think of Netscape as a "read-only" word processor.

Is it really that simple?

Yes it is. Of course you'd have little use for a read-only word processor if all you ever loaded in it were files from your own computer. But what if you could connect your read-only word processor to a remote computer that held a lot of documents that contained information you could use? You might be interested in loading those files even if you couldn't edit them—especially if you could print them and save them as files that could be edited in your word processor.

Now what if you could connect your read-only word processor to thousands of remote computers—located all over the planet—that held millions of documents that contained just about every type of information you can imagine? That may sound attractive, but it also may sound daunting—after all, how are you going to find information you need when it's buried in millions of documents and spread across thousands of computers?

Okay, so what if we gave you a wide variety of search tools that could help you pinpoint the information you need from among the millions of available documents? What if we gave you the ability to search for your information by browsing lists of related topics? What if we also gave you the ability to find any document on the system that contained a keyword or a combination of keywords that you specify?

What if we included in these documents graphic images, photographs, sound files, video clips, and forms that let you submit applications and make credit card purchases? Then, imagine that we threw in a real bonus. What if we cross-linked all of these millions of documents so that when you locate one document that contains some information you want, it contains links to other documents on related topics? What if we made these cross-links so easy to use that merely clicking a mouse on a word would load the related document? We'll call these links "hypertext" because they hyper-accelerate your ability to find what you need from among millions of pages of text.

Hypertext

If you become confused by the term "hypertext," don't be dismayed. It's not your fault, because "hypertext" means more today than it did when the term was coined.

The term was created as a definition for a word or phrase within a text document that provides a link to other text documents. Think about encyclopedia articles you've read that ended with a list of "Related Topics" that you could read if you dragged out about six other volumes. In an electronic encyclopedia, you merely click on any of the "Related Topics" and you see the related article—that's hypertext.

Your first exposure to using hypertext, however, might be to click on a graphic image that jumps to another graphic image. Or you might click on a graphic image that downloads a sound file. "How," you might ask, "is that 'hypertext?'"

Sorry about the confusion. But a long, long time ago—way back in 1991—no one had any idea that hypertext would become what it is today. Obviously the people who coined the term hypertext were better computer programmers than seers. That's not a complaint, though, because no one saw this coming. If the term were to be coined today, it might be called "hyperlink."

The bottom line is that hypertext is like magic. It is revolutionizing communication. You'll be able to click on words, buttons, or graphic images, and be swept off to any region within cyberspace that the author wanted you to see—other documents, images, sound clips, video clips, forms, software, and tables of data. And you easily will be able to create your own hyperlinked documents, thus being able to jump your readers off to any region within cyberspace that you'd like them to see.

Finally, what if we also gave you the ability to put your own information on this system so that anyone connected to it could find your information by topical index or by a keyword search, and gave you the ability to cross-link your information to other documents on related topics? You wouldn't object if we made you look at these documents in a read-only word processor, would you? If not, then you'll find this to be an exciting chapter that will revolutionize the way you think about the world.

Every feature we've listed above—and many, many more—are available today when you use Netscape to browse the Web. We'll devote the rest of this chapter to helping you learn to use Netscape, your read-only word processor, to load and browse through documents from all over the world.

Hands On

The global community

"Once a photograph of the Earth, taken from the outside, is available... a new idea as powerful as any in history will let loose."
Sir Fred Hoyle, 1948.

On Christmas Eve, 1968, Apollo 8 orbited the moon. It showed us an "earthrise" for the first time—twenty years after Sir Fred Hoyle made his prediction that such a view would loose a "new idea as powerful as any in history." Many of the people who saw that earthrise were building a computer networking system that today brings you the World Wide Web.

Certainly the Internet qualifies as Sir Hoyle's new idea. It is as powerful as any idea in history.

Is it a coincidence that the Internet was created by the first generation to see an earthrise? Absolutely not. Is it a coincidence that in 1995, as the Web swept the world, that we all saw the earthrise again in the year's biggest movie, Apollo 13? Absolutely not. The timing is perfect. The events are linked.

We all want to be connected—it's a natural part of human nature because, truly, "We all are one." The hypertext links on the World Wide Web are rapidly creating a physical manifestation of our longing for unity—to become one.

"In a real sense all life is interrelated. All persons are caught in an inescapable network of mutuality, tied in a single garment of destiny. Whatever affects one directly, affects all indirectly... I can never be what I ought to be until you are what you ought to be, and you can never be what you ought to be until I am what I ought to be. This is the interrelated structure of reality."
Martin Luther King, Jr.

King probably wasn't thinking of the Internet when he wrote about the "network of mutuality," but it's possible—the Internet had been born. Whether or not he knew it then, today we have an unsurpassed network of mutuality that will have joined together everyone on this planet by the end of 1996. As we write this book, one of its authors, Eric Engelmann, is helping the World Bank establish its Web presence in Africa, the only populated continent that doesn't yet have complete Internet connectivity. But soon, global Internet service will be in place and the planet will be able to act as a unit.

The World Wide Web now gives us the ability to transform humanity into a single living organism. Think of it on a personal level first, then on a planetary level.

If you get a splinter in your finger, your whole body rallies to help the tiny area that's affected. But consider the relationship of that tiny splinter to the size of a human body and it might seem ridiculous for a person to be intensely focused on such a minuscule problem. Yet, even a 200-pound man can be stopped by a small speck. Would he forget about the splinter if someone pointed out what a tiny percentage of his body was involved? Of course not, and the reason is communication. That tiny area is able to communicate the severity of its crisis to the rest of the man's system. This is a crucial survival technique because if that tiny area goes untended, an infection could develop that would be able to shut down the whole system. So, the entire resources of that 200-pound man rally to the aid of a minuscule area and the entire system benefits.

Similarly, the World Wide Web has given us the ability to direct our energies toward even tiny areas that need the help of the entire system. And such an intense focus will help us all, because it will prevent small problems from festering into much larger ones that could harm the global population.

For example, if we all had had the benefit of "splinter-like" communication when the HIV virus first was discovered in monkeys, there likely would be no global epidemic today. Unfortunately, the parts of humanity that had the ability to stop the problem while it was only a splinter did not feel a oneness with such a small affliction. We still were suffering under the delusion that we all are separate. But the Web can help us prevent future "splinters" in the body of humanity from festering into serious, harmful problems. We hope that as you learn to use the Web, you'll bear in mind its unprecedented ability to join us as we always have been meant to be joined. If you're interested in learning more about this, visit http://www.citapei.com.

Netscape

For our Hands On Web exercises, we'll use the Netscape Navigator Web browser for Windows (see Figure 11-1). Why did we choose Netscape? Here's a quotation we pulled from the Netscape Products home page (see *http://home.netscape.com/comprod/netscape_nav.html*). It said, "Netscape Navigator has a common feature set and interface across Windows, Macintosh, and UNIX.

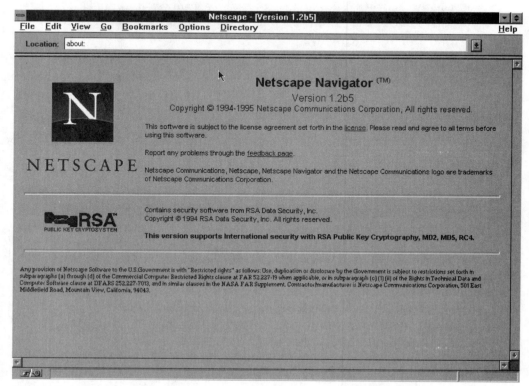

Figure 11-1

It is the most widely used network browser in the world today. Independent statistics show that over 75% of the browsers currently used on the Internet are Netscape Navigators. Today, millions of people are navigating the Internet with Netscape Navigator."

This isn't hype. Netscape is the best Web browser according to every source we've checked to date. The best testimonial we've encountered about Netscape being the de facto Web standard is the number of Web pages that have a statement similar to, "This page was designed to look best with Netscape. If you aren't using it to view this page... get it."

Getting your copy of the Netscape Web browser

If you don't have Netscape—or if you'd just like to get the most up-to-date version—you can download a free trial version from the Internet. Here is a URL that you can use to download Netscape: *http://home.netscape.com.* Find the link that leads you to download the latest version of Netscape.

The commercial version includes a printed manual that may unveil productivity-enhancing tips that you'll miss by using only the free versions. You can purchase the commercial version of the Netscape Web browser directly from Netscape by calling them at 415/528-2555, faxing them at 415/528-4140, e-mailing them at *sales@netscape.com*, or by visiting their online store on the Web at *http://order.netscape.com/order2.html.*

We wrote this chapter on Netscape the same month that the company went public and sold stock. By the time you read this, who knows how the company, its software, and its distribution system will have evolved? You will need to use the URLs we've listed here as a starting point for discovering how the company has positioned itself and Netscape today.

Creating some on-screen elbow-room

Most Web pages are too large to fit into the Netscape viewer all at once, but you'll want to see as much as possible. In our first Netscape exercise, we'll have you maximize Netscape using a Windows command, then eliminate some buttons that unnecessarily clutter the screen (see Figure 11-2), then give you keystroke equivalents to replace the buttons.

Hands On

Objective: **Maximize your Netscape viewing area.**

❏ Start Netscape with an Internet connection.

Netscape may automatically do this for you when you start it. There are a lot of ways to get an Internet connection, so we'll leave that part up to you and your computer professionals, if you need help.

❏ Double-click the title bar to maximize Netscape on-screen.

If your view already looks like the screen shown in Figure 11-2, you can skip the next two steps.

❏ Click in the **Location** text entry box.

❏ Type *http://home.netscape.com* and press **ENTER**.

Notice how this document appears on-screen, especially note how little of the document you can see at one time. Scroll through this document using your **UP ARROW** or **DOWN ARROW** keys or your mouse. Now let's improve your view.

❑ Click **Options** then uncheck **Show Toolbar**.

❑ Click **Options**, then uncheck **Show Directory Buttons**.

You don't need the two bars you just turned off. The buttons on both of them either have keystroke equivalents or are used occasionally enough that they do not merit full-time screen space.

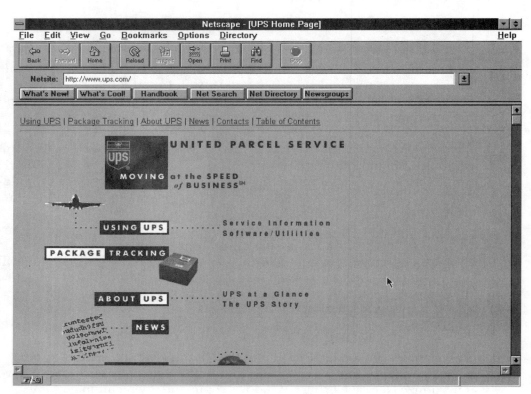

Figure 11-2

Once you've eliminated these two button bars (see Figure 11-3), you'll enjoy the increased viewing area. Of course you also can eliminate the Location bar, but that's a crucial navigation tool that you most likely will prefer to keep. Moreover, the keystrokes in the next table will give you such easy replacements for the hidden buttons that you never will miss them.

Toolbar Button	Equivalent
Back	ALT+LEFT ARROW or right mouse, Back
Forward	ALT+RIGHT ARROW or right mouse, Forward
Home	Click Go, Home
Reload	CTRL+R or View, Reload
Open Location	CTRL+L or File, Open Location...
Open File	CTRL+O or File, Open File...

▶ *Hands On*

Print	CTRL+P or File, Print...
Find	CTRL+F or Edit, Find...
Save	CTRL+S or File, Save As...
Stop	ESCAPE or Go, Stop Loading
Directory Button	**Equivalent**
What's New!	Click Directory, What's New!
What's Cool!	Click Directory, What's Cool!
Handbook	Click Help, Handbook
Net Search	Click Directory, Internet Search
Net Directory	Click Directory, Internet Directory
Newsgroups	Click Directory, Go to Newsgroups

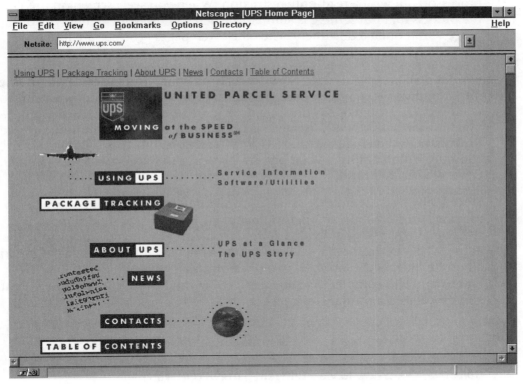

Figure 11-3

Surf the Net

Let's review. You're using the best Web browser available. You've opened up the screen for maximum viewing space and you've learned some shortcut keys. Now it's time to surf the Net. If you skipped chapter 5, "The Over-Information Age," we suggest you put a bookmark on this page and go back and read chapter 5 now. Nearly everyone is overwhelmed by the unfathomable depths and incomprehensible breadth of the resources that the World Wide Web can bring to a computer screen. But if you're ready for it... let's launch into cyberspace!

Hands On

Objective: **Start surfing the Net.**

❏ Start Netscape with an Internet connection.

❏ Double-click in the **Location** text entry box.

❏ Type *www.marketing-coach.com/mh-guide* and press **ENTER**.

❏ Click on **URL Links**.

❏ Click on **Chapter 1**.

Moving around in a Web document

What you have been seeing so far is akin to viewing documents in your word processor, but with a read-only restriction. When you see a screen on the Web, the process that put it there is similar to when you use your Windows word processor to open a document. Thus the "Web pages" you see are pages in opened documents that are available on the Web.

Besides being read-only, Netscape differs from your word processor in another important way: It can open documents from computers all over the world. Your word processor only opens documents that are on your hard drive or your organization's network. Netscape has the built-in ability to communicate with the Internet via a language called TCP/IP (see glossary). This Internet communication ability is what permits Netscape to locate and load documents from all over the world.

Since Web pages are no more than documents, let's review some shortcuts to moving around within an opened document, because you'll need to be as efficient at navigating individual Web documents as you are at navigating the entire Web. The example we'll use is a very long Web document that summarizes all of the links in this book (plus a few bonuses that we've added since the manuscript was completed). Later, we'll show you how to save this document and turn it into a primary reference source.

Hands On

Objective: **Learn how to view different parts of one Web page.**

❏ Press **DOWN ARROW** to scroll down through this document.

❏ Press **UP ARROW** to scroll up through this document.

❏ Use your mouse on the scroll bar on the right of the screen.

   Use the arrows at the top or the bottom to scroll up or down. Grab the elevator button (square box) on the scroll bar and drag it up or down to more quickly scroll long distances.

❏ Press **CTRL+END** to jump to the bottom of this document.

❏ Press **CTRL+HOME** to jump to the top of this document.

❏ Press **PG DN** a couple of times.

❏ Press **PG UP** a couple of times.

Remember these keystrokes throughout all your Web surfing. When your computer is pushing the limits, using the mouse places a strain on your Windows resources. If the mouse acts sluggish or skittery, try using these keystrokes instead.

Finding the information you need

All the power that's built into Netscape would be nearly useless if it weren't for the existence of a wide variety of Web search engines. In fact, Netscape has several features that have spurred the search engine creators to make their services user-friendly. Thus, search engine development has been a two-way street, with Netscape increasing the demand for more search engine power while at the same time contributing to the very power increases that it demands. The result has been to bring you an array of fast, powerful, and comprehensive search engines that will help you locate nearly any topic in cyberspace.

HYPERJUMP

Search engines

Software applications that help you find information within computer information files are called search engines. They have two basic functions. The first is to run through the information files word-by-word and build an index of the words it finds—much like the index in the back of this book. The second function is a user interface that accepts keyword input that the search engine uses to locate information that contains the specified search request.

We cannot track all of the search engines that are available on the Web. We constantly see new services emerge. We're going to profile two of them for you here because they both are highly popular, powerful, and representative of basic Web search techniques. Once you've used these two, learning the others will be a snap. In the Continuing Education section at the end of this chapter (and on the Web page you just loaded), we'll give you URLs and summaries for several others.

There are two reasons to try alternative search engines: 1) the others may better suit you personally than the two we'll profile; 2) the ones we're profiling may be too busy. Put an array of search engine URLs on your Bookmark List under the category "Search Resources" so you always will have them handy to answer your research demands.

Lycos

Lycos is a creation of Carnegie-Mellon University in Pittsburg (see Figure 11-4). It is oriented toward keyword searches and offers several search options. This engine is fast and comprehensive, though at times you might believe that it's slow. Just remember, you are sharing this service with millions of people around the world. Consider the wonder that it works at all!

We'll run through an exercise to demonstrate how to use Lycos to look up a specific topic.

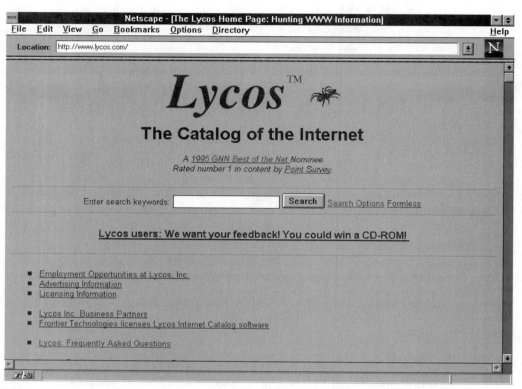

Figure 11-4

 ## Hands On

Objective: Learn to search the Web with Lycos.

❏ Double-click in the **Location:** text entry box.

❏ Type *http://www.lycos.com* and press **ENTER**.

❏ Click **Search Options** to get a more comprehensive search form.

❏ Click in **Query** and type *hot air balloon*.

❏ Select **Match All Terms (AND)** and **Good Match**.

> This means that Lycos will give a higher score to documents that contain all three terms you entered.

❏ Under **Display Options** select **10 Results per page** and **Detailed Results.**

❏ Click **Search** and wait.

> When we performed this search in January, 1996, Lycos gave us this report, "Found 61,439 documents matching at least one search term. Printing only the first 10 of 47 documents with at least scores of .0500 and matching 3 search terms." Browse through the listing you received and see your results.

❏ Press **CTRL+END** to jump to the bottom of this lengthy page.

❏ Click the right mouse button and click **Back**.

> You could click **Home** but you didn't get here from the home page, so we only needed to go back one page. Note that you also could click on **Next 10 hits** to continue displaying more of the listings that matched all three terms.

▶ *Hands On*

❏ Try some searches on topics that interest you.

    Reset the **Options** if necessary.

You can read more about using Lycos by clicking on some of the links on its home page. You can get details on the searching mechanism itself by clicking on **Search language help** on the search form page.

Yahoo

Yahoo is one of the earliest Web search engines (see Figure 11-5). Yahoo's primary search orientation is topic-based. Instead of looking for your information by a keyword search, you can scan broad categories to find things that catch your eye. Yahoo also includes a keyword search similar to Lycos— currently better in some ways than Lycos—but we'll just demonstrate its topic-based searches.

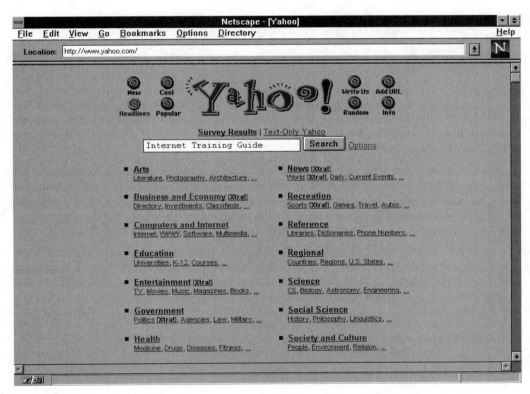

Figure 11-5

Hands On

Objective: **Learn to search the Web with Yahoo.**

❏ Double-click in the **Location:** text entry box.

❏ Type *http://www.yahoo.com* and press **ENTER**.

    This page offers more options than Lycos, but still includes a keyword search text entry box. You can click on **Options** to tailor your search more precisely. For now, though, we'll explore some of the other search methods that Yahoo offers.

❑ Click on any major topic or subtopic and follow the thread.

> For example, click on **Business and Economy**, then click on **Marketing**, then browse the list.

❑ Click on the **Yahoo!** graphic to return to the home page.

❑ Click on any category that interests you.

> Check out some of them if you want to.

❑ Click on the **Yahoo!** graphic to return to the home page.

❑ Click **Extra** to see news categories.

> Click on a news category to see related headlines. Check out some that interest you.

❑ Press **CTRL–HOME**.

❑ Click on **New** to see the latest additions to Yahoo.

> Note that Yahoo is growing by hundreds of links per day.

❑ Press **CTRL–HOME**.

❑ Click on **Cool** (the cool "shades").

> You'll find on this page a dazzling array of unrelated links. Try a few and have some fun!

❑ Click on the **Yahoo!** graphic to return to the home page.

> Remember, if you can't see this graphic press **CTRL+HOME** to return to the top of the current page.

❑ Click on **Random** (the dice).

> This is for those days when you just can't decide what to read. Sit back and leaving the driving to Yahoo!

❑ Press **ALT+LEFT ARROW**.

❑ Click on **Info** (the "I").

> Be sure to check out **Yahoo Help - Quick Tips on Using Yahoo** so you'll do even better on searches when you really need to find something specific and find it fast.

❑ Click on the **Yahoo!** graphic to return to the home page.

If your organization is not yet indexed on Yahoo, be sure to click on Add URL so that Yahoo can take your organization's Web contact information. Expect to be able to find your organization via Yahoo about a week or so after adding your URL.

Remember, there are many other good search engines at the end of this chapter in the Continuing Education section as well as on Yahoo's home page. To see some others now, click on **Options** on the Yahoo home page, then press **CTRL+END** to jump to the bottom of the options page. Last time we checked the bottom line of this screen listed: "Open Text," "Web Crawler," "Infoseek," "Dejanews" and "More..."

Electronic bread crumbs

With the power of such amazing search engines at your fingertips, it's easy to wander off into the vast forest of cyberspace and get yourself lost. You'll be jumping from one hypertext link to another, ever more deeply probing the depths of cyberspace and then you'll decide you want to return to a screen you saw earlier. But you'll have no idea how to find it again because you never actually saw or typed the URL—it was just the result of choosing one of the dozens of hypertext jumps you've made. All you've got is a vague memory of how the screen looked, and now you want to see it again.

Fortunately, the Netscape folks experienced this lost feeling enough times that they created an electronic trail of bread crumbs to mark our path through the cyberspace forest. So, Netscape includes several tools that let you quickly return to screens you've seen before.

Back and forward

The simplest bread-crumb features are Back and Forward. Netscape includes three methods to activate these two features, but we'll show you only two because one method is the Toolbar buttons that we had you remove earlier—no need to waste screen space when there are such convenient alternatives. Here are the other two:

Hands On

Objective: Activate the Back and Forward features.

❏ Click the right mouse button anywhere on the current Web page.
❏ Click **Back**.
❏ Click the right mouse button anywhere on the current Web page.
❏ Click **Forward**.
❏ Press **ALT+LEFT ARROW** three times.
❏ Press **ALT+RIGHT ARROW** three times.

View history

If the document to which you want to return is a long way back, these may become tedious navigation tools, although you can jump back very rapidly using the ALT+LEFT ARROW keystroke. Still, there are more direct routes back to pages you have previously viewed. Let's practice using them now.

Netscape caching

When you use these Back and Forward commands, you may notice that the screens load more quickly than they did originally. That's because Netscape stores downloaded screens (called "caching" in computer talk) so that it doesn't have to download them from the Internet again if you decide to return. The larger the cache size, the more screens Netscape can hold, and the faster your system will respond to Back and Forward. Netscape has two caches: one in RAM memory, and another on your hard drive or network that it uses once the RAM cache is full.

The default cache sizes that are set in Netscape are compromises to accommodate computers that have little free memory. Hard disk prices have dropped so dramatically that you may now have more free disk space *after* everything is loaded than you used to have when your hard drive was freshly formatted. RAM memory remains expensive, so it's not likely you have a lot of free RAM going to waste. You can increase both cache sizes to improve speed by following the steps in the next Hands On.

Hands On

Objective: **Increase Netscape's cache size.**

❏ Click **Options, Preferences...**

❏ Click on the **Cache and Network** tab (see Figure 11-6).

❏ Double-click in the **Memory Cache** text entry box.

> If you've got 16 megabytes of RAM, you can try setting this to 4000 kilobytes (4 megabytes). If you run a lot of other applications at the same time, you might have to live with a smaller Netscape memory cache, perhaps 2 megabytes. Whatever your computer's memory cache, you'll have to balance this setting against other memory demands.

❏ Double-click in the **Disk Cache** text entry box.

❏ Type *32000* and click **OK**.

> The version of Netscape that we used for this book accepted a maximum disk cache of 32 megabytes. You can try more on your system if you like—perhaps they've updated this feature—but when we set ours above 32000 kilobytes, Netscape changed the setting to zero (0). If you attempt to set your disk cache greater than 32000, be sure and return to see if Netscape accepted the higher setting.

❏ Click **Options, Save Options**.

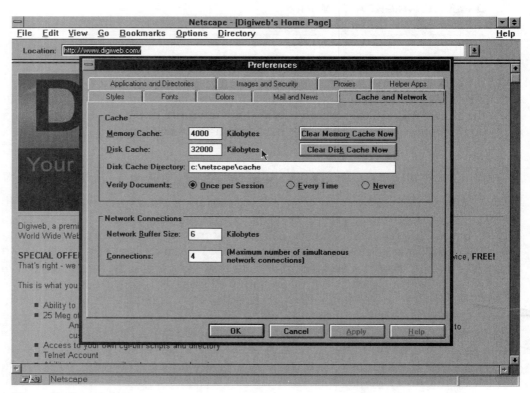

Figure 11-6

Hands On

Objective: Use the Netscape History list to find previous pages.

❏ Press **CTRL+H** to view History.

❏ Use **UP ARROW** or **DOWN ARROW** to scroll to any document.

❏ Press **ENTER** to return to that document, then press **ESCAPE** to close History.

> Those steps used the keyboard, now let's try two different methods that use the mouse.

❏ Click **Go, View History...**

❏ Click on any other document, click **Go to**, then click **Close**.

❏ Click **Go** then click on our URL Links document.

> If you activated this menu with **ALT+G**, you might prefer to make your selection by pressing the underlined number of the document you want to see.

What if you need another application while you're surfing?

Remember that Windows simulates full multitasking ability. That means that it can perform more than one function at a time. Here are two techniques to keep in mind when you're surfing the Net.

Switch applications

You can switch to other open Windows applications by cycling through them with the ALT+TAB key or by pressing CTRL+ESC to see the current Task List. This is particularly valuable when you hit during peak hours a Web site that uses extensive graphics. You can ALT+TAB to another application and get a little work done while Netscape continues to download. For example, you could jump to Eudora and compose an e-mail message. It's not much, but at least you can save a little time instead of watching the hourglass.

Run multiple Netscape sessions

You can open multiple Netscape Windows, although this certainly is not a solution to long download times. But it does permit you to see two Web pages at once—or three Web pages, or more! When you create multiple Netscape sessions each occurrence is a separate Windows task that will appear on the CTRL+ESC Task List and to which you can switch using ALT+TAB. Follow these steps to open an additional Netscape window (see Figure 11-7).

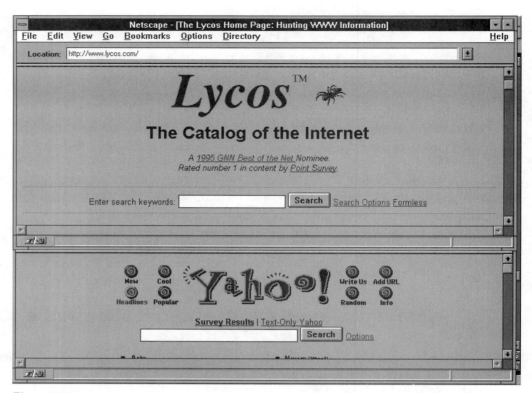

Figure 11-7

Hands On

Objective: **Learn to open multiple Netscape windows.**

❏ Click **File, New Window** or press **CTRL+N**.

> This opens a new Netscape window that loads your default home page. You will be able to see the first session in the background. You can navigate in either one now, setting them both to different URLs. If you can see both of them, you can use your mouse to switch back and forth. It's probably best, however, to run them both maximized, so let's do that now and learn how to switch between them when they're maximized.

❏ Double-click in the title bar of the new Netscape window.

❏ Press **CTRL+ESC** to see both of them on the Task List.

> You'll see the title of the current page in each session in square brackets after "Netscape."

❏ Double-click on the first Netscape session you had open.

❏ Press **ALT+TAB** once to return to the new Netscape window.

❏ Press **ALT+TAB** once again to return to the first window.

❏ Press **ALT+TAB** once to return to the new Netscape window.

> Of course you don't have to run these windows maximized. You might want to use the Restore command and then size them so that you can see both Web pages at the same time, perhaps to compare two Web sites.

❏ Click **File, Close** to close the new window.

> Notice that **Close** is a new menu item—you still could select **Exit** to quit Netscape, but when you open multiple windows, you get this extra item to close just this window.

Closing one will not terminate your Internet connection, because you still have the first Netscape window open. Be sure you still have our document loaded that lists all the URLs in this book.

Finding information on a Web page

Many of the hypertext Web pages that you'll view include jumps to bookmarks within the same document. You'll be able to tell if you've jumped to another spot within the same document because the URL will not change except for the very end, onto which will be appended a pound sign (#) and the bookmark name.

But you won't always find the information you want by using hypertext jumps and you'll need to search the full text of the current Web document. Netscape has a built-in Find feature that we'll practice now. For this exercise, let's say you wonder if we've given you any URLs that lead to weather information.

Hands On

Objective: Learn to use the Netscape Find feature.

❑ Make sure you're in the URL Links document you found earlier

❑ Press **CTRL+F** or click on **Edit, Find**.

❑ Type *breathing space* and press **ENTER** to jump to that phrase.

> This only finds text within this specific document. This is not searching the Web itself. It's not even searching other documents that may appear to be the same as this document, but which actually are other documents on the same server. It finds text only within this single Web document.

❑ Click **Cancel**

Using the information you find

Finding an important business lead, tip, or idea can bring value to your organization. Finding some research material you've been seeking can be a huge relief. Coming across exciting information on the Web that you never knew existed is absolutely exhilarating. But what good is any of the value, the relief, or the thrill, if all you can do with it is to read it on the screen? Getting it on your screen is a good start, but we're now going to show you how to transfer it into your system in a useful format. There are numerous options and you probably will use them all, depending on the information you've found and on how you want to use it at the time.

Copying and pasting Web pages

Probably the quickest, simplest, and most overlooked option for transferring Web text is by using the Copy and Paste commands with the Windows clipboard. If you can see it, you usually can paste it into your word processor. This gives you the ability to reshape and reformat the text, embellish it with nice fonts, and print it as part of a larger document.

Hands On

Objective: Learn to transfer Web text into your word processor.

❏ Use **ALT+TAB** to cycle back to the Program Manager.

❏ Start your word processor.

❏ Use **ALT+TAB** to cycle back to Netscape.

❏ Drag your mouse to highlight the listing you just found about Breathing Space.

❏ Press **CTRL+C** to Copy it to the Windows clipboard.

❏ Use **ALT+TAB** to cycle to your word processor.

❏ Press **CTRL+V** to Paste the copied text into a blank document.

> You now could go back to Netscape and grab more text from this Web document, or get more from any Web document in the world!

You won't be able to grab all of the text you read on the Web, because some text actually is part of a graphic image. In those cases, you won't be able to grab the text you want by simply dragging your mouse over it. You'll know it's not regular text characters because, as you drag your mouse, the text will not highlight.

Printing Web pages

If you only need to read the document and don't need to use it in your word processor, you can print the document directly in Netscape. This is a quick way to get a hard copy of Internet information, but it is (of course) completely inflexible; you can't reformat it.

Netscape offers optional embellishments for printed Web pages that include headers and footers with name, date, and URL. We'll run through the printing setup options later (see Figure 11-8).

Printing a Web document is perfect for things like airline schedules and data tables, when all you need is a quick print-out and the information is more important than the formatting.

Hands On

Objective: Learn to print a Web document.

❏ Click **File, Print Preview** then use **Zoom In** and **Zoom Out**.

> Zoom in to better see the header and footer on each page. Use **Two Page** and **One Page** to change views and use **Next Page** and **Prev Page** to turn document pages. You can print from the preview screen by clicking on the **Print...** button, but instead let's return to the regular browsing screen and choose some page setup options.

❏ Click **Close**.

❏ Click **File, Page Setup...**

> The best settings for **Page Options**, at the top-left, will depend upon the printer you're using, so we'll let you experiment with those. The same applies to the **Margins** settings.

❏ Click **Document Title** if you want to remove the title from the header of each page.

❏ Click **Document Location (URL)** if you want to remove the URL from the header of each page.

❏ Click **Page Number**, **Page Total** and **Date Printed** as desired for the information you want included in the footer of each page.

❏ Click **File, Print...** then select options as desired.

❏ Click **OK** to print our URL Summary.

Or you can click **Cancel**.

Saving Web documents

You can use Netscape to save a Web document, but if you're not careful, the document will be saved with all of the hypertext markup language (HTML) codes. In your word processor, you'll need to clean out the extraneous codes to get down to only the text you need. Check out the sidebar on how to get and use a macro for WordPerfect for Windows that we've developed that will clean all of the HTML codes from a WordPerfect document. We will show you an option, however, that cleans the HTML codes from the document as it saves. Still, the macro will be useful because sometimes, one way or another, you're going to end up with documents that have a lot of embedded HTML codes that you'll want to clean out.

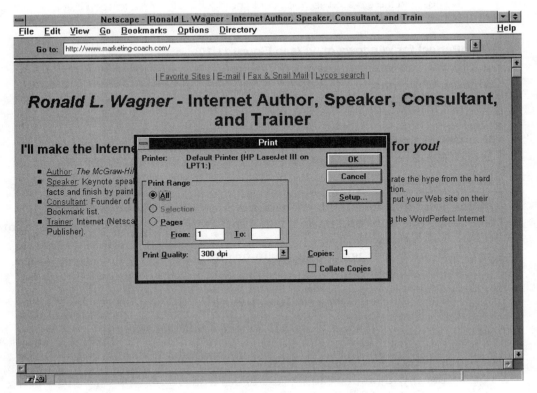

Figure 11-8

Hands On

Objective: **Learn to save a Web document.**

❏ Click **File, Save as...** or press **CTRL+S**.

Netscape creates a name for you that's extracted from the title of the Web document, then it appends the extension "htm," which is DOS-syntax for hypertext markup language (HTML). You can, of course, change the name as desired.

The key to cleaning out the HTML codes is to click on the **Save File as Type** drop list and change to **Plain Text (*.txt)** (see Figure 11-9). You don't have to actually use the *txt* extension—the document will be saved as plain text even if you keep the *htm* extension, as long as the file type has been set correctly.

Use the **Drives** and **Directories** windows to set the desired path.

Put this document in a directory that you commonly use for word processing, because we're going to open it later in this exercise. Please write down or remember the directory. If you're on a network, you can click the **Network** button to access your available network drives.

❏ Click **OK** to save the document.

❏ Use **ALT+TAB** to switch to your word processor.

If your word processor is not running, use **ALT+TAB** to switch back to the Program Manager and then start it.

❏ Click **File, Open...** or press **CTRL+O**.

Navigate to the saved Web document and double-click on it to open it and display the conversion dialog box.

WordPerfect for Windows only: (see Figure 11-10)

❏ Click the drop-list arrow to get a list of formats.

❏ Select **ANSI (Windows) Text CR/LF to SRt** and click **OK**.

❏ Click **File, Save** or press **CTRL+S** then click **OK**.

Microsoft Word for Windows only:

❏ Click **File, Save** or press **CTRL+S**.

At this point, the document you had in Netscape now has been saved in the format of your word processor. If you didn't switch to plain-text you'll see a lot of HTML codes, but we've given you a quick way to remove those. Or, return to Netscape and save it again in the plain-text format.

Cleaning HTML codes from saved Web documents

If you don't switch Netscape into the right saving mode, or if someone sends you an HTML document, cleaning out the HTML codes will be an agonizing task. But if you don't clean out the HTML codes, you won't have easy access to the plain text. So, to make your HTML documents more useful, we've written a macro for WordPerfect for Windows 6.0/6.1 that automates this tedious task and will clean an HTML document in seconds.

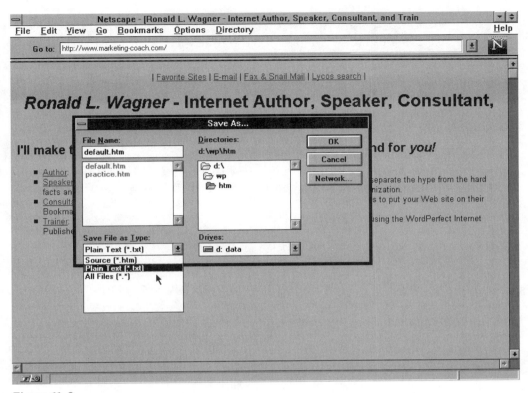

Figure 11-9

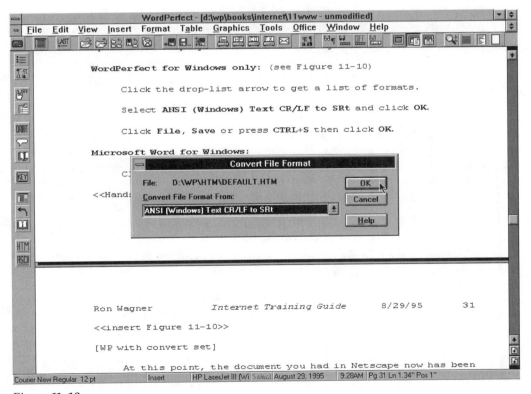

Figure 11-10

Of course, before you use such a document, consider carefully the document's copyright. Documents placed on the Web do not lose their copyright. Read appendix A on copyrights if you aren't sure what rights you have to use this document. Your best bet, however, is to be up-front about using it and e-mail the copyright holder for reprint permission. People often are glad to grant permission, especially if you cite their URL in the document in which you use their text.

Our HTML cleaning macro (*htmclean.wcm*) is available from this book's home page at *www.marketing-coach.com/mh-guide*. The Web page contains complete details on how to download the macro and use it in WordPerfect. (It also includes a link for you to send us a similar macro for Word if you write one.)

Hands On

Objective: **Run the WordPerfect for Windows HTML-Clean macro.**

❑ Open a document that contains HTML codes.

❑ Press **ALT+F10**, type *htmclean* and press **ENTER**.

   This will take from a few seconds to a minute or more, depending on the document's size. You can click on **Cancel** or press **ESC** to abort early.

❑ Click **File, Save** or press **CTRL+S**.

❑ Click **OK** to save the document in WordPerfect format.

You now have a plain-text version of the original Web screen. Before you run this macro, though, make sure that you don't need anything inside any of the HTML codes. Sometimes all of the copyright information or the contact information for the original source is contained in hypertext. When you clean out the codes you will lose everything that's between a pair of angle-brackets (<sample HTML code>).

Saving images

The last method you have for extracting Internet information into useable formats is to save graphics files. Netscape makes this very easy. All you have to do is click your right mouse button on any Web page graphic and choose the right save option.

Hands On

Objective: **Learn to save a Web page graphic image.**

❑ Double-click in the **Location** text entry box.

❑ Type *http://www.internext.com* and press **ENTER**.

❑ Click the right mouse button over the graphic image (see Figure 11-11).

❑ Click **Save this Image as...**

   Select a directory in which to save it.

❑ Click **OK**.

▶ 212   *Hands On*

The image has been saved in the Graphics Interchange Format (compressed graphic images). At the time this book was written, neither Microsoft Word nor WordPerfect for Windows could handle GIF or JPEG files directly. Because the Internet is strewn with millions of images in these two formats, we imagine that both Novell and Microsoft will have updated their word processors to handle GIF, JPEG, or both by the time you read this. If they haven't, let them know you need these important capabilities.

Right mouse button bonuses

If you used the right mouse button in the last exercise when you saved a graphic, then you may have noticed that the menu had several other shortcuts. We'll run through one of them with you now in case you missed them or didn't save a graphic. To see these commands actually function, you'll need a Web page that has a graphic image. You can use the Internext home page we used earlier.

Copy a link location

Netscape also uses the right mouse button to give you an easy method to copy the URL of a hypertext link into your Windows clipboard. You then may use ALT+TAB to cycle to your word processor or to your reserved URL storage file (see chapter 7, Windows Wide Open) and paste in the URL. As you've seen, some URLs are a real mess to retype, so this method may save you a lot of time, aggravation, and mistakes. We'll again use the Internext home page for this exercise.

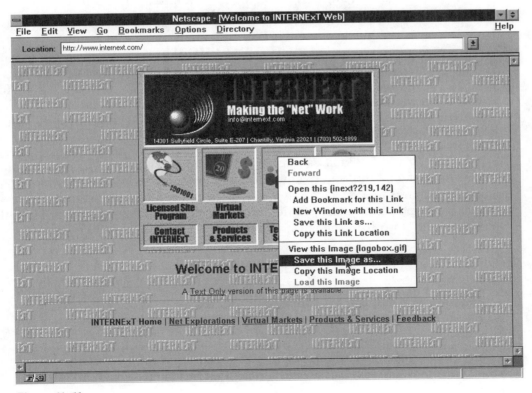

Figure 11-11

Hands On

***Objective:* Save a link location to the Windows clipboard.**

❑ Start with the Internext home page.

❑ Click on **Net Explorations**.

❑ Place the mouse over **The Web Crawler** link, but don't click.

    Read the link's URL on the status line at the bottom of the screen. You don't want to type that, do you? Remember, these Web addresses are case-sensitive; you would have to get every character exactly right!

❑ Click the right mouse button and click **Copy this Link Location**.

    The URL is now in the Windows clipboard. If you wanted to paste it into another Windows application you now would use **ALT+TAB** to switch applications, then press **CTRL+V** to paste it.

Bookmarks

Bookmarks are the next step beyond leaving yourself an electronic bread-crumb trail. Bookmarks create a permanent file that saves the URL of any Internet document and assigns it a plain-language name. You can pop up your Bookmark List any time and quickly jump to all of your favorite sites.

We'll learn four different Bookmark features: 1) adding Bookmarks, 2) editing Bookmarks, 3) modifying and arranging the Bookmark List itself, and 4) turning the Bookmark List into your own personal "home page."

Add a bookmark

There are two ways to add personal Bookmarks in Netscape. The first is so easy we don't even need a Hands On exercise to learn it. Whenever you see a site for which you want easy access, simply press CTRL+A for the "Add Bookmark" command. Using the mouse, the steps are: click Bookmarks, Add Bookmark. The current URL is added to the default Bookmark category.

You also can add Bookmarks directly to the list (see Figure 11-12). This has the advantage of enabling you to enter Bookmarks for sites you've yet to visit, or to add Bookmarks to a selected category. The next three lessons assume you have at least Netscape 1.2. If yours is older than this, check out the sidebar earlier in the chapter and download the latest version.

Hands On

***Objective:* Add a Bookmark directly to the listing.**

❑ Press **CTRL+B** or click **Bookmarks, View Bookmarks...**

❑ Click on the top folder on the list.

❑ Click **Item, Insert Header...**

❑ Click in the **Name** text entry box and delete "New Header."

- ❏ Type *Practice* and click **OK**.

  This creates a new folder under the main folder.
- ❏ Click on the folder "Practice."
- ❏ Click **Item, Insert Bookmark...**
- ❏ Click in the **Name** text entry box and delete "New Header."
- ❏ Type *ILC Glossary* and press **TAB** to jump to **Location (URL)**.
- ❏ Type *http://www.matisse.net* and press **TAB** for **Description**.
- ❏ Type *Internet Literacy Consultants Glossary* and click **OK**.
- ❏ Click on the folder "Practice."
- ❏ Click **Item, Insert Bookmark...**
- ❏ Click in the **Name** text entry box and delete "New Header."
- ❏ Type *Lycos* and press **TAB** to jump to **Location (URL)**.
- ❏ Type *http://www.lycos.com* and press **TAB** for **Description**.
- ❏ Type *Carnegie-Mellon Lycos Search* and click **OK**.
- ❏ Click in the **Name** text entry box and delete "New Header."
- ❏ Type *Yellow Pages* and press **TAB** to jump to **Location (URL)**.
- ❏ Type *http://www.yellow.com* and press **TAB** for **Description**.
- ❏ Type *Yellow Pages* and click **OK**.
- ❏ Click on the top folder on the list.
- ❏ Click **Item, Insert Header...**
- ❏ Click in the **Name** text entry box and delete "New Header"
- ❏ Type *Internet Resources* and click **OK**.

  This creates another new folder.
- ❏ Click on the top folder on the list.
- ❏ Click **Item, Insert Header...**
- ❏ Click in the **Name** text entry box and delete "New Header"
- ❏ Type *Directories* and click **OK**.

  You can continue the lesson now by adding folders for your own categories. Here are a few more suggested headings that you could create now:

  Search Resources

  Reference Resources

  Corporations

  Universities

  Miscellaneous

Now that you've set up all of these headings, we'll give you a short exercise that will let you choose a new default Bookmark category. This is the category under which all Bookmarks will be added when you use Bookmarks, Add Bookmark or press CTRL+A.

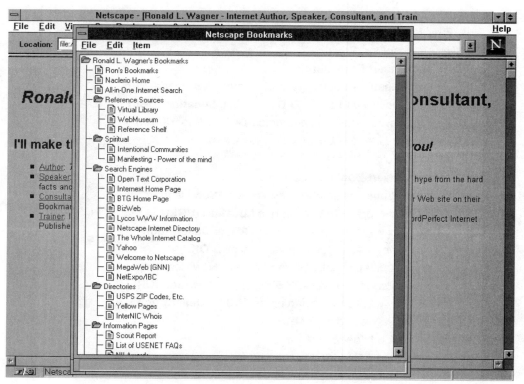

Figure 11-12

Hands On

Objective: **Set the default Bookmark category (see Figure 11-13).**

❏ Click **Bookmarks, View Bookmarks**.

❏ Click **File, Preferences...**

❏ Click the drop list under **The Add Bookmark Menu command adds to:**.

❏ Select the header you want as your default category.

❏ Click **OK**, then click **File, Close**.

❏ Click **Options, Save Options**.

To place a new Bookmark in a category other than this default, you first must add it the list under the default. Then you can press CTRL+B to open the Bookmark List and then drag and drop the new Bookmark onto the desired category.

Edit an existing bookmark

Sometimes a URL for which you've created a Bookmark will change, or you'll get some new information about a Bookmark site that you'd like to add to the description. Netscape makes Bookmark editing a snap. Here are the steps:

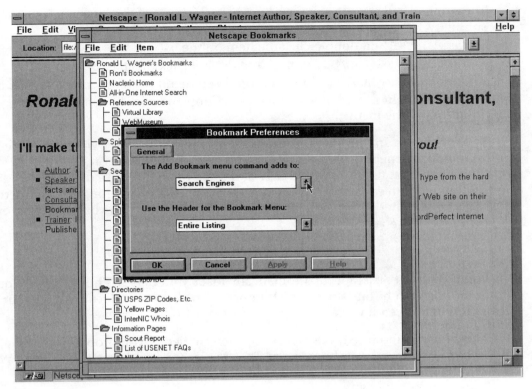

Figure 11-13

Hands On

Objective: **Learn to edit a Bookmark.**

❏ Click on any existing Bookmark.

❏ Click the right mouse button then click **Properties**.

❏ Make any necessary changes, then click **OK**.

Modify the bookmark listing

The order of the folders and the document references under each folder can be rearranged at any time simply by dragging any entry either to a new folder or to a new location under the same folder.

Hands On

Objective: **Modify the bookmark listing.**

❏ Drag and drop "ILC Glossary" on the "Internet Resources" folder.

❏ Drag and drop "Yellow Pages" on the "Directories" folder.

❏ Click on the folder "Practice" and delete it by pressing **DELETE** or by clicking on **Edit, Delete**.

❏ Double-click the control menu box or press **ALT+F4** to exit the Netscape Bookmarks window.

There are several ways to use your Bookmark List to surf the Internet. Here's a summary:

- Press CTRL+B and double-click the item on the list.
- Click Bookmarks, View Bookmarks... and double-click the item on the list.
- Click Bookmarks and click on the drop-down menu or sub-menu of Bookmarks.
- Click the right mouse button on your desktop and click Bookmarks at the bottom of the menu.

Bookmarks are an important feature of Netscape because they will greatly speed your work by enabling you quickly to save any URL you find on the Internet. Please note that the Bookmarks are not limited to saving URLs of Web documents. You can use a Bookmark to save the URL of anything on the Internet: FTP sites, Gopher sites, newsgroups, and local documents on your organization's own network server.

Create your own "home page"

When you start Netscape, it automatically loads your default "home page." Your home page can be any site on the Internet or any hypertext document on your own system, even if you are using a stand-alone PC.

If you haven't modified Netscape since you installed it, you probably have their Web page set to be your home page. They're nice folks and they have a good Web site, but you can turn your Bookmark file into a tailored home page that can boost your productivity. Here's how:

Hands On

Objective: Turn the Bookmark file into your home page.
- ❏ Click **Options, Preferences...**
- ❏ Click on the **Styles** tab.
- ❏ Click **Start With:, Home Page Location:**
- ❏ Click in the text entry box immediately below this button.
- ❏ Type *file:///c:\netscape\bookmark.htm* and click **OK**.

    Note there are *three* slashes after the colon (see Figure 11-14).

    Now every time you start Netscape it will load your Bookmark List in hypertext. The folders will show up as bolded headings and each entry will show up as a hypertext jump. If you place your mouse—without clicking it—over a highlighted jump, you can read the URL in the status bar at the bottom of the screen. Any descriptions you manually entered on your Bookmark List will show up as regular text under its associated hypertext jump entry.

The McGraw-Hill Internet Training Guide home page

Now that you know how to change Netscape's default home page, you may have better ideas than using your bookmark file as we showed you in the last exercise. For example, you might find a really terrific hypertext document somewhere that contains a treasure trove of fabulous Web sites. Wouldn't that be nice? We thought so; that's why we've created our URL Summary document.

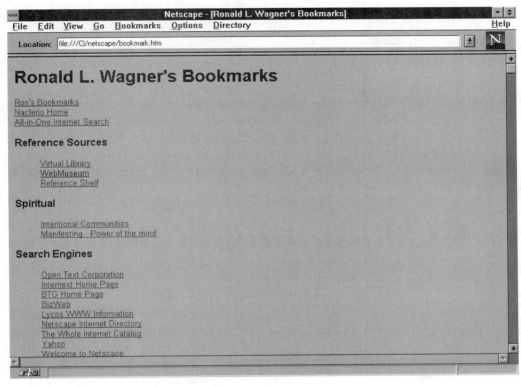

Figure 11-14

 Hands On

***Objective:* Use our URL Summary as your default home page.**

❑ Go to *http://www.marketing-coach.com/mh-guide*.

❑ Click **URL Links** and then click **Download Summary**.

❑ Click **File, Save As...** or press **CTRL+S** for the save dialog box.

❑ Change to your Netscape directory.

❑ Click **OK** to save *mh_links.htm*.

❑ Click **Options, Preferences...**

❑ Click on the **Styles** tab.

❑ Click **Start With:, Home Page Location:**

❑ Click in the text entry box immediately below this button.

❑ Type *file:///c:\netscape\mh_links.htm* and click **OK**.

Now every time you start Netscape it will load *The McGraw-Hill Internet Training Guide* URL Summary as your home page. You later might modify this file to add your own links and remove some that you don't find useful. Or, you can·return regularly to the book's Web site and download and save updated versions. Feel free to copy and distribute this list to anyone—you have our permission.

Now that we've covered the technical aspects of using Netscape to navigate us around in cyberspace, we've covered all the basic Internet tools that you'll need. You'll spend most of your Internet time using Netscape. You frequently will use e-mail (most likely Eudora). And you occasionally may need WS_FTP to transfer files or WSIRC to set up an Internet conference. Now that you've learned how to use all of those tools, the Hands On phase of this book is complete. Thanks for sticking with us.

In the book's final phase we'll give you some important information and tips that will help you create your organization's Web presence. The next two chapters will help you plan your own cyberspace presence by analyzing some examples of powerful, useful, and user-friendly Web features that you may want to employ in creating your own Web site. The remaining chapters will cover Internet money issues and computer security, and then we'll close the book with technical help on creating your own Web presence.

 # Continuing Education

All-In-One Internet search

http://www.albany.net/allinone

Awesome! That's the only word that can describe our candidate for the best research tool on the Internet today—of course, by the time you read this, who knows! It's a compilation of various forms-based search tools found on the Internet that have been combined to form a consistent interface and create a convenient "all-in-one" search engine (see Figure 11-15). If you can't find it through this site, it isn't worth finding.

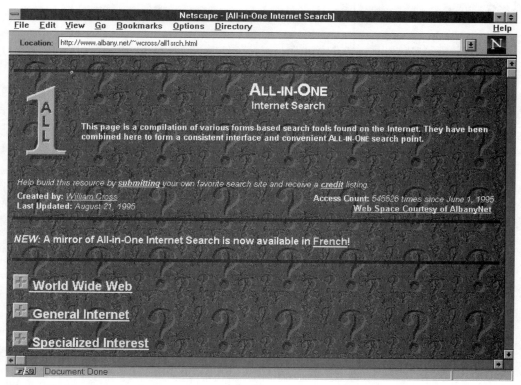

Figure 11-15

WWW FAQ

http://sunsite.unc.edu/faq

This online Frequently Asked Questions site is an excellent site for new Web users. Most of the other sites listed here are information-searching resources, so you might want to try this site first to get a better overview of what's out there waiting for you in cyberspace.

Open Text Web index

http://www.opentext.com/omw/f-omw.html

An excellent search site that provides both simple and compound search strings. Click on "Open Text Web Index" to get to their "Simple search" engine. This site also enables you to search the Web in several languages besides English: Deutsch, Français, Italiano, and Nihongo (Japanese). Check the options you want, enter a keyword or phrase and click on Search. You also can select more detailed searches using the optional hypertext links to Power Search and Weighted Search. Like other search engines, Open Text is growing rapidly as they index tens of thousands of Web pages per day.

Web searching tips

http://www.opentext.com/omw/f-hints.html

This page—actually a link on the main Open Text search page—offers some excellent tips on how to maximize the results of Web searches. The question is: Do you really need to find more information?

Yahoo directory

http://www.yahoo.com

This is a staple Web search engine. It's got just about everything you could want. The search mode is based upon your browsing through hypertext-linked tables of contents to find topics that appear to match your area of interest. It's getting plenty of competition now, but it was among the pioneers and deserves a look simply because of the huge number of people who learned from the early work that Yahoo did.

Lycos

http://www.lycos.com

This Internet search tool was created by Carnegie Mellon University (located in Pittsburgh) and is one of the most popular sites on the Internet. It's based upon a vast index of keywords that it has pulled from HTTP, Gopher and FTP files all over the Internet. At the beginning of July, 1995, while we were writing this book, Lycos had indexed 4.7 million documents; one month later the total had climbed to 5.5 million pages! Go see how many pages it's indexed today.

The Lycos index searches document title, headings, links, and keywords to build a reference against which you can search the Internet. You find topics by entering a keyword or a string of keywords that Lycos compares against its index. The results of the search are reported to you with a score based upon how many of your keywords it finds, the number of occurrences, and how far into the document the words are found.

InfoSeek

http://www.infoseek.com

InfoSeek is a new full text search service that makes finding information easy. It enables you to search Web pages, Usenet News, more than 50 computer magazines, newspaper newswires and press releases, company profiles, medical and health information, movie reviews, technical support databases and much more. Internet Magazine called InfoSeek the best search tool on the Internet. It functions much like Lycos. This is a commercial service, but the costs are reasonable. Check out their Web page for current pricing structure.

WWW Virtual Library

http://www.w3.org/hypertext/DataSources/bySubject/Overview.html

Here's a topic-oriented Internet reference site. Instead of keywords, you look for topics that interest you, or ones that intrigue you; there's something here for everyone. This is not like other topic-oriented sites like Yahoo; it really is an online hypertext library.

Web Museum

http://sunsite.unc.edu/wm/

This truly is a treasure trove of Internet resources (see Figure 11-16). It's a free art museum created by Nicolas Pioch, a student studying economics at the Ecole Nationale Superieure des Telecommunications in Paris. It's a personal creation that has no support, no funding, no manpower. The WebMuseum is a

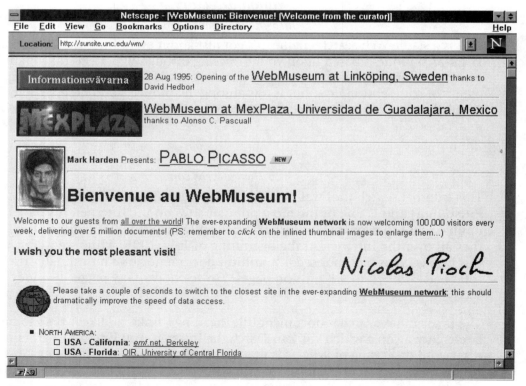

Figure 11-16

collaborative work that encourages its visitors to contribute to expand and improve the WebMuseum. This site won a "Best of the Web Award" in 1994.

MegaWeb

http://gnn.com/gnn/GNNhome.html

When the research for this book was compiled, this service was in beta test. It's probably up to full speed by now, so check it out. Click on "The Whole Internet Catalog" under their "Best of the Net" category.

World Wide Web yellow pages

http://www.yellow.com

Here's an easy to remember URL that should find its way onto thousands (millions?) of Netscape Bookmark lists. You can use this page to search for a wide range of businesses with a Web presence. World Wide Yellow Pages is a trademark of Home Pages, Incorporated.

UIUC Web

http://www.atmos.uiuc.edu/wxworld/html/top.html

Welcome to Weather World. This is the Web version of the popular University of Illinois Weather Machine Gopher service. Here you'll find a comprehensive collection of current weather information. The main menu presents a convenient one-page summary with links to popular, weather-related items. Everything else is on lower-level menus.

BookWire library index

http://www.bookwire.com/index/libraries.html

Here's a powerful listing of Web-accessible libraries from around the globe. This is an excellent model of what the Internet does best. In fact, if you haven't read chapter 5, "The Over-Information Age," this particular page may make you run screaming from your computer. You literally could spend the rest of your life exploring just the links on this page and still tap into but a fraction of all that it offers.

You can use this Web page to tap into almost any information you want from libraries in these basic groups: Asia, Pacific, Canada, Europe, Latin America, and United States. For example, tracking down the European option on this page can lead you to hundreds of world-wide resources through the Bodleian Library at the University of Oxford.

Project Gutenberg

http://jg.cso.uiuc.edu/pg/pg-home.html

Project Gutenberg "etexts" are public domain works distributed by Professor Michael S. Hart through the Project Gutenberg Association at Illinois Benedictine College. Among other things, this means that no one owns a United States copyright on or for these works, so the Project (and you!) can copy and distribute them in the United States without permission and without paying copyright royalties. Special rules apply, however, if you wish to copy and distribute etext under the "Project Gutenberg" trademark.

Galaxy

http://www.einet.net/

Galaxy is a guide to Web information and services and is provided as a public service by EINet and a variety of Galaxy guest editors. Be sure to click on the "Add" jump because it will let you enter your own home page URL and other information so that other users can use Galaxy to find you.

Britannica Online

http://www-lj.eb.com/

This is a commercial site. Its only free services are demonstrations and accounts for educational institutions. Full searches require a fee payment, but you get the full resources of *Britannica Book of the Year*, *Nations of the World*, *Merriam Webster's Collegiate Dictionary*, and the *Propaedia*.

Federal Government

http://www.fedworld.gov

FedWorld is a hypertext menu of various Federal Government computer resources (see Figure 11-17). The National Technical Information Service (NTIS) introduced FedWorld in November 1992 to help with the challenge of accessing U.S. Government information online. Most of the links are to other Web sites, but it also includes Telnet links to several Federal computer systems. You'll find most links under the "Index of Subject Categories," but you will also find direct links to some popular sites, including Web, FTP, Gopher, and Telnet sites. The

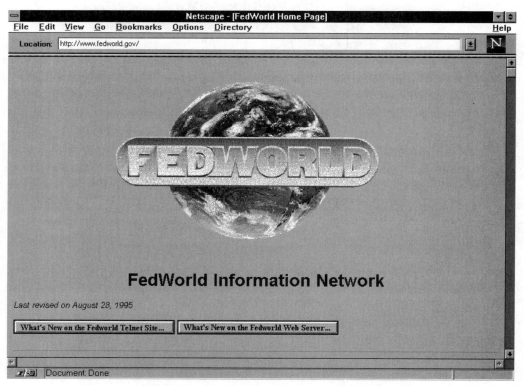

Figure 11-17

Hands On

IRS isn't yet on this site, but we happen to know that it soon will be. Ron Wagner, one of this book's authors, is helping the IRS to rewrite the entire tax code using WordPerfect for Windows and to convert it into hypertext—this could be up to 60,000 pages of text! Helping with the IRS conversion will be Ron's next job as soon as the manuscript for this book is completed.

Truly awesome Web stuff

http://www.clark.net/pub/journalism/awesome.html

"The glory and the grandeur of the Internet all on one site" is their claim-to-fame. They've got the "Truly Awesome" list (last count: 29 sites) and the merely "Awesome" list (last count: 97 sites). Be sure and check out the latest update at this address. From here, you can spend your entire life surfing the Web—of course you still will be farther behind than you are today, but at least you will have a fun trip.

PHASE 3
The rest of the story

PAUL HARVEY, the longest-running radio commentator of all time, opens the final segment of his radio programs with his legendary phrase, "And now—the rest of the story." Paul Harvey and one of this book's co-authors, Ron Wagner, are fellow graduates of Tulsa Central High School. So, now—to borrow from a fellow Tulsa Central graduate—here's "the rest of the story."

Learning how to wield an artisan's tool doesn't make anyone a skilled artist. Skills must be developed with practice over time. Only then can tools convey the artist's expressiveness. So, now that you've learned how to use the tools of the Internet, we want to help you develop the necessary skills to express yourself on the Internet.

Internet technology changes daily and the pace of those changes is ever increasing; this phase of the book is intended to be a starting point for you—a foundation for the knowledge base you're going to build. We'll present the overall context, basic principles, and some of the secrets behind doing business successfully on the Internet. But the "Continuing Education" references at the end of each chapter represent a wealth of resources that can boost your Internet success and will be necessary for the evolution of your skills.

Only you can decide

There is no single solution for all companies. The strategy employed by a small company in a small town will be vastly different than the one employed by a multinational corporation with offices in dozens of major cities. You'll need to use the information in these chapters to decide how your company will proceed with its own presence in cyberspace.

No one can decide for you, nor can any individual provide enough information upon which to base a sound decision. We wish we could tell you otherwise, but it simply isn't so. You always will need to cross-check and track Internet technology changes.

Let's consider some examples:

- A small company might need to hire a consultant because it lacks the internal expertise—not to mention the learning time—to create a Web site. On the other hand, a small association may serve its members well with a simple Web page that easily can be created in WordPerfect.
- A large corporation may have the internal expertise already on staff that can handle the move into cyberspace. On the other hand, a large corporation might need to create a truly world-class image that will involve pulling together a team comprised of current staffers, as well as outside advertising and technical consultants.

You'll face some hard decisions, because learning the Internet is much like learning chess. You can get the basics quickly and put up a simple Web page using some slightly advanced word-processing skills. But mastering the Internet to world-class levels can be a full-time job. This book, however, will prepare you to choose the best route for your organization's particular circumstances.

The rest of the story

We'll begin the rest of the story by walking you through an analysis of some good examples of Client-centered Interneting. You'll learn to focus—as you create your company's Web presence—on the needs of those who will use your Internet services. The principles you observe in the first chapter of this phase will lead nicely into the chapter on Client-centered Interneting in which we'll present some principles and tips for making your Web site not only useful, but popular.

Keeping customers informed on the Internet is one matter, but collecting money from them is another. We've got a chapter that covers money issues from both angles: income and expenses. These both are rapidly changing environments, and (more than with other areas) you'll need our "Continuing Education" section to stay abreast of Internet technology changes.

Closely related to money issues—and changing just as rapidly—is the issue of internal computer security. Believe it or not, people today are earning a living running computers that "sniff" Internet traffic for keywords that are of interest to their clients. We'll show you how to stay on top of this.

We'll wrap up with a chapter on Internet publishing. We'll discuss publishing your own Web pages and then we'll close with some pointers that will help you handle the technical aspects of creating your own Web site.

Your home on the Web

WE'LL BEGIN Phase 3 of your Internet training by giving you some pointers on constructing a good Web site. We want you to see some well-done Web sites that will spark the fires of your imagination. Our approach will be to analyze one site, give you a Top 10 List of good uses for a Web site, and then point you to several other Web sites that employ techniques your organization may adopt.

One of the most important factors in Web site design is to focus on the needs of your visitors. In other words, one of the most important factors in Web site design is Client-centered Interneting, which we introduced in chapter 2, "Internet reality check." We'll directly discuss Client-centered Interneting principles in the next chapter, but in this chapter you'll begin to see it in action.

The Web enables you to make available massive amounts of information in a nonlinear format. This book, in contrast, is in a linear format—we only can give you access to its information one-page-at-a-time. Publishing information in a set of footnoted, indexed reference books gives readers an improvement over a linear format, but readers must flip pages and drag out multiple volumes to obtain nonlinear information access.

Breaking old restrictions

The hypertext markup language (HTML) upon which the Web is built frees you from presenting your information in a linear format. The site that we will profile, the Fairfax County Economic Development Authority, presents, in an easily accessible format, volumes of text that otherwise would be an avalanche of linear information. The nonlinear structure of hypertext documents means that each reader gets a tailored version of your information, structured according to the links that each chooses to follow rather than structured according to the way you decided to present the information.

The Web enables us to get to know each other on our own terms by bringing a new perspective to the old adage, "You never get a second chance to make a good first impression." Hypertext documents will present different first impressions of your organization to different people, because each will see what they want to see rather than what you believed would appeal to the majority of a mass audience. Thus, hypertext enables your organization to present a good first impression to a wide variety of visitors.

Fairfax County
Economic Development Authority

The Internet can provide a tremendous boon to governments and to government agencies. We're going to analyze a site that combines both (see Figure 12-1), an agency of the government of Fairfax County, Virginia, near Washington, D.C. It's run by the Fairfax County (Virginia) Economic Development Authority (FCEDA).

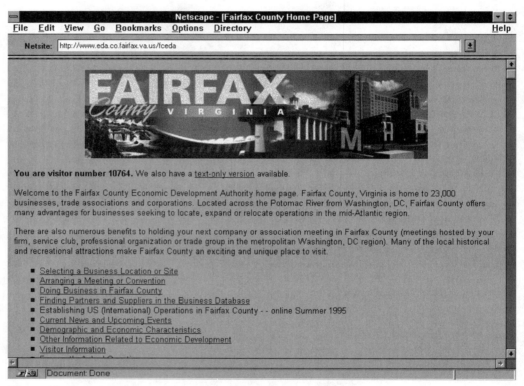

Figure 12-1

This site definitely will give different first impressions to a variety of visitors. For example, if you visited this site because you wanted to hold a business conference in Fairfax County, you'd see a different site than if you visited this site because you wanted to know how to obtain a business license and open a branch office.

Why Fairfax County? Here are five good reasons.

⊚ This is a well-done Web site.
⊚ Fairfax County is extremely prosperous: The top county in the U.S. for average education levels and usually placing in the top two or three counties in the U.S. for per capita income.

The rest of the story

- Fairfax County has generated business from this Web site.
- We wanted to profile a noncommercial site.
- One of the authors lives in Fairfax County (that's a very good reason)!

Hands On

Objective: **Analyze a Client-centered Web site example.**

❑ Start Netscape with an Internet connection.

❑ Double-click in the **Location:** text entry box.

❑ Type *http://www.eda.co.fairfax.va.us/fceda* and press **ENTER**.

Text-only version

You can't assume that every visitor will appreciate your graphic images. Graphic images required far more bandwidth than text, and can make your site annoyingly slow. Until you know that all your visitors have cable modems, you should offer a "text-only" option at the top of your home page. FCEDA has done that. Click on text-only version to see how this page is simplified (see Figure 12-2).

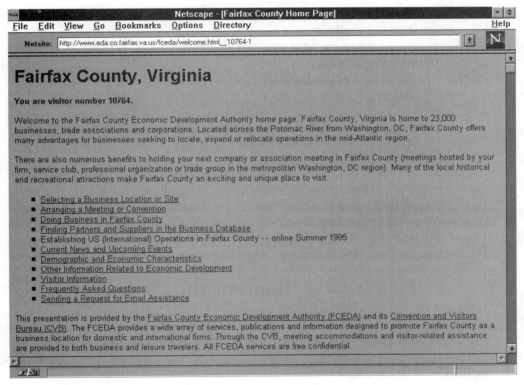

Figure 12-2

Adding this option is not much extra work, and it may generate repeat business from a valuable client with a slower connection. Even if most users in the U.S. had high-speed modems, a text-only version still would make sense for the

FCEDA because they are attracting international businesses to Fairfax County. Overseas connections are going to be slower, and often the phone systems are not on par with the U.S. phone systems.

Click the right mouse button, then click Back to return to the original, graphics-based page.

Check out different views

A well-done Web home page will look good in Netscape with a variety of different viewing options selected. You cannot predict how your users will have their broswer configured, so assume they have turned on every option and thus have reduced their screen space to the minimum. Let's view this page at both extremes.

Hands On

Objective: **Learn to test a Web page in different views.**

❑ Click **Options**.

Make sure that all three of these options are checked:

Show Toolbar

Show Location

Show Directory Buttons

The page still shows the most important information.

❑ Click **Options, Show Toolbar**.

❑ Click **Options, Show Directory Buttons**.

This probably is the best way to run your Netscape browser. You don't need the two bars you just turned off, because they have keystroke equivalents or are used only occasionally and do not merit full-time screen space. See chapter 11, "The World Wide Web," for a table of Netscape's shortcut keystrokes.

Now use the scroll bar or the UP and DOWN arrows to see what's on the home page. Most well-done sites use a brief home page with hypertext links to other pages and to other Internet resources. This page fits that pattern. Scroll all the way to the bottom and note the row of hot buttons. There are several features at the bottom of this page that are good examples to model. Let's discuss them.

Home button

Note the "Fairfax Home" button (see Figure 12-3). That's a good item to have, even though you technically haven't left the home page. (Note that the URL has not changed from what you entered in the Hands On exercise steps.) This button actually just takes you to the top of this page. Be sure and make this easy for your visitors.

Configure button

Here's a rarely seen feature. This "Configure" button enables the user to customize the display and offers more choices than the usual toggle between text-only and full graphics options. Let's see how it works.

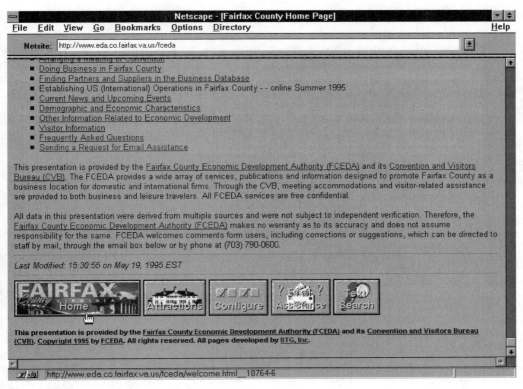

Figure 12-3

Hands On

Objective: **Test the Configure button.**

❏ Click **Configure**.

❏ Under the Icons option, click **Text** then click **Make Changes**.

❏ Press **CTRL+END** to jump to the bottom of the page.

   Note that the buttons have been replaced by normal hypertext jumps.

❏ Click **Configure** again.

❏ Click **Default Values** to restore the original settings

❏ Click **Make Changes**.

❏ Press **CTRL+END** to jump to the bottom of the page.

"Configure" is a nice bonus feature, but it's something you can't expect to be able to implement on your own without training that's beyond the scope of this book. Check with your Internet service provider, a consultant, other Internet books, or some of the sites we list in this chapter's Continuing Education section.

E-Mail button

Every Web home page you create should have an e-mail link so users easily can contact you. Don't ever make them work hard to reach you for more information. After all, you started this whole Internet adventure to increase contacts.

There are several ways to implement an e-mail request. Click on this button to see the FCEDA solution. It is not actually e-mail, though. It's a form that will transfer information from you into their system (see Figure 12-4). You'll find true e-mail replies by visiting other sites we've listed, which is a simple solution that nearly anyone can implement.

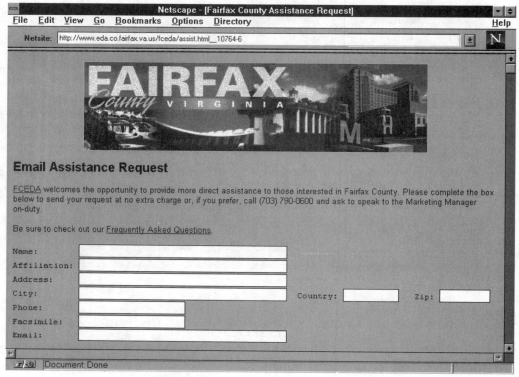

Figure 12-4

Hands On

Objective: **Examine a form that accepts user information.**

❏ Click **E-Mail Assistance**.

> Note the URL change. You're in the same "fceda" directory, but Netscape has loaded a different page.

❏ Scroll through the screen and check it out.

> Because it's a single page, you can use your **UP** or **DOWN** arrows to scroll, and you can use **CTRL+END** and **CTRL+HOME**.

❏ Click the right mouse button and click **Back**.

❏ Press **CTRL+END**.

The method the FCEDA uses here is more technical than using a regular e-mail reply, because it provides a customized reply form. Completing this form places the information in a database on the FCEDA server. While more difficult than

The rest of the story

e-mail to implement, it improves user-friendliness by providing a list of check boxes that can save users some time by making information requests that require only a mouse click. You also can ensure you get the information from each visitor that you want.

Text search button

On some sites, text searches are optional, but on an elaborate Web site such as this one, it's a necessary example of Client-centered Interneting. If you were considering doing business in Fairfax County, you might want to locate information that would help you establish your business. Getting this information by phone might waste a lot of time and long-distance charges while you're getting switched to the right person, but the FCEDA transferred the burden to themselves by creating a Web page that lets you quickly look up whatever you want and print it once you've found it. That's Client-centered.

Let's try it. If you were going to start doing business in Fairfax County, you might want information about obtaining a business license. We'll find out if the Internet has made that easy for us.

Hands On

Objective: Demonstrate a Web site text search feature.

❏ Press **CTRL+END** to drop to the bottom of the current page.

❏ Click on the **Text Search** button.

❏ Click in the **Search Keyword(s)** text entry box.

❏ Type *license* and press **ENTER**.

  The first item on the list is a hypertext link to a Frequently Asked Questions (FAQ) file that will help us.

❏ Click on **Frequently Asked Questions**.

❏ Click on **What do I need for my firm?**

❏ Click on **Doing Business in Fairfax County**.

❏ Click on **Licenses, Permits and Regulations**.

❏ Click on **Business, Professional and Occupational Licenses (BPOL)**.

  Read about how you could obtain the forms necessary to apply for a business license in Fairfax County. As you can see, you could click on a hypertext link and also read information about Fairfax County business taxes.

This is a terrific example of the power the Internet is bringing to us all (see Figure 12-5). How would you otherwise even begin to locate information like that about a county? Someday, perhaps all progressive local governments will make economic development information available via the Internet. When that day comes, we all will be able to find speedy answers to obscure questions.

Within two months of this site going online it had attracted at least four companies that were interested in dong business within Fairfax County. One prospect (that never before had heard of Fairfax County) was planning to relocate there based upon what it discovered from this Web site.

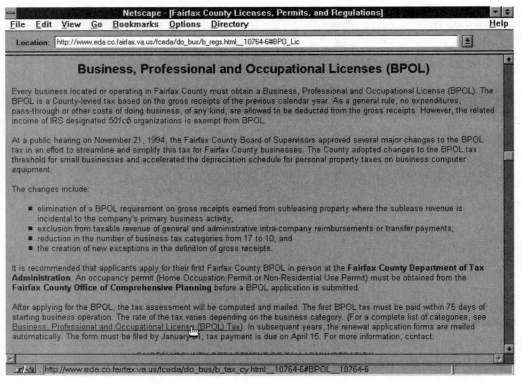

Figure 12-5

The Web site not only attracted the interest of the relocation prospect, but the Web site itself was a factor in that company's decision because the Business Directory at this site would direct other businesses to services that the new company planned to provide.

What if you're in a small organization?

So, your organization is not as large as Fairfax County, and you want to know how you can put up such an elaborate site without maintaining your own Web servers? No problem. Fairfax County doesn't have its own Web servers, either. The FCEDA site is maintained on servers at the BTG Corporation, the company that developed the FCEDA site.

You'll have no trouble finding service providers who will maintain your Web site. You can establish your own domain name and get an Internet service provider (ISP) to set up your site as *www.yourname.com*. For example, Jeff Davidson, who contributed much of the material for chapter 5, "The over-information age," is the founder of The Breathing Space Institute. Jeff used *www.digiweb.com* to register his domain name and place his Web site at *www.brespace.com*. His site is maintained via FTP.

If you don't need your own domain name, another option is to tag onto a larger Web site. All you need is a directory on someone else's server. You'll find far more providers who can handle this service and the cost will be surprisingly low—adding your page is very little trouble for someone who already has an established domain. We put this book's Web site at an existing site whose addresses is *www.marketing-coach.com*. All we had to do was create a new directory /mh-guide. Thus the book's Web URL is *www.marketing-coach.com/mh-guide*.

FTP to upload

Your service provider will give you a directory into which you can upload files for your Web site. You won't be able to do this with Netscape—at least with the version that was out when we finished this book. You'll need a stand-alone FTP application that gives you these crucial capabilities on the remote computer: upload files, create and remove directories, and delete and rename files. Many sites won't let you upload directly into your web page. This is required if you are to create and frequently update your own documents. Many providers also restrict programming and image-map applications. Shop around.

In chapter 9, "Basic Internet Research Tools," we covered the use of a popular, full-featured FTP application known as WS_FTP. If you skipped the optional exercises when you did that chapter, you may want to return soon so you'll be able to speak the language when you talk to ISPs about setting up your organization's Web site.

Leased lines

Another option for a Web site is to lease a full-time, dedicated line and set up your own Web server software on one of your own computers. Until recently, of course, that option has been prohibitively expensive for anyone but a major corporation, but it rapidly is evolving and may soon become a solution even for very small organizations. Check with ISPs today and ask about leased lines and Web server software. It may be quite affordable by now. Also, check in chapter 16 for help on creating your own Web server.

Let's close this site analysis with one more Hands On exercise that demonstrates another service you may want to provide for your clients, customers and prospects. Fairfax County maintains a database of registered businesses that includes company information and a description of each registered business' services and products. Let's take a look.

Hands On

Objective: **Demonstrate a database search.**

❏ Press **CTRL+END** and click on **HOME**.

❏ Click on **Finding Partners and Suppliers in the Business Database**.

❏ Click on **Perform a search**.

❏ Scroll down to and click in **Description keyword(s)**.

❏ Type *McGraw-Hill.*

❏ Click on **Perform Query**.

Now you can browse through a list of Fairfax-based companies that provide Internet consulting services (see Figure 12-6).

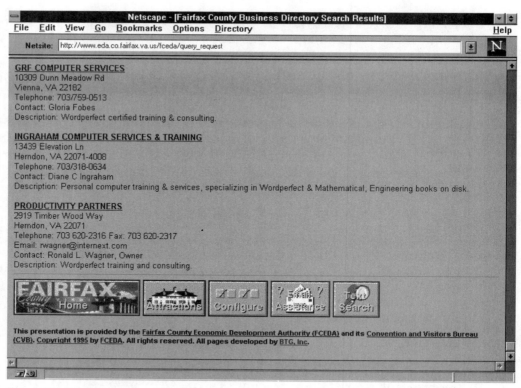

Figure 12-6

There are many uses for similar services within your Web site. For example, if your organization represented public speakers, you could maintain a database of your clients and have a search engine similar to the one on the FCEDA site. When meeting planners contacted your site seeking information about public speakers, they could perform a keyword search on topics of interest to their own organization and get a list of candidates for speaking to their group. Let's consider some other Web site usage ideas.

Top 10 uses for a Web site

Here's that Top 10 list of Web site ideas that we promised earlier. Perhaps these Web ideas will help you add value to your organization's Internet presence.

10. Personal

Family newsletters, announcments, favorite Web links, friends on the Internet, favorite photos, and résumés.

9. Clubs and groups

Event schedules, membership information, membership rosters, links to related Web sites, alumni clubs, reunion schedules with directions and maps, volunteer coordination, by-laws, notices of rule changes, meeting minutes, club announcements, nomination of officers, elections, book reviews, recipes and cookbooks, trip directions and maps, travel suggestions, and travel stories with photos and maps.

▶   *The rest of the story*

8. Local sports teams

League schedules, team standings, player and coach rosters, volunteer coordination, weather contingencies and postponements, and links to sponsor home pages.

7. Politics and government

Campaign information, schedules, events, community news, party platforms, candidate standings, poll results, online candidate debates, online voter discussions, voter forums, candidate slates, constituent newsletters, pending legislation, representative's newsletters, FAQs pages, voting information, registration information, voting locations and times, and election results.

6. Community information

Local laws and regulations, civic promotion, homeowner's associations, building codes, event schedules, school sports events, plays and schedules, school lunches, voting information, poll locations and maps, transportation information, schedules and maps, disability information and ADA compliance, community service, and announcements.

5. Entertainment

Theater schedules, play schedules and review, restaurant takeout menus and ordering, concert schedules, ticket availability and ordering, restaurant suggestions, menus, prices, reservations and maps, restaurant reviews, movie reviews, and movie schedules.

4. Online publishing

Customer newsletters, industry newsletters, political commentary and campaign information, special-interest magazines, daily updates, and consumer alerts.

3. Working together

Joint projects, sharing documents, online scheduling, online statistics, company calendars, company special events, employee-of-the-month awards, special recognition, conference information, schedules and maps, and meeting minutes.

2. Customer support

Frequently Asked Questions (FAQs), online assembly instructions, online manuals, parts lists and ordering, sales, tips and ideas for using your products, other Internet sites that will help your clients and customers, reporting software bugs and distributing fixes, and product release notes.

1. Business presence

General business information, hours of operation, phone and fax numbers, mailing address, directions and maps, online brochures, product brochures, order forms, surveys, forms, and an internal, employees-only Web page.

Intranet

The *largest* use of hypertext technology today, you may be surprised to learn, is for internal web servers in large organizations. We'll refer to these as a lowercase "web," and we'll use their generally accepted name, "Intranet." Every document, spreadsheet, graphic presentation, help file, customer database, etc. can be linked together and presented on a web server in simple menus. Because they run on a high-speed local area network (LAN), they are FAST!

Eric Engelmann, one of this book's authors, currently is helping the World Bank with its web servers, both Internet and Intranet (see Figure 12-7).

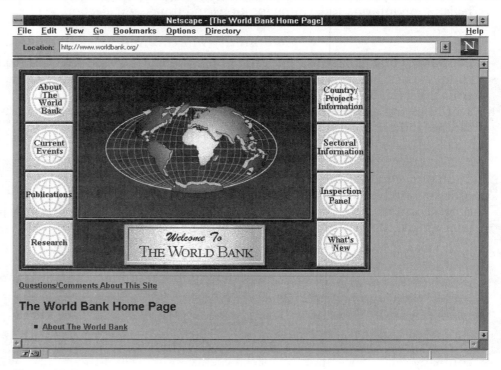

Figure 12-7

Internal web servers at the World Bank get far more hits than does the public Web server. The World Bank's Intranet includes a complete online directory of the 8,000 World Bank staff. It's searchable by first or last name, organization and location. All the bits and scraps of corporate information that are published internally (newsletters, policy directives, how-to files, etc.) are published in color at lower cost in terms of money, environmental waste, and filing manpower.

HTML also can be used to produce CD-ROMs for sites that truly are remote. For example, Eric is sending copies of the World Bank's internal web server to 28 regional field offices in Africa. Even companies or field offices with no immediate plans to connect to the Internet and contribute to the Web can benefit from an Intranet if they have a LAN. Windows-based Web servers, discussed in chapter 16, have simplified the technical aspects of Web site creation so that no Unix programming is required.

Other Web examples

There are so many! But we knew you'd want to see more well-done sites, so here are a few that we've found.

- Southwest Airlines (*http://www.iflyswa.com/*) This site features a picture of an airport gate. You "walk up" to and click on what you want—even a painting of the company president! But, honestly, it's not Client-centered Interneting. You'll find it hard to use because you can't tell in advance where the different hot spots will take you.

- Valvoline Racing (*http://www.valvoline.com/*) The Valvoline Company put this one on the track during the 1995 Indy 500 Memorial Day race. In addition to being well-done, it's a lot of fun and it includes a complete technical run-down of the hardware and software behind the scenes, plus photographs and short biographical sketches on the people who created it. You not only will learn from this site, but you can contact its creators to help you create your own organization's Web site (see Figure 12-8).

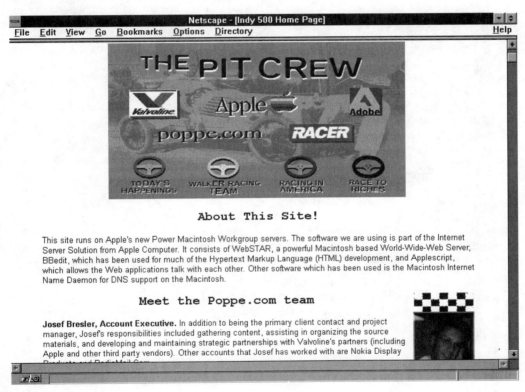

Figure 12-8

- United Parcel Service (*http://www.ups.com/*) You'll learn from this user-friendly site and discover a nice addition to your Bookmark list. Notice how it's structured perfectly to display in Netscape with both the Toolbar and the Directory Buttons turned off. If those are showing, the home page is cut short and you have to scroll to see the bottom two features.

- FedEx (*http://www.fedex.com/*) Another user-friendly and valuable Web page. Be sure and check out the link to CommerceNet at the bottom of the page.

- United States Postal Service (*http://www.usps.gov/ncsc/*) We included this one because it demonstrates how technology can be made available over the Web. Click on ZIP+4 Lookup Form and enter this exact address: Delivery Address *1600 penn avenue*, City State and/or ZIP Code *washington, dc*, then click on Submit. All spelling and capitalization errors will be fixed, the comma removed, the address converted to its full form and a full Zip+4 will be added. Remember, the result you see is in a Windows document (see Figure 12-9), so you can use the clipboard to Copy an entry from this screen and Paste it into your word processor or database. (Until recently, this service required you to buy a CD-ROM subscription that cost more than $1000 a year.) Enter your own address but include a few small errors, such as entering "Dr." if you're on a "Rd" or simply omit an "St" at the end.

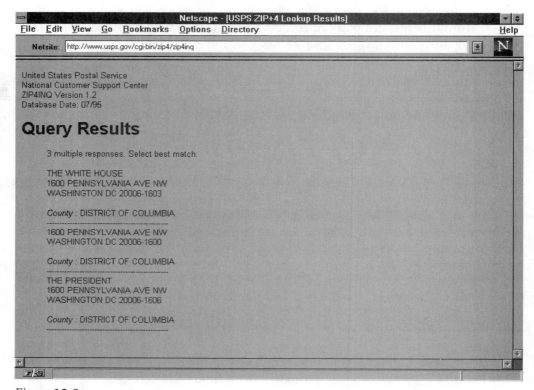

Figure 12-9

Summary

The Continuing Education section at the end of this chapter will give you a lot of help in building your own Web site. This is an area in which technology is changing more rapidly than any individual can track. Even these Web sites won't be enough to keep you totally up-to-date, but from each of them you'll find links to more sites and you can build your own self-updating reference library by creating a Netscape bookmark folder entitled, "Building a Web Site," and placing under it links to sites that you want to emulate. Chapter 14, "Money Issues," will give you some pricing guidelines on what you can expect to pay to establish various levels of a Web presence.

The next chapter, "Client-centered Interneting," is going to apply some market-proven business principles to your organization's Internet presence. The remaining chapters of this book will give you an overview of other important Internet principles and, most importantly, it will give you more URLs to track any of the topics that you need to follow.

 # *Continuing Education*

Creating Net sites
Help, how to create Web services

For this one, you don't even enter a URL—Netscape does it for you if you'll simply click the two commands listed above on their own Help menu: click Help, then click How to Create Web Services. That action will jump you to one of Netscape's Web documents that has an extensive listing of Web resources to help you get started with your organization's Web site.

The World Wide Web
http://www.w3.org

This site is maintained by the World Wide Web Consortium (W3C) that promotes the Web by producing specifications and reference software. It provides a wealth of Web information, such as how to put up a Web site, Web conferences, Web mailing lists, newsgroups, and a FAQs file. The W3C is funded by industrial members but its products are freely available to all users. The W3C is run in collaboration with CERN (where the web originated) by MIT, with INRIA acting as its European host.

Setting up your own server
http://www.digex.net/papers/webhost/

Here's some informative material from Joe Peck, Internet Server Product Manager at Digital Internet Exchange (DIGEX), a Maryland-based Internet services provider. Joe presents a detailed list of selection criteria for choosing a Web hosting service. This could be one of the most important decisions your organization makes—be sure to gather all the information you can before committing your resources.

Internet literacy consultants
http://www.matisse.net/

The Internet Literacy Consultants (ILC) have a Web page that includes a jump called "Services & Prices." This is one of the most extensive pricing guides you'll see. Many ISPs do not want you to see price lists like this up front. You may appreciate the candor of this list. ILC is based in San Francisco, so their prices will give you an idea of prices in major U.S. cities—last time we checked, their rates seemed to be on par.

Domain naming system structure

ftp://ds.internic.net/rfc/rfc1591.txt

When your organization establishes its Web presence, you'll want your own domain name. This document can answer a lot of your questions about domain names.

A beginner's guide to HTML

http://www.ncsa.uiuc.edu/General/Internet/WWW/HTMLPrimer.html

This is a primer for producing documents using the Hypertext Markup Language (HTML), the basic language used by documents on the World Wide Web. It's from the National Center for Supercomputing Applications (NCSA). Browse around while you're there, they also have sample style sheets they've developed so that everyone at the NCSA who creates a Web document can use the same styles to achieve a unified on-screen appearance. You may need to adopt a similar standard within your organization if you will use multiple authors for Web page material.

A field guide to home pages

http://gnn.com/gnn/netizens/fieldguide.html#homestead

Here's a discussion of Web page theory that offers a series of hypertext links to pages that display different aspects of using the Internet. The samples represent a wide variety of Web-page philosophy, including a look at some home pages designed by elementary school children, which may present a fresh, unfettered approach to Web site design.

Setting up shop on the Internet

http://www.netrex.com/business.html

This page is by Andrew Dinsdale (with Netrex) and features a list of hypertext jumps that will help you with numerous Web technology questions. Here are some of the topics you might use as you are preparing to launch your own Web site: Introduction to Electronic Commerce, Commercial Use Strategies, The Do's & Don'ts of Online Marketing, Get Connected, Security, Employees, and finally, Government Involvement. As you would expect, each of these topics not only offers its own information, but serves as a jumping-off point for a vast array of other sites around the Web. Starting with this one address alone, you could build a substantial library of Web technology documents.

BTG Incorporated

http://www.btg.com/

The Web site of the Fairfax County Economic Development Authority was created by BTG. BTG was among the original builders of ARPANET, the predecessor of today's Internet. Their home page will connect you to some other excellent Web sites and tell you about BTG's professional services. If it can be done on the Web, BTG can handle it for you, including maintaining your Web site on BTG's secure servers.

Netscape

http://home.netscape.com/assist/net_sites/index.html

Home. Mecca. The Center of the Earth. And they even can help you with your Web site. Did you expect any less? 'Nuf said.

▶ *The rest of the story*

Client-centered interneting

REMEMBER the founding principle beneath the Internet: the Internet is an information distribution system. When your Internet site becomes a distributor of valuable information, Internet users will find it, use it, return to it, and tell others about it.

Fortunately, the Web gives you the leverage to deliver value faster and better than ever before, but only if your Web site focuses on your clients and customers, and *not* on making your organization feel good about itself. Your organization's core strategic goals are to:

- Create a Web site and systems for distributing and delivering information that your customers and clients will regard as valuable. To paraphrase a popular slogan, your Web site needs to be the "gift that keeps on giving" to its visitors.
- Continuously increase the promotion and delivery of perceived and acknowledged value to your key clients, customers, and targeted prospects.

Dick Connor, cmc

We've asked Dick Connor, Certified Management Consultant (cmc), to share his ideas for making a Web site more user-centered. Dick specializes in assisting his clients in developing and delivering value to their clients through a system that he founded that's called "Client-centered Marketing." To meet the marketing demands of clients who wish to market on the Internet, Dick has teamed with Ron Wagner to create a cyberspace version of Client-centered Marketing that they call "Client-centered Interneting."

The principles behind Client-centered Interneting are derived from the lifelong work of Dick Connor. Dick, one of only 2,500 Certified Management Consultants in the world, also is the author of three marketing books published by John Wiley and Sons, *Marketing Your Consulting and Professional Services*, *Getting New Clients*, and *Increasing Revenue From Your Clients*. The latter is Dick's sole authorship; the first two were co-authored with Jeff Davidson of the Breathing Space Institute, who contributed to chapter 5, "The Over-Information Age."

In this chapter, we've summarized the key principles and action ideas from Dick's books as they apply to Client-centered Interneting. These principles also are the foundation of a client-analysis software application called *Your Marketing Coach*, available at *http://www.marketing-coach.com*.

Client-centered Interneting

The marketing task has changed from promoting your services to providing client-perceived, value-creating solutions to needs and problems. This change is profound; it's from checkers to chess. The play and strategy are different and more complex.

As you learned to use the Internet in the Hands On phase of this book, you probably noticed a few Client-centered Interneting principles, but most obvious is the severe lack of such user-oriented principles. Too much of the Web is self-serving hype about the Web itself—it's time to move beyond the "gee whiz" of Web technology and employ Client-centered Interneting to make the Web create value.

Value

Value is the worth your service adds to the existing information and knowledge base of your clients and customers, as well as to their organizations and their markets. Satisfying today's clients and customers means adding more value than ever, more knowledge than ever, more experience than ever, and more solutions than ever.

Value is a function of a need being met in ways that meet or exceed the client's expectations. In other words, your clients must feel that they earn a suitable return on their investment in visiting your Web site. And you get about 5 to 10 seconds to convince visitors that you offer value in return for their time.

The attributes of value

Now that you've started surfing the Net, you probably have been struck by its amazing abilities to deliver previously obscure or hard-to-locate information. The prime goal for your Web site is to help your clients and customers find the obscure and hard-to-locate information that consistently will add value to their organizations. Consistently adding value to your clients requires answering the key question, "At this time, what defines value for my clients and customers?"

Let's consider some client-sided value attributes:

- Client-defined—Value always is defined by the recipient, never by the provider. Value is in the eyes and emotions of recipients, and always is founded on their personal and organizational needs.
- Benefits—Distribute information that enhances performance, improves profits or improves the client's working environment. Value-added solutions are the tangible and intangible benefits that your service delivers.
- Hope—Clients don't purchase your services and products, they buy the hope that you will help them create a more favorable future, as they define it.

▶ *The rest of the story*

- Justification—Value is perceived in the "gut." People then justify a buy/no-buy decision to themselves and to others by the use of such things as competitive proposals and testimonials that support their decision.
- Other Resources—Track and recommend resources that can help your clients when they have needs that you cannot meet. Remember, when someone in search of a solution visits your Web site, you need to make sure that your site provided what they wanted. Even if you do not directly profit from the solution, they'll remember you as a value-added provider.

Quantity and quality are not value-adders

Clients are not satisfied by your quantity or quality—how much you put on your Web site or how good it looks—but by the value they perceive during the delivery and after using the information you provide. Your Web site is a source of potential value that must be translated and made visible for your clients on their terms.

At best, quality is only an entry fee to play the game. An ingenious, humorous, or attractive Web site may draw a slew of first-time curiosity seekers, but no one will return often if they discover no perceived value for them at your site.

Build a gift that keeps on giving

Do you want a quick example of a value-added Web service? Subscribe to a stock market reporting service such as Quote.Com at *http://www.quote.com/* (see Figure 13-1). With Quote.Com, you can track hundreds of stocks, com-

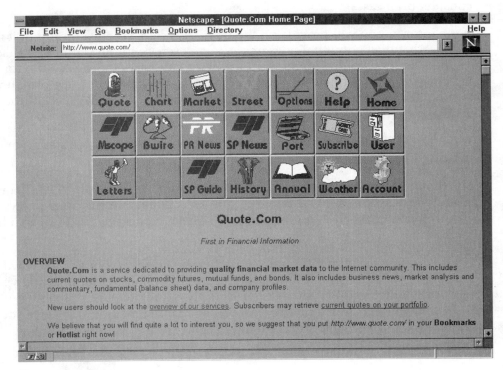

Figure 13-1

modities, mutual funds, and news pages. But you don't need to own stocks to track them. Instead, you can use these reporting features to create a value-added service for clients and customers by tracking stocks that affect their industry and their competitors.

- Portfolio quotes—Retrieve quotes for your entire portfolio with one command, using e-mail or the Web. Use this to stay abreast of your clients and customers and their competitors, as well as your own competitors.
- Alarms—You may set upper and lower trigger points for each item in your portfolio. Quote.Com will monitor them during the trading day and send you an e-mail notice if the alarms are triggered. Wouldn't your clients and customers like to know that your Web site will help them understand the meaning behind a dramatic swing in a prime competitor's stock?
- News alerts—Subscribe to MarketScope or BusinessWire, PR Newswire, or S&P News and they automatically will send you financial news items that impact the industries you track for your clients and customers.

Once you receive any of these reports, you immediately would write a value-added analysis and put up the analysis on your Web site. You would e-mail key clients to alert them to the update on your Web site.

Regularly update your Web site

Valuable information often is extremely time-sensitive. The value visitors find today may be worthless next week. Of course that's not always true, but let's consider both cases.

If the information you provide on the Internet is static, then you can put it up and nearly forget about it. For example, in an exercise in the Hands On phase, we showed you how to download the documents you need to file a request for information with the Federal government under the Freedom Of Information Act (FOIA). Because these forms remain unchanged for years, that aspect of the Federal government's Internet site requires little oversight.

You rarely will have that luxury. Government reporting forms are static; your industry likely is not.

Much of the information that makes your organization valuable to its clients and customers has a short shelf-life. Make sure every client and customer knows that you are a source for fresh information that's been repackaged in a way that brings them value.

Users who find exciting information on their first visit to your site likely will return in a week or two. If they find the same information on the second visit, most still will visit again. But three visits to the same old page probably is your limit, and you may lose a prospect forever. Perhaps some users may give you another look in a few months, but maybe not.

Relationship development

Client-centered Interneting essentially is relationship development. The relationship is based on both technical and personal factors that create interdependence— you need your clients and customers, but they need your Web site.

The cultivation of a satisfied Internet client requires much more than an eye-stopping Web site. Satisfying clients and customers requires building a value-perceived relationship. To build this relationship, you need to understand your clients' industry and target markets, their business goals, needs, restraints, and areas of potential growth in their markets. Then you need to use this specialized knowledge to create value-added solutions for your clients and customers.

Professionals who are effective marketers have learned to develop special relationships both with organizations and individuals with whom they jointly serve the needs of clients and customers. On the Web, this means cross-linking with related sites. Once the special, cross-linked relationships are established, the primary task is jointly to sense, sell, serve, and satisfy the needs and expectations of clients and customers in ways that are mutually profitable.

 NET TIP Remember that the Internet is international in scope. You soon may be building relationships with people from all over the world—it's not much harder to work with someone who's in Paris, Texas than it is to work with someone in Paris, France. You may have to do some more homework before you can understand the needs and expectations of all the people who are drawn to your site.

Develop an Insider's Understanding

An important tool for the Client-centered Interneter is to possess an Insider's Understanding of the business, environments, and expectations of your clients and customers. Client-centered insights about the dynamics of surviving and thriving in the client's industry niche enable you to add value to their operations. When you are aware of a client's industry, environments, and technology, you will be a highly-valued information source.

Once you have an Insider's Understanding of your clients' industry, you can raise industry issues that demand their attention, even if the issue will not directly affect them today. Your Web site can raise these issues and include links to sites that offer or discuss solutions.

Effortlessly build an Insider's Understanding

To develop an Insider's Understanding of your clients' and customers' industries, you need to track industry developments, both within your own industry and within their industry. You also need to track their competitors as well as your own.

An information service such as Farcast can give you, your clients, and your customers the competitive advantage you need. Farcast is an agent-based personal news and information service. Farcast lets you browse and search its collection of news, press releases, and reference material. The service is available interactively 24-hours-a-day, or you can contract with Farcast to automatically send you news articles from a wide range of topics. You also can create your own information robots ("Droids") that search more than 5,000 articles daily to retrieve news that will help you build an Insider's Understanding within targeted industry niches.

Be sure you subscribe to newsgroups and mailing lists that affect the industries of your clients and customers. And, be sure you constantly check out their Web sites as well as the Web sites of their competitors. Your clients and customers need to know that you know their industry as well as they do.

Save visitors from the over-information crunch

New Internet users universally report they are stunned by the amount of information that the Internet makes available. The impact on people of such an avalanche of over-information is serious enough that we devoted a chapter on handling its effects. (Be sure you didn't skip chapter 5, "The Over-Information Age.") You can provide a valuable service to your Web site visitors merely by sorting and repackaging information, and then providing links to the information they most need to see.

The effects that the Over-Information Age has on people actually can work in favor of your business. You now have an opportunity to rescue your clients and customers from the electronic avalanche by giving them a safe haven where they quickly can tap into that minuscule portion of information that they find valuable. The key to your success lies in a feature of Netscape: the Bookmark List (see Figure 13-2).

How to know when you've become a Client-centered Interneter

As a marketer you need to understand the significance of the Netscape "Bookmark" feature. When Internet users encounter an exciting or valuable site they can, with a couple of mouse clicks, add that site to their Bookmark List. Think of this as similar to television remote controls that have a "favorite channel" feature. Bookmarks enable users to return with a couple of mouse clicks—no matter how deeply they've strayed into unfriendly cyberspace—to a comfortable, favorite site where they can count on finding value.

Make your site easy to find

Until they put your site on their Bookmark List, clients and customers may have difficulty locating your site. Don't make them work hard to find your organization. Here's a couple of tips that can help:

Structure your Web site and documents for search engines

In an exercise in the Hands On phase, we walked you through an information search on the Web using the Lycos search engine. You may schedule your own URLs (or nominate other URLs) for exploration by Lycos—this alerts the Lycos web explorer to your home page so it can add your Web text to its search index.

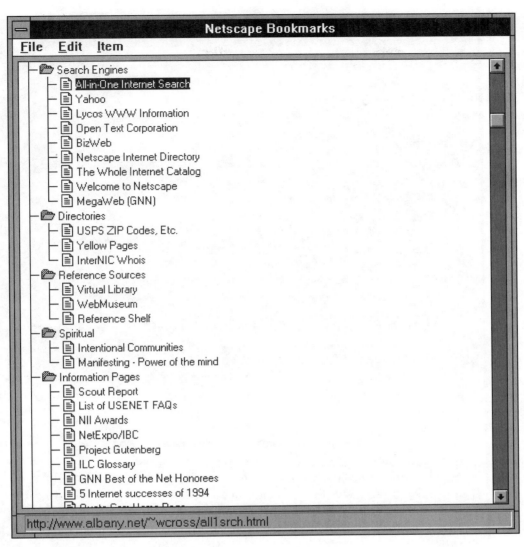

Figure 13-2

Lycos scores words by how far into the document they appear. Thus keyword "hits" in the title or first paragraph are scored higher. For each document it indexes Lycos keeps the title, headings, subheadings, links, the 100 highest-weighted words, and the first 20 lines. Make sure your title and opening paragraph contain the keywords upon which you expect people to search when trying to find your site.

Most Web sites waste the title on something generic, such as, "Welcome!" No one is going to locate your service because they searched Yahoo for sites with "welcome" in the title. Here's a good example, done by Eric Engelmann, one of this book's authors. Notice the square brackets after "Netscape" in the Title Bar (see the mouse arrow in Figure 13-3). After being indexed on the Web like this, the Wine Rack quickly began generating business from around the world—the carefully targeted title was a key factor. This is your one shot—don't waste it by making your title read "Our Home Page."

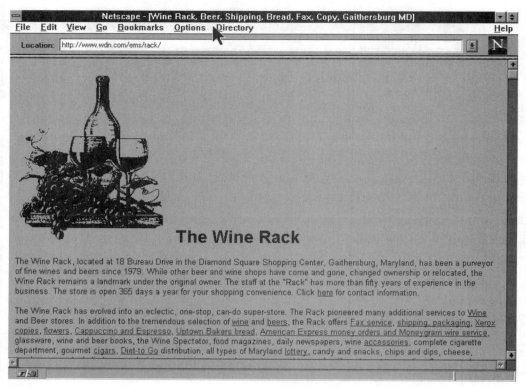

Figure 13-3

Register your own domain name

Using your own domain name is an important factor in helping your clients and customers find and remember your Web site. For example, Ron Wagner and Dick Connor established a Web site for their Client-centered Interneting, which is based on a software application called "Your Marketing Coach." An Internet service provider (DigiWeb at *http://www.digiweb.com*) registered the domain name of *marketing-coach.com* for Ron and Dick. The Yahoo Web search engine searches for strings in URLs, so our URL makes "marketing" as easy to find as we could make it!

When your clients and customers see your site and click **Bookmark, Add Bookmark**, then you'll know that you've embodied Client-centered Interneting. If your Web site gets assigned to lots of Bookmark Lists, then your organization is cruising in an express lane on the information superhighway.

Of course, once you're in that fast lane, you can't slow down. People can change lanes pretty quickly. It only takes a couple of mouse clicks to remove a Bookmark, too. If you've let your information go stale, then when a client finds another hot site and notices that his or her Bookmark List is getting full, you can get bumped.

▶ *The rest of the story*

Ban the hype

At times it seems that the Web is a last-chance outlet for press releases that otherwise never would be seen by a single public eye. The "opportunity" to read a puffed-up press release does not create value for your clients and customers.

Business consultant Marcus Bogue says, "...it doesn't matter how good you are; it only matters how relatively good you are. If someone else is better than you are, it doesn't matter how good *you* are." Web site visitors don't care about how good a press release says you are—they'll judge your site based on how it delivers perceived value. You might put one short "pull-quote" from your press release on the home page and include a link to the full text. But always remember that people will sell themselves based on how much your Web site improves their lives or their business.

Tips for staying on the bookmark list

Update your Web information at least weekly, but don't expect your clients and customers to return out of curiosity. Your Web page needs to tell visitors that you update the page regularly and when they can expect new material. Television channels and movie theaters always tell you what's coming next and when it will be available. Part of maintaining a client-centered Web site is providing these previews—your current information may not interest them, but you might make some Bookmark lists because they want to return for one of your "Coming Attractions" or for a "Tip of the Week."

Don't try to impress Web visitors with a lot of breathless hype about your products and services. Most consumers today are well-informed and have long-ago learned to ignore the hard-sell. In other words, what visitors find on your site must appear to benefit them first.

If visitors perceive your site as valuable, your clients and customers will do some of your sales work for you. People want to be well-informed, and your organization's online presence can let them learn exactly what they want to know—and to learn it on their terms.

Winston Churchill made an apt quotation that describes how most people feel toward learning: "I love learning, but I hate being taught." Your clients and customers will love learning from a site with depth, but they don't want to be taught by hyped-up press releases.

Less fun is more

It's a good idea to make your site fun to visit as well as valuable. But be careful. In chapter 2, "Internet Reality Check," we related in a sidebar story about how computer games are adversely affecting corporate productivity. The challenge for you is to make your site something that an employee could use during business hours without fearing that the boss will walk in and "catch" them on your site. Be wary of providing "cool stuff" links to game sites around the Web as an enticement to attract visitors. You might poll some of your clients and customers about this concept. If your site passes the "boss walking in" test, then it most likely is client-centered.

Top 10 ways to build a successful Web site

We'll close with a Top 10 list of some of the best things we have found for leveraging your Web site. Remember, the design focus must be client-centered— never technology-centered. Create value through depth, avoid hype, and let visitors discover for themselves the value your site provides.

10. Keep visitors from getting lost

Make sure that every page on your site includes a link back to your home page. If visitors get lost or sidetracked while exploring your site, you don't want them to move on to another site out of frustration. Make sure they quickly can return to something familiar and comfortable.

9. Go easy on the graphics

We've seen some Web sites that truly are works of art by master graphic artists. But during peak business hours, bandwidth limitations might actually make it impossible for some people to access your site. At a minimum, use interlaced graphics and offer a "text-only" hyperlink at the top of the document so visitors quickly can select a faster option if they are not willing to wait for your art to download.

8. Include multiple contact links

What a waste of your time and resources if a visitor decides to contact you and can't locate the necessary information. Every page should include links that jump back to the home page as well as a jump to your contact information—e-mail, fax, snail mail address, and phone numbers, if appropriate.

7. Test it personally

Test your site regularly to see how it looks and feels to clients. Check it out using different settings (toolbars and directory buttons on and off), different hours (peak and off-peak), different modems (try slow and fast), different browsers (Netscape for Windows and Macintosh, for example), and different screen resolutions.

6. Build it with professional designers

You don't have to hire a consultant if your organization has design and advertising professionals on staff. If not, however, investing in a professional designer and ad copywriters may be some of the best money you ever invest in your business.

5. Submit it to indexers and directories

Contact every Web indexer. Make sure they've got your URL, and make sure you've placed keywords high in your document. And don't waste that valuable title text on "Welcome to our Home Page!"

4. Link, link, link

Cut deals with everyone you can whose site relates to your business. Get your link on as many other pages as possible. Of course, you will reciprocate, but multiple links makes your site more valuable because your clients will know that you are a source for fresh, valuable, related sites from all over the Web.

▶ *The rest of the story*

3. Preview regularly scheduled updates

The movie theaters do it. The cable movie channels do it. Television stations do it. Even magazines do it. You simply must include on your site a preview listing of upcoming topics. You never know when a visitor might find nothing at your site today, but notices something important in the preview that will bring him back next week.

How do I update my site if my visitors don't need news tips?

So, you don't need the information services we've profiled earlier? Your clients and customers need in-depth research instead? Then try the most comprehensive information on the Internet: NLightN at *http://www.nlightn.com/* (see Figure 13-4).

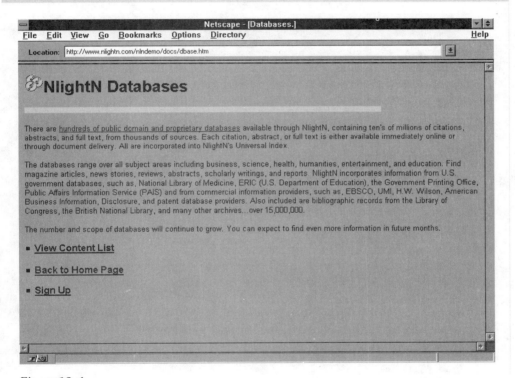

Figure 13-4

If you think Lycos is comprehensive, prepare to be dazzled—or overwhelmed. NLightN is so vast that Lycos provides only about five percent of the information resources that NLightN has indexed. The NLightN index lets you search a universal index that's 20 times as large as Lycos! It includes 10 million books, 1 million dissertations, 1 million patents, hundreds of thousands of wire service records from more than 20 wire services, tens of millions of journal articles, book, movie, and audio-visual reviews, and informal and formal searches of the full text of encyclopedias, dictionaries, and standard reference works.

This is a fee-based service and you'll have to sign up for a membership. But prices start at only 10 cents. Take a trial run at this site and then brainstorm ways you can use it to put value-added services on your Web site—you're sure to find something here that your clients and customers will appreciate finding on your Web site.

2. Start now and grow

You probably already have seen some Web sites that are "under construction." Don't be shy about applying this caveat to your own site (see Figure 13-5). If you've got valuable information, get it out there right away. Any moderately advanced user of WordPerfect for Windows or Microsoft Word quickly can create some basic web pages. Get the site up and running and let the search engines start indexing your keywords. Actually, your site needs to constantly offer new features and information anyway, (see Item #3) so why wait until you think it's "done?"

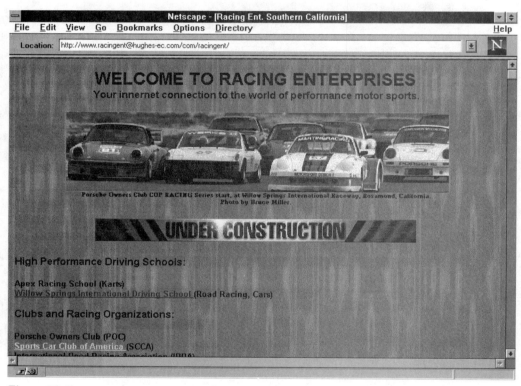

Figure 13-5

1. Make it client-centered

And the number one factor in a successful, business-oriented Web site is to focus on the needs of others. Provide value that rewards your visitors and they will reward you. Remember, your clients and customers are being crushed under the onslaught of the Over-Information Age—make your site a safe haven for them. You can add a rejuvenating break to their day by linking to *http://www.brespace.com* for a daily "Breathing Space" tip.

The rest of the story

Continuing Education

Client-centered Interneting

http://www.marketing-coach.com

This site will be your most up-to-date source of information for client-centered Interneting. It includes links to marketing books for professional service providers, such as *Marketing Your Consulting and Professional Services* and *Getting New Clients*, both by Dick Connor, cmc and Jeff Davidson, cmc. It will let you download the latest version of software that will guide you through using client-centered Interneting principles, *Your Marketing Coach*, as soon as it becomes available. The site also contains links to other Internet sites that can help your organization fulfill its business marketing needs.

Internet Business Guide

http://www.intuitive.com/taylor/#books

Here's a sample chapter from a business book on the Internet by Dave Taylor, the founder of the Internet Mall. Dave has posted this chapter in the hope that you'll by the book. Here's a chance to sample a book at your leisure before you buy. The full, printed version of the book has a wealth of top-notch Internet business principles.

Small and home-based businesses

http://www.ro.com/small_business/homebased.html

The fastest-growing segment of our economy is the home-based business (see Figure 13-6). Downsizing and outsourcing is creating a revolution in home-based businesses. Here's a Web site that can help you serve the needs of this booming market niche, or help you create new marketing ideas to sell the services of your clients and customers to home-based businesses. Here's what this site says about itself: "Small and home based business info: Small and home-based franchises, business opportunities, small business reference material, information to help run and market your small or home-based business, small and home-based newsgroups, searching tools, services for small business, just about anything related to small and home-based business can be found in these links. Enjoy!"

Internet marketing discussion list archives

http://www.popco.com/hyper/internet-marketing/

This site is a source both for information you can use and information you can repackage after putting your industry-specific spin on it for clients and customers. It discusses appropriate marketing of services, ideas, and items to and on the Internet. When we wrote the manuscript for this book, more than 4,500 people and sites—involved in all aspects of marketing, sales, programming, journalism, and other fields—were active in this forum. This site is a good source for organizations that want to create Web sites, market products and goods electronically, develop payment systems, or write about industry developments.

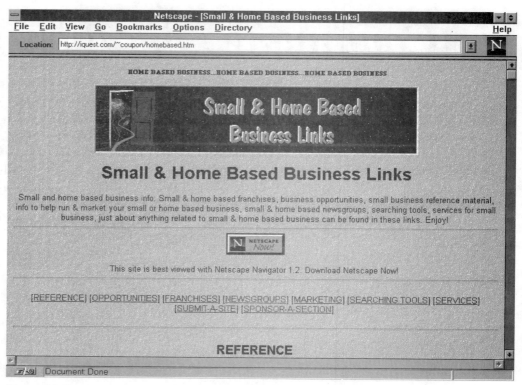

Figure 13-6

DigiWeb

http://www.digiweb.com

Here's the fastest-responding Web services provider we have met (see Figure 13-7). DigiWeb registers your unique domain name, sets up a Web site (up to 25 megabytes, plus 10 megabytes of e-mail), forwards mail to your new domain to an existing e-mail address, and provides FTP service for unlimited updates. As of the fall of 1995, DigiWeb charged only $25 for setup and $20 per month for all of this, and the site was up in hours—other providers we tried didn't come close. At those rates, even a sole proprietorship can afford a personalized domain name and a Web site.

Direct FTP uploading is a must—never contract with a Web service that promises to transfer your updates "soon" after you send them in. Any delays by your provider will prevent you from offering some of the Client-centered Interneting features we profiled in this chapter.

World Wide Web yellow pages free listing

http://www.yellow.com/cgi-bin/online

Check out this URL right away! For a limited time, they're giving away yellow page listings. Fill in the on-screen form and provide the URL to your own home page. World Wide Yellow Pages is a trademark of Home Pages, Inc.

Figure 13-7

Internet size

http://www.netrex.com/business/basics.html

The Internet connects some 35 million (figures debatable) users and is the fastest-growing communication resource on the planet. In January 1995 "Wired" magazine cited the Internet Society as reporting a third-quarter 1994 net growth of 21 percent. Based on these figures, the number of Internet hosts will hit 100 million by 1999. Hosts in the U.S. grew from 16,556 to 24,861!! The links on this page may help you determine for yourself the potential size of your markets in cyberspace.

Money issues

MONEY makes the world go around, and someone has to pay to produce and maintain the information content on the Internet. If you've built a truly client-centered Web site, there's a good chance you'll need to know how to handle financial transactions across the Internet. As an electronic merchant, of course, you can expect to become one of those who produces and maintains the Internet's information content.

We'll cover money issues from two angles that will affect your organization: income and expenses. We'll explore the income angle so you'll understand how organizations get paid across the Internet, and we'll discuss the expense angle so you perhaps can decrease your organization's electronic communication expenses. Let's begin with the fun part—getting paid.

Simple credit card purchases

While there's been a lot of press about maintaining credit card security on the Internet, this is just a small part of exchanging funds on the Internet. But it's the simplest concept, so we'll address it first. The problem with giving someone a credit card number on the Internet is that you can't be sure where your credit card information will travel and who might copy the information while it's en route. Because conventional data transfer on the Internet isn't encrypted, an experienced Unix hacker might create a program that grabs and saves for later analysis any data that looks like #### #### #### #### ##/##. The hacker then could build a database of credit cards numbers and, supposedly, use them to buy things for himself or fence the numbers to professional credit card thieves.

Unsafe at any speed

Although Internet credit card number theft certainly is possible, and occurs occasionally, it's not a serious threat. Consider other credit card transactions and you'll realize that there are plenty of easy ways for people to collect and sell credit card numbers without having to learn to hack the Internet. When you buy a mail-order lava lamp or even hand your credit card to a waiter, you are risking theft by people who need far fewer skills than experienced computer professionals. You are a lot more likely to have someone intercept your mail or trash for credit card fraud.

Besides, the Internet has technology that makes credit card transactions far safer than handing your card to a waiter. The basic technology is called "public-key cryptography." When you access a secure document with Netscape, you'll see a warning before it loads. When the document is loaded, you'll see a variety of clues that let you know your're viewing a secure document (see Figure 14-1):

- An unbroken skeleton-key in the lower-left corner of the screen—normally, this key is broken to indicate you are viewing an insecure document.
- Look closely for this one: the thin bar beneath the Location text entry box now is blue. On normal, insecure documents, this bar is gray.
- The URL has changed from "*http://*" to "*https://*".

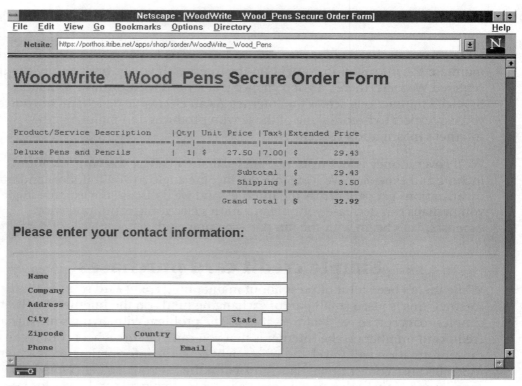

Figure 14-1

More on security in the next chapter.

Public-key cryptography scrambles numbers and other personal or corporate data before it's sent, then enables the receiver to unscramble the original information. New technology being planned by credit card companies will let buyers pay by credit card without merchants ever knowing the buyer's card number. This will make credit card usage on the Internet even safer than using it in a restaurant.

Collecting tolls on the information highway

The real challenge to the Internet and the information age is how to get very small payments to creators of intellectual property without making everyone on the information superhighway run through countless electronic toll booths. It can be done, and we'll discuss later some emerging technology that will make possible very small payments (micropayments).

Site sponsors

One toll-collecting method would be to employ advertising, as is done in other electronic media. This is a rapidly growing phenomenon. You'll see Web pages sprinkled with logos that advertise "site sponsors" who help the site owner cover the costs of maintaining a database, newsletter, or a search engine. In exchange, the sponsors get to place a link on the site—usually a graphic of their logo—so that visitors quickly can get information on the sponsor's product. You may be able to help finance your Internet costs by selling space to sponsors. You also may be able to increase traffic at your site by sponsoring well-done, related sites that already have high traffic. Yahoo, for example, sells some of its premium space so that visitors will see your logo. If your organization has a high traffic flow, others will want to pay for electronic billboards that your visitors will see.

Internet cash

Another option is to dispense Internet cash that can be collected in very small amounts any time you get a piece of information. Internet cash also has the benefit of being able to keep all transactions private. When paying by Internet cash, even the merchant you pay may not know who bought their information. Some early companies that offer online payment plans are:

- First Virtual (*www.fv.com/html/fv_main.html*);
- DigiCash (*www.digicash.com/ecash/ecash-home.html*);
- Cybercash (*www.cybercash.com*) (see Figure 14-2);
- ATS (*www.versanet.com*).

The other side of the Internet coin

Privacy cuts two ways, though. Criminals are eager to find new ways to hide and launder income from illegal activities. Terrorists want to eliminate money trails that can lead authorities to them or their sponsors. The U.S. government is exploring ways to monitor transactions, but Internet privacy systems—especially secure data-encryption and digital cash—would make their mission much more difficult. No one knows how this conflict will play out, or whether an acceptable compromise can be found between Big Brother and anarchy. Meanwhile, as the government is pondering options, the Internet is rapidly creating its own monetary system—let's learn more about this phenomenon.

Internet commerce systems

Many potential merchants are anxious to sell information, search services, software and audio or video clips on the Internet—perhaps your organization is among this group. And an eager cadre of potential clients and customers is ready

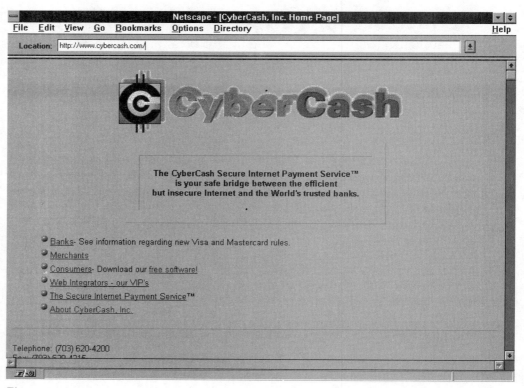

Figure 14-2

to buy. Today, however, because nearly everything on the Internet is free, owners of intellectual property have little incentive to make their valuable "information goods" accessible through the Web.

Several entrepreneurial groups are developing Internet commerce mechanisms that will bridge this gap between sellers and buyers and create an Internet marketplace. Let's consider some of the features your organization may need in a commerce system.

Micropayments

The Internet marketplace must support *micropayments*—which means merchants can sell information for as little as 10 cents. To support these *micromerchants*, the system will need to feature extremely low accounting and billing costs. Micropayment transaction costs can be as little as one cent for a 10-cent item. Internet commerce systems will enhance the quality and variety of information products sold and bought on the Web. Those selling the information—even micromerchants selling a single page of information—at last will receive fair compensation for their products, which will enable them to remain in business.

Security

Internet commerce systems have to provide secure transactions for both your organization and your clientele. When you sell products via the Internet, you'll need assurance that hackers cannot sniff your traffic for passwords that will enable them to download products without paying. Your clients and customers will want to know that their credit card information remains a private matter between the two of you.

In client/server systems such as the Internet, transaction security is a two-way street. Both your system (the server) and the buyer's system (client) must use software that includes security features. The Netscape Web browser has built-in security features already, so most of your buyers will have the required software.

Netscape security fiasco

During the late summer of 1995, a flurry of news stories about Netscape Communications Corporation's server security threw a scare into people who relied on Internet commerce. The news hype portrayed Internet transactions as a risky business that would open us all to wanton electronic looting.

First, the bad news. There is no such thing as absolute security—with computers or otherwise. Anyone with physical access to your computer can get information from it. Security measures can force hackers to expend vast resources to crack a system, but security will not make your system hacker-proof.

Now, the good news. Internet commerce is no more risky than any other credit card transaction. Most businesses will lose far more to "shrinkage" and insider theft—guests and employees can steal from within heavily secured homes and businesses—than to fraud from intercepted Netscape credit card sales. Most computer users never will experience any serious computer security problems. We've not uncovered any accounts of serious Internet credit card fraud.

So why was there so much news about Netscape having a security flaw? Mostly to sell papers and advertising.

Here's a quick wrap-up of what really happened:

Netscape uses a Secure Sockets Layer (SSL) protocol on its commerce servers to ensure communications security when exchanging credit card or other private information with Web browsers. With SSL, a random number is generated and then used in a mathematical formula to create a "session key" for encrypting information to be sent across the Internet.

The U. S. version of Netscape's Web browser software uses a complex session key (128 bits in length) that is extremely difficult to crack. The export version of Netscape (yes, the U. S. military still thinks computer algorithms are munitions, and subject to export control) uses less complex keys of only 40 bits. A hacker with access to lots of networked computing resources can crack a 40-bit key in about a week or more.

But David Wagner and Ian Goldberg, at Berkeley, discovered that the random numbers that Netscape used to generate its session keys were not truly random. They noted a trace of a predictable pattern that let them put a foot in the locked door of Netscape's security. This breach placed even the complex 128-bit keys at risk of being cracked, because it no longer was necessary to check every possible key combination.

Once alerted to the problem, Netscape quickly released revised versions of their software that eliminated this weakness by using a more truly random number. They also hired a team of world-class computer security experts to foil future problems. So, don't worry about Internet security too much. Someone eventually will find a way to crack just about any security system, but your odds of experiencing a loss are very low.

Certified delivery

Another Internet commerce requirement is for "certified delivery" of online transactions. Certified delivery protects both sellers and buyers, especially when the product's value is time-sensitive. The seller's system will transmit electronic products only after valid payment is confirmed. Conversely, certified delivery also means that your clients and customers are charged only when the information actually is sent.

Automated flexible pricing

Few businesses charge the same price for the same product for all buyers. Your Internet commerce system needs to offer discounts and handle premium pricing. A lot of factors can affect your pricing. Here are some pricing factors that you may need for your computerized commerce system to consider:

- Discounts, perhaps even free copies, if the buyer is part of a site license group that has paid a flat rate.
- Volume discounts for individual purchases, or if a buyer is part of a special consumer or user group.
- Premium surcharges during peak-hour access and discounts for off-peak access.
- Price quotations for buyers who are shopping, but not ready to buy. The system needs to record quotations with the records of your prospective buyers so there won't be price confusion when it's time to close the sale.

A typical commerce group

The NetBill project describes itself as a business model for a commerce server (see Figure 14-3). A commerce server is a set of standards and software that enables buyers to pay online merchants. The NetBill project has teamed with strategic business partners, Visa International and Mellon Bank Corporation. NetBill research, however, is funded in part by a grant from the National Science Foundation (NSF). While NetBill has a growing full-time and part-time staff—drawn mainly from the ranks of Carnegie Mellon University (CMU)—much of its development has been completed by students in project courses taken as part of CMU's graduate program in Information Networking.

A commerce group—such as NetBill—maintains commerce server accounts that link to financial institutions for both your organization and for your clients and customers. These links not only handle the actual financial transaction, but they certify the delivery of both product and payment. NetBill's project group handles both sides of certified delivery.

NetBill uses a financial transaction protocol that supports flexible pricing; it can calculate customized quotes for individual buyers and handle pricing approvals. It also uses digital signatures to protect account security on both sides of the transaction. You digitally sign orders using a key that is never revealed to the merchant, so eavesdroppers cannot intercept credit card numbers and approval authorizations.

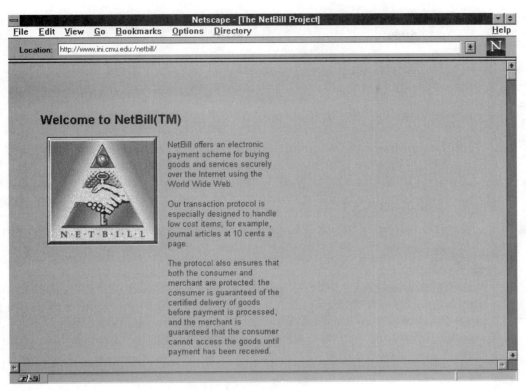

Figure 14-3

Tracking a commerce server sale

When you request an information product from a merchant, your client software sends a digitally-verified purchase request to the merchant's server. The product is sent to you in an encrypted format. Encryption transforms data into a format that is unreadable by anyone without a secret decryption key that will "unlock" the information and restore it to a readable format.

The information server computes a cryptographic checksum—a series of arithmetic operations that detect whether a file has been damaged or modified—on the encrypted message. After sending you the product, the server then sends an electronic payment order (EPO). At this point, you cannot yet decrypt the goods, but you have not yet been charged.

Your system calculates a checksum and sends a reply to the server. When the server receives the EPO reply, it compares its checksum against the one computed by the client library, which ensures that the encrypted goods were received without error. If the checksums match, the merchant creates a digitally-verified invoice that includes the price, the checksum, and the decryption key for the product. The merchant sends both the EPO and the invoice to a commerce server, which verifies that the product identifiers, prices, and checksums all match. The commerce server debits your account (which you have prefunded) and credits the merchant's account, logs the transaction, and saves a copy of the decryption key. It then sends the merchant a digitally-verified message with an approval code, or an error code if the transaction failed. Finally, the merchant forwards the commerce server's reply and the decryption key to your client software, which enables your software to decrypt the information product you've purchased.

This may sound like a hopeless mess that's way too much trouble. To computers, however, it's not complicated, and the whole process takes but a few seconds.

Multiple users and accounts

NetBill supports "many-to-many" relationships between consumers and accounts. This means that a single corporate or academic account may authorize many users to charge against it and obtain special pricing. Also, individual consumers may maintain multiple personal accounts. One user on every large account will be the account owner, and one will be the administrator. An authorized administrator can use a standard Web browser to open an account, view and change an account profile, authorize a funds transfer into the account, or view a current statement of account transactions.

Account information checks by administrators are treated as regular financial transactions to ensure authentication and security. Account creation is one of the largest costs associated with traditional credit card and bank accounts, but automating account creation for both consumers and merchants helps to limit costs.

Account types

A commerce account may be prepaid (debit model) or postpaid (credit model). In the debit model—used by DigiCash and Cybercash, for example—funds must be available in the buyer's commerce account to cover purchases. You first would deposit green cash with DigiCash or Cybercash, and then go surf the net with electronic money burning holes in your electronic pockets.

In the credit model, used by traditional credit card vendors, transactions are accumulated and payment to the commerce account is triggered at a certain time (billing period) or when a preestablished dollar limit is reached. With either model, both merchants and consumers will have online access to transaction status and statement activity.

Other uses for commerce servers

So far, we've considered purchases of goods and information. A good commerce model, such as NetBill's, can support other types of purchases and payments.

- Utility payments, such as an electric bill or gas bill, and local tax payments.
- Online video and audio, although at the present time, this conflicts with the safeguards in certified delivery.
- Software application rental. Software could incorporate the client library in any application. Periodically, the software would ask users to approve another purchase to get the next month's activity or "issue" of new software.
- Ticketing for events and for airline reservations. The airlines are setting the stage for this as they begin developing ticketless flights. Your ticket might be just a printed receipt with a code number that agents would match with their computer.

While most of the information exchanges on the Internet may continue to be free, creators and producers of information goods now will have incentive to supply more and better products. And we all will benefit from the improved quality and increased quantity of new goods available on the Internet.

Costs of setting up shop

If you want to know more about how your organization can conduct financial transactions across the Internet, you'll need to refer to the URLs we've provided in the Continuing Education section at the end of this chapter. For now, we're going to switch to the other angle on money issues: how much you might have to spend to get an Internet connection that will enable you to conduct Internet commerce. Again, you can't get all the answers from a single source, but this is a starting point that includes references to other sources.

Off-site Web services providers

If you work in a small organization, or perhaps even a home-based business or a sole proprietorship, you're not likely to maintain your own Web servers and the required, dedicated Internet connection. The necessary capital equipment could represent a large portion of your organization's budget, and you simply can't afford to put your business on hold while you learn to set up a Web site that can handle financial transactions.

Instead, you can call in the experts and let them set up your Web site while you continue to generate revenue doing what you do best (see Figure 14-4). A start-

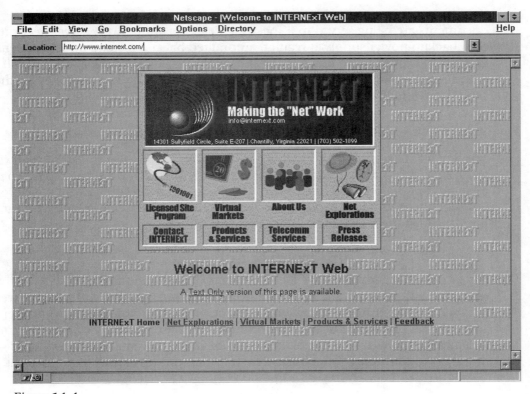

Figure 14-4

up fee, a base monthly fee, and a transactions fee can buy you a turn-key Web site. Here are three basic solutions with approximate costs as quoted in the summer of 1995. (Note that these costs are for complete *turn-key* systems and assume that the provider does all of the work for you. If you can create your own Web pages, you can buy Web server space for $20 per month. For example, check out *www.digiweb.com*.)

- Basic Web Presence—E-mail account via a PPP connection, up to five Web pages with one scanned graphic per page, a hyperlink on your Web page to your e-mail. Price guideline: $500.
- Enhanced Web Presence—All Basic features, up to 10 Web pages with 10 scanned images anywhere within those pages, one hyperlinked image map, autoresponder mail system for information inquiries, one form page, registration of your own domain name. Price guideline: $2,000 to $3,000.
- Virtual Store Front—All Enhanced features, up to 30 Web pages with 20 scanned images anywhere within those pages, two hyperlinked image maps, four form pages, high-capacity server, transaction encryption for your customers who use Netscape. Price guideline: $6,000 to $9,000 plus $300 per month.

On-site Web servers

Many Internet providers custom-build Web servers on-site. Be sure that the one you use offers a range of servers according to your needs and budget. Their server development team should be able to help you select a server that best fit your needs (according to size of documents, processing needs, and the amount of expected traffic).

Your Web servers need to be closely monitored to ensure that all of the documents are being served in a speedy, efficient fashion. Every server needs its own backup power supply, a regular, automated backup system, and an assigned technician to make sure that the server remains up and running at all times. If your company can handle these functions on-site, and has the resources for the capital investments, then you won't need to contract for an off-site server.

The cost of connectivity

Sending a slice of your revenue to a commerce server is only one factor that will gnaw away at your profit margin. You may be surprised at how much you'll need to spend to obtain the online connections required to handle full-time electronic transactions. Numerous services are available, and you'll need to balance your needs against these different service and cost options.

International leased lines

For those businesses that have large amounts of international telecommunications traffic, many services offer a secure, affordable alternative to the traditional public switched telephone network. Leased-line solutions offer companies a private, dedicated communications pipeline at a flat monthly rate. This pipeline may carry multiple channels of voice, fax, data, video traffic, or—a major boon to international business—full-time online financial transactions.

You'll find many providers that offer leased lines of various capacities to accommodate virtually any business need. In addition, some of these providers will install your network virtually anywhere in the world and maintain it 24 hours a day, 365 days a year. Whatever capacity your company chooses, it pays the same flat rate regardless of usage. Thus, you no longer pay a penalty even for micropayment transactions, because no individual sale incurs a direct communication charge.

 NET TIP Speaking of saving money—always shop around for all Internet services. You easily can be overcharged. We wish this weren't true, but here's one quick example: The first service provider we contacted to price autoresponder service quoted a $50 setup fee and $30 per month. The next one quoted free setup and $10 per month. We've seen many similar pricing discrepancies.

Let's consider some leased-line options.

Packet-switched networks

Medium-sized organizations that do not have the transaction volume to justify a dedicated, leased-line network may choose a *packet switched network*. This solution, which is priced according to actual usage, offers the same reliability and security of leased-line networks, without tying you to heavy volume commitments, though each transaction incurs a communication charge. Packet-switched networks may prohibit profitable micromerchant sales.

Internet connectivity with a private network

Private networks can be interconnected with the Internet, enabling your company to partake directly in the cyberspace revolution. This level of service is reaching into the major leagues and can help your company create an impressive world wide Internet presence. Yet you may find start-up costs to be surprisingly low and your investment payback coming quickly.

Savings example

To demonstrate how much savings you might attain with a private network solution, let's use an example of an import/export company with offices in Copenhagen, Denmark and in New York City. Voice, fax, and data traffic between the two offices is heavy, because they depend upon one another for vital information. A few years ago, such services were so costly as to preclude profits on many small-scale international ventures.

Today, however, a single 56kbps line can provide this example company with six simultaneous communication channels for voice, fax, or online financial transactions. Including all necessary equipment and line costs, this private network would cost the import/export company about $7,000 per month. While that may seem like a high figure, let's evaluate how much they might spend on traditional solutions.

If both offices previously were using publicly switched networks for only 16 minutes of usage per day on each of the six communications channels on both sides of the Atlantic, the private network would pay for itself in less than six months. From that point on, the initial investment would continue to improve profits. Moreover, revenues from micropayments likely would rise, because a leased line eliminates any transaction-based cost-burden. And you can count on their usage going way beyond the previous 16 minutes per day.

Summary of money issues

From both angles—income and expenses—Internet money issues are changing at hyperspeed: credit card transactions, digital cash, commerce servers, encryption, communications capabilities, and communications charges. A book only can take a snapshot of one moment in history, so you won't be able to rely upon any Internet book for up-to-date information on any of these topics. Hence, you'll need to use the URLs in the Continuing Education section to track current technology, and you'll need to check with Internet professionals for the latest updates.

Do not rely on a single source, though. Be sure to cross-check information you read on the Web, and get second opinions from professionals you interview.

The next chapter will present another Internet topic that is changing just as rapidly as the ones we've covered here: computer security. Security is closely tied with money issues, so you may end up using the same source for solutions to both your money and security issues.

 *Continuing Education*

Netscape commerce server software
http://merchant.netscape.com

All of your online credit-card sales can be kept absolutely secure by using the Netscape Commerce Server software. Netscape has RSA security built-in, using public-key encryption. This Web site probably always will be an excellent starting point for learning more about Internet security and for tracking technology updates and breakthroughs.

Contact NetBill
http://www.ini.cmu.edu/netbill/

Here's the Web site for Carnegie-Mellon's NetBill commerce server project that we profiled earlier in this chapter. NetBill's research is funded in part by a grant from the National Science Foundation (NSF), one of the founders of the Internet.

Digital cash
http://www.digicash.com

Digital Cash (Digicash) is pioneering a new system for transferring money via the Internet; it effectively creates a new monetary system. Digicash vendors accept payments from customers in the form of "e-cash" money. For your customers to use this service, they first have to transfer some actual cash from their bank into e-cash at Digicash. With this account established, buyers then can shop Internet vendors who accept e-cash. This system has more advantage for the vendor than for the client. But if your business is suffering collection problems, check out DigiCash (see Figure 14-5), because when a customer makes a purchase, their e-cash goes straight into your bank—you don't have to worry about credit card verification.

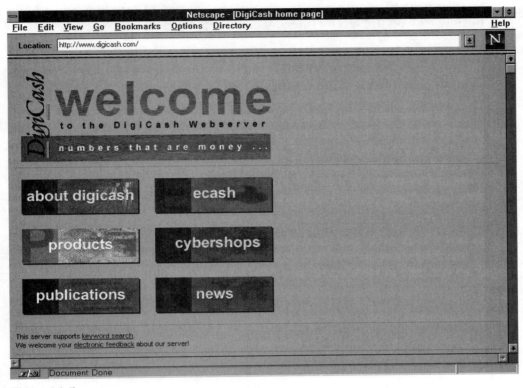

Figure 14-5

Cybercash

http://www.cybercash.com

CyberCash offers banks, merchants, and consumers the Secure Internet Payment Service (SIPS). SIPS protects consumer credit card numbers used for shopping on the Web, and enables merchants to safely process credit card transactions over the Internet. By 1996, SIPS will enable consumers to use their own money for Internet payments. Check out this Web site for details on how your organization can use their system. CyberCash encryption software has been approved for worldwide export by the U.S. Government.

Open Market commercial sites index

http://www.directory.net/

Open Market, Incorporated develops and markets software, services and custom solutions that facilitate electronic commerce on the Web. Open Market applies both advanced technology and a business perspective to the expansion of business into an electronic marketplace. They offer solutions that address the needs of small companies and global businesses alike. Check out this site for a bonus look at some other neat technology.

Miscellaneous Web business sites

http://www.owi.com/netvalue/v1i1l1.html

Here's a list of miscellaneous, interesting Internet business sites that you can visit to see how they handle money transactions. Instead of searching for specific businesses, you'll select by category, such as Financial Services, etc.

Internet security

INTERNET security parallels "real world" security in many ways. The advent of motor highways and the anonymity of 20th-century life made crime less risky than in earlier eras. The anonymity and global reach of the Internet is doing the same on our electronic highways. A European hacker can ride the Internet to a U.S. business for fun and profit, without investing in plane tickets or showing his identification to curious government officials. And he won't worry about clearing his burglar tools through customs.

Because your hottest new project and ideas may now traverse cyberspace, every worker needs to know about hacker tools such as "sniffers" and "snoopers." Computer hackers today earn a living breaking into computer systems. They have special computers that "sniff" Internet traffic for keywords that are of interest to their clients. They also play a game called "door rattling." It's the equivalent of snooping through a neighborhood and rattling doorknobs to see if anyone forgot to lock up. Door rattling thieves aren't after your company in particular—unless it's your "doorknob" that turns.

If you've got secret information, you have to make it secure. You may be surprised at how little you need to do—often simple encryption is sufficient—because most Internet bandits are in for the quick buck. There are plenty of easy marks and unprotected data floating around the Internet.

Still, not everyone snooping the Internet is a door rattler. You may be at risk because your competitors can hire bounty hunters to track down your trade secrets and pull them off the Internet. In other words, someone may pay a hacker to break your encryption. When electronic bloodhounds find their quarry, your most private information quickly can be transferred and hackers collect their bounty. But we'll show you how to protect your priceless information and make the bounty hunters look for another target—or wish they had.

Inside, outside, all around the house

Browsing some of the Usenet newsgroups will show you some horror stories that illustrate the dangers the Internet can present to company secrets. And there's another angle on security breaches: People who don't lurk outside to sniff your data; they reach inside and take want they want. The Internet has spawned a whole industry that trades inside information on "soft sites"—companies with lax computer security that are easy targets for spying or just plain mischief. We'll tell you about "firewalls" and other security measures that ensure you haven't left open the door to the vault.

There's more—even if you implement the best security measures, *you* might end up doing yourself in. Remember the fable about the Trojan Horse—the victims brought in the "gift" that encased the seeds of their own destruction. Computer viruses often are disguised within modern-day Trojan Horses—programs that are interesting or useful, but that damage systems or spawn a computer virus. A computer virus is a self-replicating program that damages computer operating systems or data files. The Internet will entice you to pull in lots of outside files. If your company doesn't have virus protection, you're running on the edge. If it does, make sure you don't short-circuit the safeguards to save a few minutes.

Look, it's not actually all that bad. You just need to take some precautions—besides, ever since the 1990s started, it seems the watchword of our society has been precaution. You take all kinds of precautions in almost everything you do. Now you'll need to extend those practices to your Internet adventures as well. So, let's get the keys and start locking those doorknobs.

Sniffers and snoopers

Have you ever wondered how hackers can break into your organization's system? The easiest way is to get the ID and password of a system administrator.

How do they get that? Often from inside sources, but also by using snoopers and sniffers to find passwords that can gain them entrance onto a system where the system administrator's password may be found.

A sniffer is an Internet program that monitors Internet traffic looking for data that it suspects might contain IDs or passwords used to log onto its targeted systems.

When you log into a remote host using Telnet or FTP, your ID and password travel across the Internet unencrypted. Most e-mail also can be monitored the same way. Any sniffer that has targeted your organization's Internet traffic can pick out IDs from e-mail. If you e-mail a password to a colleague or business associate, you may also be inviting in a host of hackers.

Spoofing

A hacker can pretend to be a trusted user by changing his or her host IP address to match a user's. Then he or she can force their data to take a particular path through the Internet using "source routing," and having the last link in the route be the trusted user's system. Data sent back to the trusted user's host is then sent on to the hacker's system. Such masquerades, as well as the creation of bogus e-mail messages, are called "spoofing."

Thus, even if you receive a direct e-mailed request from someone you trust, you have to consider that the message could be a spoof. Before you e-mail sensitive data, at the very least be certain that the trusted individual actually sent the message. For maximum Internet security, never send any sensitive data without encryption.

Top 10 Internet security problems

Believe it or not, your organization's worst security enemy is itself. Here, in approximate order of occurrence, are the Top 10 Internet security problems.

10. Government agents

It hasn't happened often, but in a few cases the FBI has raided computer sites and confiscated everything. Can't happen to your organization, right? Are you sure you know everything that everybody is doing on your system? If one of them posts secret information on the Internet, then you could hear a knock on the door anytime and see a band of Federal agents with moving vans and warrants to remove your equipment.

9. Sniffers and snoopers

Unless your organization maintains a cache of sensitive information, you're not likely to be a target for sniffers and snoopers. But any research-oriented organization could attract eavesdroppers. Budget cuts have forced many companies to slash R&D spending—but a few bucks spent on hackers who monitor your data transmissions could replace a competitor's shut-down research laboratory.

8. Credit card fraud

From what we've seen, most horror stories of credit card fraud are unfounded. First, people don't need the Internet to steal credit card numbers—trash bins behind strip shopping malls have plenty of credit card numbers, and no one can backtrack to find out who got them. Besides, we simply have not found widespread reports of credit card numbers being ripped off.

7. Youthful hackers

Kids enjoy a challenge, and your system might be an inviting target. Kids, however, rarely are out to steal your data, and usually lack the fencing contacts for it if they did download something sensitive. They have, however, reformatted a lot of hard drives and deleted a lot of files.

6. Professional hackers

This is an international problem. In August, 1995, a group of Russian computer hackers was accused of stealing more than $10 million from Citibank accounts in the U.S. These people not only enjoy their work, but they also enjoy the potential for enormous rewards. And if they're smart and are willing to work on the run, they're hard to catch.

5. Internal credit card fraud

This always is a problem for any business and it probably will grow. The advent of the Internet and the expansion of credit card usage over mailed checks has created a ripe environment for employees to obtain and sell the credit card numbers of your clients and customers. No firewall will prevent this, of course; just good internal corporate security, and being alert to the possibility of fraud.

4. Inside jobs

Current employees easily can be tempted to upload some or your organization's sensitive data. With a few mouse clicks in a Windows FTP application, an employee can circumvent all your firewalls and do the work of legions of snoopers, sniffers, and hackers. Disgruntled former employees, too, may have left with sensitive secrets, or with passwords to come back in and get them later. In this era of rapid downsizing and outsourcing, you'll need to direct a lot of your security efforts toward employees whose jobs may soon be eliminated—after all, they might consider taking your data merely to be a fair severance package.

3. Viruses

This one is high on the list, but not because of data loss due to corruption by computer viruses. Viruses actually cause little data loss. Organizations of all sizes, however, have spent vast sums on virus prevention, monitoring and cleaning. The cure usually is much more costly than the problem. Nonetheless, it is a necessary business expense, because if you don't spend the money to protect your computer systems from virus intrusion, you will one day lose data to a computer virus.

2. Hardware theft, fire, and failure

This problem far outstrips all the others we've listed so far. As computer consultants, we've seen companies dropped to their corporate knees by theft, fire, and hardware failures. These security risks are not threats, nor are they theories—they are real and they happen every day. A regular routine of simple tape backups and off-site storage will give your organization a 100 percent insurance policy against these losses. Unfortunately, human nature and the laws of metaphysics have proven that the Friday when someone is too rushed to run a backup and take the tape off-site is the same weekend your computers will be stolen, or the office will burn to the ground. We're not kidding.

1. Computer users

And the number one cause of computer losses is: computer users. They cause:
- Bad password choices and compromised passwords
- Accidental reformatting
- Unintentional file deletions
- Mistakes with software that publicly post sensitive data instead of sending it securely to the proper site
- Flame wars by employees that generate negative attention or law suits

- Failure to run regular backups (see #2)
- Intentionally circumventing firewalls or other security measures because someone is in a hurry—and that was just the opening that someone's sniffer or snooper was waiting to find.

Internet security measures

The hardest part of connecting to the Internet in a large organization might not be financial resources or technical expertise; it might be convincing management that corporate data will be safe. The only truly secure system is one that isn't connected to the Internet, and that even trusted employees can't use. Of course, a truly secure system also is useless.

Network security measures try to create a compromise, balancing business needs against risks. Even modest security measures can keep out the bad guys, permit the good guys to use the Internet, and cool the fears of management. There are a lot of different solutions that depend on the size of your organization. Fortunately, the Internet itself has plenty of sources from which you can learn the latest in Internet security measures that will fit your organization (see Figure 15-1).

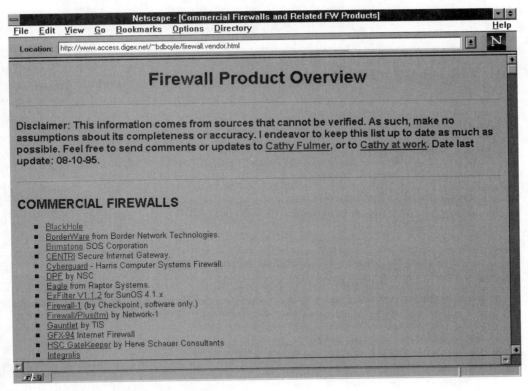

Figure 15-1

Small organizations can protect themselves from most security risks by contracting with outside providers to maintain a Web site on a remote system. No one can enter your system through a remote Web site, because it has no direct connection to your system. Large organizations, however, will need to employ one or more security measures.

Firewalls, restricted routers, and proxy servers are devices used to control data traffic while allowing fairly free visits to external systems. Let's consider all three.

Host-based firewall

A host-based firewall is a firewall where the security is implemented in software running on a general-purpose computer of some sort. Security in host-based firewalls is generally at the application level, rather than at a network level.

Router-based firewall

This is a firewall where the security is implemented using screening routers as the primary means of protecting the network.

Screening router

A screening router is used to implement part of the security of a firewall by configuring it to selectively permit or deny traffic at a network level.

Bastion host

A bastion host is a host system that is a "strong point" in the network's security perimeter. Bastion hosts should be configured to be particularly resistant to attack. In a host-based firewall, the bastion host is the platform on which the firewall software is run. Bastion hosts are also referred to as "gateway hosts."

Dual-homed gateway

This is a firewall consisting of a bastion host with two network interfaces, one of which is connected to the protected network, the other of which is connected to the Internet. IP traffic forwarding is usually disabled, restricting all traffic between the two networks to whatever passes through some kind of application proxy.

Application proxy

An application proxy is an application that forwards application traffic through a firewall. Proxies tend to be specific to the protocol they are designed to forward, and may provide increased access control or audit.

Screened subnet

A screened subnet is a firewall architecture in which a "sand box" or "demilitarized zone" network is set up between the protected network and the Internet, with traffic between the protected network and the Internet blocked. Conceptually, this is similar to a dual-homed gateway, except that an entire network (rather than a single host) is reachable from the outside.

Terms Glossary from USENET FAQ, Copyright (c) 1995 Trusted Information Systems, Inc. Reprinted with permission.

Firewalls

An Internet firewall performs the same functions as a firewall in a townhouse development or apartment complex—damage can be prevented from spreading. Firewalls force all communications with the outside world through a single machine. The firewall creates a single entry point that monitors, and therefore can control, all external communications.

Restricted routers

Restricted routers block the function of certain protocols that hackers frequently use to break into computer systems. Limiting the kinds and sources of data traffic allowed on your system makes the hacker's job more difficult. When you try to install the latest videoconferencing, telephone, or other software on your PC, and discover you can't get it to work, it may be that your Internet experts have restricted this type of data traffic for security reasons.

Proxy servers

Proxy servers are applications that act as a proxy between your secure network and the external Internet (see Figure 15-2). When you want to FTP a file, for example, your request goes to the proxy server, which sits outside of your system's firewall. The proxy gets the file for you and then sends it to you. This is safer than a direct Internet connection, but also slower and more expensive to install.

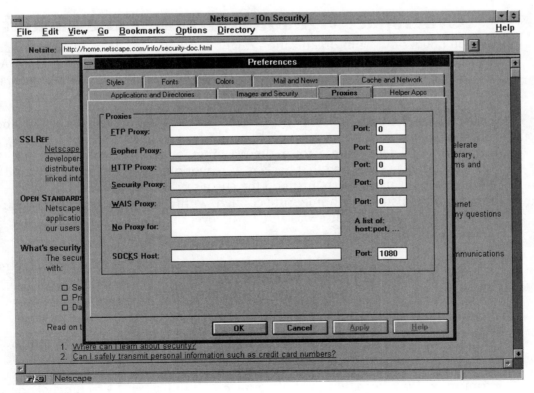

Figure 15-2

NET TIP About viruses: Even the best firewalls can't protect users against viruses they find and bring home while surfing the net. That's because viruses enter a computer system disguised as normal information. The firewall will allow the information to pass, because a valid user has given authorization. Your only protection against computer viruses is to regularly check your entire system and to check all programs that you obtain from the Internet.

Passwords

Among the top security problems on the Internet is that of passwords that are easily broken. If a hacker can get a foothold in your network—either by guessing a password or by using low-security public access—they can search for words that could be used as passwords by users with high-security access.

Passwords that are found in dictionaries, or that are used in documents, e-mail, or Web pages, are ready prey for hackers. Passwords like "TOPP$DOG," which can't be found in a dictionary but are still easy to remember, are a safer choice.

Consider combining the case-sensitivity of UNIX and the diversity of languages other than English to further enhance your password security. For example, your mail password could be as simple as "coRReo," the Spanish word for mail. Even if you had a Spanish surname and a hacker used that as a clue to guess the word, he still would have to test thousands of uppercase and lowercase combinations.

Cyberspace vigilantes—tracking the hackers

If you believe that your organization might be a target for door-rattling hackers, your Internet service provider can help you protect your organization's data. At the same time, you can become a cyberspace vigilante, riding the superhighway 24 hours a day to stop hackers.

Rick Garvin, an Internet security expert at BTG Corporation, told us a story about how he helped a client become a cyberspace vigilante. A BTG client—a government defense contractor in the Washington area, with tons of secret, sensitive data— suspected that hackers were working at night to access their data. BTG set up an alarm mechanism on the client's system that would alert the system administrator at home. Sure enough, within a few days the alarm went off at 2 a.m. The administrator was able to discover their location and report the incident to authorities.

Your data security needs may not warrant your being jarred out of bed at 2 a.m., but that is one possible solution, and it has a ripple effect throughout the industry. Thanks to one system administrator's efforts and BTG's technical assistance, one hacker paid a price for merely attempting his dirty work.

Perhaps BTG prevented that hacker from rattling your door next. That's the way we believe security should be handled, because we all are in this together. The security problems you experience today could become our security problems tomorrow. We all can, however, discourage a lot of hackers by routinely and regularly following Internet security discipline. The success of your entire organization may depend on it.

The rest of the story

Continuing Education

Netscape security features

In Netscape, click Help, On Security

Netscape has contributed greatly to Internet security by including built-in security features (see Figure 15-3). When you see at the beginning of the URL in the Location text entry box the string, *https://* instead of the usual *http://*, you know that Netscape is displaying a secure hypertext document. You also will notice the small skeleton key in the lower-left corner of the screen no longer is broken—a complete, unbroken key also is a clue that you're in a secure document. You can read about the latest Netscape security developments at this site.

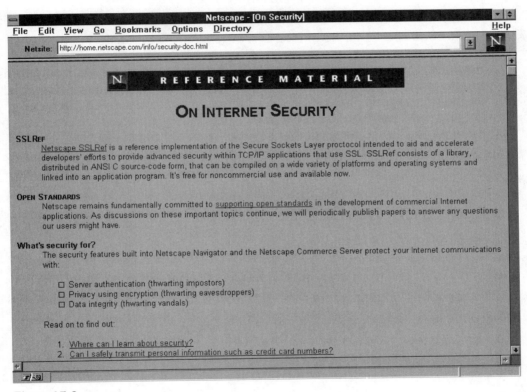

Figure 15-3

Computer security newsgroups

comp.security.announce

comp.security.misc

comp.security.UNIX

You can access the Usenet newsgroups on computer security information and read security solutions posted by the Computer Emergency Response Team (CERT).

Computer security mailing list

cert-advisory-request@cert.org

You can get mailing list announcements on Internet security by sending a subscription request to this address. E-mail with a blank subject line and with "subscribe" in the body of the message.

Firewall product overview

http://www.access.digex.net/~bdboyle/firewall.vendor.html

This site could be considered to be a one-stop source for Internet security measures for your organization. Posted by Cathy Fulmer of Panasonic Corporation, it's a long list of hypertext links to sources of Internet security hardware, software and consultants.

An introduction to firewalls

http://www.soscorp.com/products/BS_FireIntro.html

Be sure and check out the link on this page titled "Introduction to Firewalls" that is produced by SOS Corporation, a New York City-based UNIX systems management company. SOS can provide experts in computer security, systems programming, network administration, and systems management. They produce an Internet security application called Brimstone, a full-featured Internet firewall. We've singled them out here, however, because they also produce Freestone, a freeware firewall application that includes parts of Brimstone.

PGP encryption

http://www.mantis.co.uk/pgp/pgp.html

You can use this site to download a copy of an Internet encryption program titled PGP (Pretty Good Privacy). It's available for Windows, Macintosh, DOS and UNIX.

Site security handbook

http://www.first.org/secplcy/rfc1244.txt

A huge document (259,129 bytes in length) on Internet security that you can download via FTP. It's the product of the Site Security Policy Handbook Working Group (SSPHWG), a combined effort of the Security Area and User Services Area of the Internet Engineering Task Force (IETF). It also is available through the Web page of the Internet Society at *www.isoc.org*.

Computer security resource clearinghouse

http://csrc.nist.gov/

A Web page maintained by the National Institute of Standards and Technology in Gaithersburg, Maryland near Washington, DC. There's a jump on the home page called "Training" that brings up a page titled, "Training, Awareness, and Resource Publications" that is a directory of a variety of resource material for the computer security professional or trainer.

Computer security alerts

http://csrc.nist.gov/secalert/

If you're concerned about tracking the latest information on Internet security, be sure and add this site to your browser's bookmark list. Its listings of security bulletins and incident advisories can help you see trouble coming. Hopefully, of course, you will read this page often enough that you never will have anything to contribute to it.

How to prepare a work statement for computer security

http://www.first.org/nistir/ir4749.txt

This is a document titled "Sample Statements of Work for Federal Computer Security Services: For Use In-house or Contracting out," that may give you a quick boost if you're trying to learn about computer security.

Site security handbook

http://www.ietf.cnri.reston.va.us/html.charters/ssh-charter.html

This Web page actually is titled, "Site Security Handbook (SSH) Charter" and gives an overview of site security issues from the Internet Engineering Task Force (IETF). It has a hypertext link that will FTP the actual handbook, titled, "Site Security Handbook for System and Network Administrators" (127,445 bytes).

Computer virus newsgroup

alt.comp.virus

Here's a newsgroup that provides an open forum for users to discuss computer virus issues. You can read this group regularly, or perhaps include it in your specifications to a news service company that will scan this group for you and pull out articles that contain only the information you want to track.

Publishing on the World Wide Web

BEFORE 1995, writing hypertext, HTML-language home pages for the World Wide Web required a programming expert with a mountain of skill and patience. But the field is being leveled and now you don't have to scale a steep learning slope. HTML programming can be as simple as using a word processor.

You now can produce World Wide Web documents within WordPerfect for Windows and Word for Windows. Both companies offer free add-ons that greatly simplify the once-monumental challenge of creating simple hypertext documents. We'll show you how to take along an old friend on your cyberspace trek, highlighting both their strengths and weaknesses so you'll know if you need a more advanced Web editor.

But there's more to writing for the World Wide Web than producing hypertext documents—knowing how to use the tools doesn't make you a skilled craftsman. Because your writing instantly will broadcast your company's image worldwide, you'll want to ensure it's right the first time.

We'll tailor our home page tips to organizational size so that you will know what *your* company can do in-house and when you need a consultant. When you've finished this chapter, you'll be fully prepared to become a major player in the electronic world of cyberspace business.

Tools, tools, and more tools

In the course of just one year, the available tools to help you publish Web hypertext documents has gone from almost none to too many to count. Before the last year's dramatic expansion of Web tools, only programmers and computer specialists were qualified to create Web pages. But the Web's popularity explosion has prompted major software developers to create tools that enable mainstream users to create Web pages.

Developing World-class Web pages still will require a technical expert, because the leading edge of technology always stays ahead of the mainstream user. Someone always will be pushing existing technical limits, and if you want to play on that level, you'll need the services of a full-time professional. But today, most advanced word-processor users can create attractive Web pages.

We'll cover basic Web-development tools in several categories:

- Add-on packages
- Conversion programs
- HTML editors
- Graphics software
- CGI tools
- Hot Java

We'll cover each category in subsequent sections.

Add-ons to word processors

WordPerfect for Windows, Microsoft Word for Windows, and AmiPro for Windows all let users create a document and then use the "Save As" command to create an HTML-formatted document that's ready to view in Netscape. Many desktop publishing programs also offer HTML support—those that do not soon will. These add-on packages are ideal for casual publishers and for documents with lots of text.

For example, the IRS is using WordPerfect for Windows to rewrite its entire 60,000-page tax code in hypertext (see Figure 16-1). They don't need interactive graphics or sound files, so WordPerfect is an excellent choice for the IRS

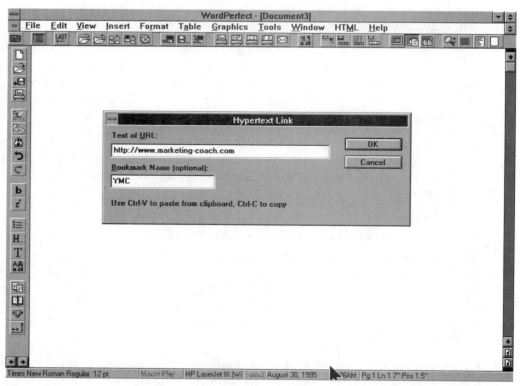

Figure 16-1

assignment; nearly everyone involved in rewriting the tax code is an experienced WordPerfect user.

In fact, it's possible that most of the rewriting on the IRS project will be done in WordPerfect 5.1 for DOS! The powerful Styles feature in the trusty old 5.1 version (dating back to that ancient year 1989) enables its documents to automatically be turned into hypertext by WordPerfect for Windows. Such backward compatibility also may be an important factor in your organization, because so many writers can't be dragged away from 5.1 even by the wild horses of Windows. The WordPerfect for Windows Internet Publisher, therefore, enables you to allow almost anyone to be involved in writing text for your Web site— even those users who refuse to give up DOS.

Conversion programs

These programs will convert existing documents, databases, and other file types to HTML format. They often do a better job than the word processor add-ons. This can be quite important if you are converting lots of existing documents. One example is Skisoft's Web Publisher (*http://www.skisoft.com*). This application is a super plus for organizations converting reams of documents. It's not perfect, but it's a big leap up from the Internet Assistant add-on for Microsoft Word.

HTML editors

These are stand-alone programs in which you create HTML files. They generally offer more hypertext features and flexibility than the word processor add-ons. But they require a greater learning curve than add-ons, and they lack some of the advanced word processing features you've come to expect in Windows applications. This book's authors both use "HotDog Pro" (see HotDog's home page at *http://www.sausage.com*). Eric also has used SoftQuad's "HoTMetaL Pro" (see Figure 16-2).

Some applications are appearing that are a cross between a stand-alone HTML editor and a word processor. These third-party add-ons may bring the advanced features of a stand-alone inside the familiar environment of your current word processor. These eventually may be the best solution—that is, until Novell and Microsoft each buy one of them and build the technology directly into WordPerfect and Word.

It may be easy, but how do I get started?

Analyzing the source code of programs that other persons have written is a commonly used learning tool for programmers. It's much easier to learn to program by example that it is to start from scratch. The same applies to writing HTML-encoded Web pages—you can learn a lot by example.

When you see a Web page that has a feature you would like to implement, click View, Source to see its HTML source code. The default is to display the code in Netscape's internal source viewer. This should be used unless you need to edit the page or display documents that are too long for the internal viewer. You can designate any editor on your system, but the Windows Note-

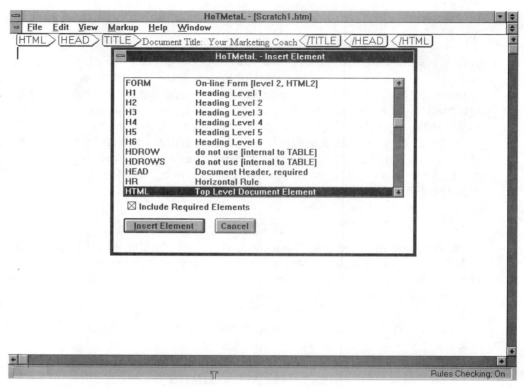

Figure 16-2

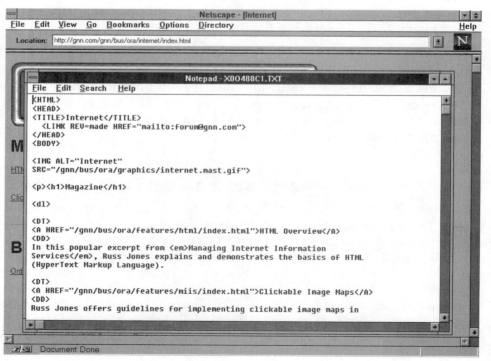

Figure 16-3

The rest of the story

pad application is a good choice (see Figure 16-3). To set the HTML editor, follow the steps in the next Hands On exercise:

Of course if you want to save the source code to any Web document, remember to click File, Save As... and use the dialog box with the Save File as Type set to Source (*.htm).

Hands On

Objective: Learn to set Netscape's HTML source code viewer.

❏ Start Netscape with an Internet connection.

❏ Click **Options, Preferences...**

❏ Click the **Applications and Directories** tab.

❏ Click in the **View Source** text entry box.

❏ Type *c:\windows\notepad.exe* and click **OK**.

> You can enter any other Windows editing application instead. If you don't know the application's full path and filename, click on **Browse**, select an editor from your system, then click **OK**.

❏ Click **Options, Save Options** to save the change.

Graphics software

Graphics tools help make Web pages attractive and interesting. These tools help you create image maps so that users can click on images and buttons for hyperlinks, instead of limiting your site to text-based links.

The popularity of color printers and the color graphics that now adorn millions of Web pages has encouraged development of a slew of advanced graphics programs. "CorelDraw" and "Adobe Photoshop" are popular commercial products, while "PaintShop Pro" and "LViewPro" are popular shareware products for graphic image manipulation. "MapEdit" is a good application for creating Web page image maps.

Common Gateway Interface tools

Common Gateway Interface (CGI) is a programming specification for Web servers that makes it possible to have HTML pages tell the Web server to run programs that make your Web pages interactive. Where this used to require programming in the C language, UNIX shell scripts, and Perl (Practical Extraction and Report Language)—and was strictly in the realm of computer professionals—market forces are propelling development of user-friendly tools that extend Web server functions.

User-friendly CGI tools include a wealth of valuable "pre-canned" programming scripts that can be referenced—to be called by the Web server—in existing hypertext documents. In other words, you won't have to start from scratch for every specialized function you want your Web site to perform. New, advanced tools such as "Cold Fusion" enable Web authors to create sophisticated database applications without doing any actual programming.

NET TIP You can get the URLs for these programs from the Web itself. Start with Yahoo at *www.yahoo.com* and search for the program you want. For example, PaintShop and LViewPro have downloadable versions that you can begin using right away. You also can track the latest developments with the hot program Cold Fusion. Remember, anytime you hear about anything new on the Internet, don't wonder where you can find it; just jump into a search engine and you probably will have it saved on your system in minutes.

Java

This specification, and competitive variants that are appearing, enable a Web browser to pull programming code from a Web server. This extends the functionality of your Netscape browser so that it can perform elaborate tricks that are not built-in. Leading Web sites may use Java to nearly eliminate all Web browser limitations. The programming language required to implement Java applications is not for mainstream users and development progress has been slow. But if you have an intricate, specialized idea for your Web site, you can turn to an Internet programming expert for help writing Java code.

As this book is being written, we've only seen Java demonstrations. By the time you read this, however, the use of Java may be widespread. Java makes some pretty high computing-power demands and needs a Pentium to run Java. So, until your average Web site visitor has a Pentium, don't pin your Web site hopes on implementing a Java application on your site.

HotDog

You can download the latest version of our favorite HTML editor, Hot Dog, at the Web site *www.sausage.com*. It's the most highly rated HTML editor in the world. They have two versions, Hot Dog and Hot Dog Pro. The regular version is limited to Web pages of 32K or less, while the Pro version permits unlimited file sizes. The Pro version has many advanced features, and even includes a spell checker. The home page of this book was created with Hot Dog Pro.

The regular version costs $29.95 and the Pro version costs $99.95. If you use Netscape, they can accept secure credit card payments. They also include a link to download free demonstration copies of both versions, to which you later can register.

HoTMetaL

You can download a free copy of the HTML editor pictured earlier, "HoT-MetaL Free 2.0+" by SoftQuad. Their commercial version is "HoTMetaL PRO." The current version is 2.0. They also have an advanced SGML browser and editor especially suitable for large organizations with extremely large document collections. Their Web site is *http://www.sq.com*. You can download the latest free version via FTP to the directory *ftp://ftp2.sq.com/pub/products/hot metal/windows/hmfree2.exe* and download the *.exe* file. This is a self-extracting, compressed file that will expand to about six megabytes. This version requires Windows 3.1 or later, and at least eight megabytes of RAM. Be sure and also get *install.txt* for setup instructions.

Creating your own Web server

At the beginning of 1995, putting up a Web server required the computer expertise of a professional. The learning curve required to create a Web site was too great for mainstream users. By the summer of 1995, however, new Web tools dramatically simplified Web site creation. We're not going to cover much on this topic, because it's one of the hottest areas in Internet technology and is changing too rapidly for any book to report accurately. We'll give you a report on one of the first packages on the market, created by a leader in Internet technical assistance. For further information, we'll let you rely upon the Continuing Education section at the end of this chapter.

WebSite

Created by O'Reilly Associates (see Figure 16-4), WebSite is a powerful Web server tool for small companies, and even for individuals, who want to create a Web site. We don't mean create the pages that a Web site will use; we mean create the entire Web site. This is a complete Web server. With this software all you need is a full-time Internet connection and your organization will become a part of the World Wide Web! It proves you don't have to be a rocket scientist to put your organization on the Web. See for yourself at *http://website.ora.com*.

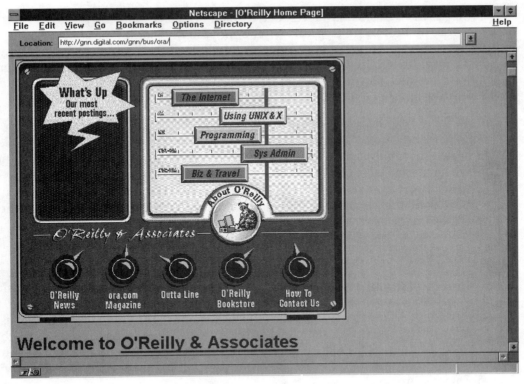

Figure 16-4

Until recently, few people were able to create Web sites because Web servers required skill in using the UNIX programming language and the servers had to run on UNIX systems—definitely not mainstream. But the advent of Windows

NT and Windows 95 ushered in the era of Web servers that could be developed and that would run under Windows—about as mainstream as you can get. Now, using a drag-and-drop interface and familiar Windows functions, any savvy computer user can create and put up a Web site.

The WebSite package includes CGI features that enable your site to display up-to-the-second information from databases, spreadsheets, or just about any document on your site. You easily will be able to put up a high-quality Web site that includes text, graphics, forms, multimedia, and indexing.

Speaking of sound

If you're going to set up your own Web server, you need to know about "RealAudio," an Internet service that permits your Web site to include real-time audio directly from your server. Check out their home page at *http://www.realaudio.com*. You've never heard anything like it.

RealAudio technology gives Internet and World Wide Web users—equipped even with only a standard multimedia personal computer and a 14.4 Kbps modem—instantaneous access to your personal audio programming. This technology raises Internet publishing to the next level of multimedia by making audio-on-demand as practical as delivery of text and graphics are today.

Progressive Networks has developed a system of three software products that employ the RealAudio technology. They are the RealAudio Player, RealAudio Studio and RealAudio Server. Your server will need the RealAudio Server and your visitors will need the RealAudio player, but they can download that from your site—of course, they may well already have it from someone else who is providing audio.

Even though audio programming has been available on the Internet for some time, significant downloading delays have prohibited its use as a part of a Client-centered Interneting strategy. The RealAudio technology provides instant audio playback because it quickly and reliably plays digital audio information in its entirety direct from your server as soon as it is transmitted. Full-motion video will be available before long, but wouldn't you like to talk directly to your clients and customers *today*?

Decisions, decisions... too many choices

How do you decide which path to choose to build your organization's Web site? First consider your existing technical and personnel resources. Do you expect 10 visitors or 10,000 visitors to your Web site each day? Do you have UNIX gurus in-house? Do you have artistic and advertising talent in-house? Will your Web site require frequent updates, or will your information be fairly static? Do you need database searches, or can you convey your organization's information with simple documents?

Depending on your organization's resources, you may decide to keep your Web project in-house, hire consultants, or outsource the entire project. Let's run through some factors to consider for organizations of varying sizes. You may benefit from reading them all, because there is some crossover.

Vast, global organization (10,000+ people)

Organizations of this size generally have lots of customers, with resources to match. They generally have advertising people who can help with focus (and control the Internet fever that may result in a slip-shod Web site); editorial staff who can ensure that grammar and writing are crisp (as long as they don't impede progress); computer professionals who can build elaborate scripts and database functions (or stall the whole project by trying to be too technical); and cautious management (who prudently, and unfortunately, may slow down the whole project).

We've found that when large organizations eventually get themselves online, their sites often provide so little valuable information that their presence is no more informative than a simple brochure, and defeats the benefits of the Web. This is because large organizations have huge investments in reputation and organizational infrastructure that require careful analysis before any action is taken on a Web site that will present the company to their customers.

The Internet also offers tremendous opportunities for an "Intranet," which lets staff use the power of the Web to access internal corporate information. Because control is decentralized and customers won't see it, each department often is free to immediately set up a Web server to ease their information storage and reporting needs. Even where field offices don't have Internet access, CD-ROMs containing data dumps of corporate Web servers can be shipped to them so that they have a (somewhat out of date) copy of the corporate databank.

Tools

Tools that might be used by a large organization—which runs the whole Web project internally—include C compilers, multiple high-end PCs, multiprocessor PCs, mini/mainframe Web server hardware, UNIX or Windows NT Web server software with on-staff technical support, advanced graphics editing tools like Corel Draw and Adobe Photoshop, document conversion tools, SGML (the parent of HTML) browsers and tools from SoftQuad, and database access tools like Cold Fusion.

Large domestic organization (1,000 to 10,000 people)

Organizations in this size range still, generally, have enough of the internal resources found in giant organizations that they can expect to handle a Web project internally. Shipping out CD-ROMs to branch offices in organizations of this size probably wouldn't be cost-effective, but a private Intranet still is a powerful productivity tool.

Tools

Tools you might find used in this size range include C compilers, multiple high-end PCs, multiprocessor PCs, minicomputer Web server hardware, UNIX or Windows NT Web server software with technical support contracts, advanced graphics editing tools like CorelDraw and Adobe Photoshop, document conversion tools, and database access tools like Cold Fusion. A single fast server probably can handle all internal needs.

Start an Intranet today

You can start an Intranet on your own network today. Begin by writing a home page for yourself, your branch, or your division. You can use the Internet Publisher for WordPerfect for Windows, or the Internet Assistant for Word. Save the file in a public directory on your network. (You may need to have your network administrator create a Web page directory for you.) Check out the page yourself by using Netscape and clicking on *File, Open File...*, then selecting the file you just saved.

Now pass the word via e-mail that your Web page is available. Remind other users that after they load your page to use *Bookmark, Add Bookmark* to create a Netscape bookmark for your site. Your e-mail also can encourage others to create a Web page and save it in the same directory.

If your network had a Web page for every individual, branch, or division and everyone had a Netscape bookmark folder called "Intranet" that listed these pages, then you would have an Intranet. Even a small office using Windows for Workgroups can create an Intranet; there's nothing elaborate about it. It's no more complicated than saving Web pages on your network and having people view them in Netscape. Pretty cool, isn't it?

Medium-sized domestic organization (100 to 1,000 people)

Organizations in this size range probably will have one or more full-time computer specialists who can meet the technology challenges of the 1990s. This person probably even will be able to handle installing an internal Web server. Expect your computer professional to be able to create Web pages with graphic images and possibly even database applications.

Depending on types of customers, it may make sense to maintain an external Web server, but at this size, an organization is in the crossover range and should consider renting space on an ISP's Web server. A tailored domain name still would be a must, however. Organizations in this size range probably will train additional staff to regularly produce simple Web documents, and will rely on the computer professional to write or supervise production of database applications.

Tools

Typical tools used in this organization will be word processor add-ons, desktop publishing programs with HTML output support, a Windows NT server, a specialized HTML editor like HotDog, a commercial Web server like WebSite, Netscape Communication Server, or Purveyor, and perhaps a database access application like Cold Fusion.

What about UNIX?

UNIX experts usually do not abound in organizations in this size range or smaller. But if you have more than one UNIX guru in-house, you may want to take advantage of the wealth of UNIX support for Web servers and Internet applications.

Never, however, ever leave your company dependent on a lone UNIX professional. Replacing a lost UNIX guru is nearly impossible to do quickly. Information on your site may go stale before you can hire a replacement who can work through hundreds or even thousands of clever improvements that your former guru made to your system. Sticking with Windows NT will give you a wealth of professionals on which to draw if you need a replacement.

Small organization (20 to 100 people)

A small company often will have a local area network (LAN) that easily can be adapted to an internal TCP/IP network and use an inexpensive Web server. Such an organization often will have a knowledgeable full-time computer specialist in-house, or a consultant who makes regular visits. This computer professional should be able to put up a simple Web site on an internal web—if your organization uses information intensely—and on an ISP's Web server for customer access. And an Intranet still makes sense on this scale.

Tools

Tools used in organizations of this size include word processor add-ons, desktop publishing software with HTML output, and tools recommended by your ISP for image-mapped hyperlinks and database applications. Your ISP almost certainly will have people in-house with enough Web development skills to create a professional Web site.

Very small organization (1 to 20 people)

Small companies and sole proprietorships nearly always lack a computer professional, thus they will need to look for a Web service provider who can develop and maintain a Web presence. Keep in mind that no one who uses your Web site knows its location, so your Web site can be maintained anywhere in the country—good to keep in mind if you find a real deal on Web server space a thousand miles away, such as Digiweb: *http://www.digiweb.com*.

Tools

Tools used in organizations of this size include word processor add-ons. Nearly anyone skilled in Windows word processor usage can put basic information on a Web page. You'll want the Internet Publisher for WordPerfect for Windows or the Internet Assistant for Microsoft Word for Windows.

After creating the basics, contract with a local Web-page designer to fill in your weak points. You also may need an ad copywriter to help with the writing, an advertising consultant and an artist to help with graphics and design. If you've used such professionals before, you probably will find that they have expanded their services to include Web technology.

If information on your Web site needs frequent changes, you can update your Web site quickly by using an ISP that permits you to FTP updates directly into the Web directory. You don't want the accuracy of the information seen by your clients and customers to depend on an ISP's schedule for updating your information. These services often are run by young people who may not understand the importance of responding to your schedule; but direct FTP capability will ensure that you have control over your Web site's content.

Summary

That's about all we can give you for now. Internet technology changes too fast to put any more details in a book. As with every chapter, we'll close this last one with our Continuing Education section that will give you valuable ongoing sources of up-to-date information as it changes.

Continuing Education

The McGraw-Hill Internet Training Manual

http://www.marketing-coach.com/mh-guide

This site is maintained by Ron Wagner and Eric Engelmann, the authors of *The McGraw-Hill Internet Training Manual*. We'll include the Continuing Education section from every chapter so you can visit any URL in this book without retyping it—except for this one, of course. We will update URLs as they change and add new, valuable URLs as we find them. Also, expect to find updates to a chapter or two in which we've made important changes. The site offers an online version of our glossary—with additional terms—and a link to download the macros we've created for cleaning HTML codes from Web pages you save. It also includes links to other good Internet books.

O'Reilly Associates

http://gnn.digital.com/gnn/bus/ora/

O'Reilly Associates has emerged as a powerhouse of technology on the Internet. They've published a library of more than 80 excellent technical reference guides that delve into details far more deeply that we have in this book. Actually, mainstream users may find the topics covered in this site to be too technical, but if you are performing or managing the Hands On work involved in publishing your organization's Web site, then you absolutely *must* place O'Reilly's URL on your Bookmark List.

Random tips and hints on constructing Web pages

http://www.nd.edu/PageCreation/TipsAndHints.html

Here's a Notre Dame University site that gives tips and hints on constructing HTML documents. Be sure to check out the "Clickable Graphics" tutorial that gives you a clickable graphic map demonstration-tutorial. This site is not an encyclopedic presentation on creating HTML documents, but it does address a number of issues that are encountered frequently.

Creating cool Web pages

http://www.mecklerweb.com/~taylor/coolweb/coolweb.html

Here's an online hypertext guide to a book titled *Creating Cool Web Pages with HTML* by Dave Taylor (IDG 1995). You'll find at least one link to a full chapter from the book.

The rest of the story

Russ Jones's HTML Overview
http://www.ora.com/gnn/bus/ora/features/html/index.html

Here's an online guide to publishing on the Web by Internet guru Russ Jones (see
Figure 16-5). Click on HTML Overview to read text that includes these topics:
"Autoflowing and Autowrapping," "HTML Tag Syntax," "Document Construction
Guidelines," "Sample HTML Document," "Hyperlinks," "Linking to Points
within Documents," "URLs," "Lists," "Graphics," "Server-Side Includes," and
finally "For More Information About HTML." Click on Clickable Image Maps to
read Russ's guidelines for implementing hyperlinked graphic images on your
Web server upon which users can click to jump to linked topics. The information
at this site is excerpted from Russ's book, titled *Managing Internet Information
Services*, which naturally has even more neat stuff on HTML publishing. The end
of this page also has links to other HTML-related Web pages.

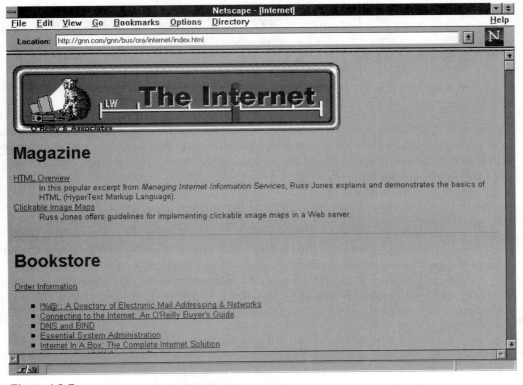

Figure 16-5

Self-taught Web publishing
http://www.lne.com/Web/Books/HTML/

This is the home page for the books *Teach Yourself Web Publishing with HTML in a
Week* and *Teach Yourself More Web Publishing with HTML in a Week*, both by Laura
Lemay. These books describe how to write, design, and publish information on
the World Wide Web. In addition to describing the HTML language itself, they
provide extensive information on using images, sounds, video, interactivity,
gateway programs (CGI), forms, and image maps. Through the use of dozens of
real-life examples and actual HTML source code, the books help you not only

learn the technical details of writing Web pages, but also teach you how to communicate information effectively through the Web.

The World Wide Web Handbook

http://www.ucc.ie/pflynn/books/wwwbook.html

This is a Web site for the book *The World Wide Web Handbook: An HTML Guide for Users, Authors, and Publishers* by Peter Flynn, published by International Thomson Computer Press. It profiles the book, including its Table of Contents and includes a downloadable version of the "HTML Reference Card" that is included with the printed edition of the book.

HTML specification 3.0

http://www.hpl.hp.co.uk/people/dsr/html/Contents.html

Here's a link to the table of contents for the complete HTML 3.0 specifications online manual. HTML 3.0 has been designed to be created in a variety of different ways. It is simple enough to type manually, and can be authored using WYSIWYG editors for HTML or generated via export filters from common word processing formats or other SGML applications.

Fill-out forms overview

http://www.ncsa.uiuc.edu/SDG/Software/Mosaic/Docs/fill-out-forms/overview.html

This site focuses on creating fill-out forms for your Web pages. One of its most valuable features is a listing of 13 forms done in HTML (at last count) that you can use as examples. They range in complexity from "ludicrously simple" to extremely advanced.

Computer graphics and visualization

http://www.dataspace.com/WWW/vlib/comp-graphics.html

A dazzling array of sources for graphics that you can use in publishing your Web page. You could spend all day at this site alone. Unfortunately, this trip—with countless graphic images to download—can be annoying during off-peak hours and impossibly slow during peak hours. Keep this URL, though, for the day that soon will come when you've got more bandwidth than you know what to do with.

U.S. government Web site

http://sunsite.unc.edu/govdocs.html

This site enables you to search for U.S. Government documents on the Web, such as press releases, speeches (including some audio and video clips), and information from the National Trade Data Bank. Take careful notes, because many of the references you find here may be good value-added links for clients and customers that use your Web site.

Top ten copyright myths

HERE'S AN answer to common myths about copyrights as applied to the Internet. It was created by Brad Templeton, the publisher for ClariNet Communications Corporation's news service, and it covers issues related to e-mail, news, research and Usenet posting. ClariNet, founded in 1989, is the Internet's first and largest electronic newspaper.

Please note that while most of the principles covered here are universal in Berne copyright signatory nations, some are derived from Canadian and U.S. law. Brad created this document to clear up some common misconceptions about intellectual property law that often are seen on the Internet. It is not intended to be a complete treatise on all the nuances of the subject.

Another note: **Do not e-mail Brad Templeton for legal advice**—use other resources or consult a lawyer. You can, however, check out Brad's personal Web page at ClariNet: *http://www.clari.net/brad* (see Figure A-1).

Copyright myths

Here's the text of Brad's Ten Big Copyright Myths, followed by a summary of the main points. Be sure and check out the Continuing Education section at the end of the chapter in which we point you to some other Internet sources on copyright issues.

1. If it doesn't have a copyright notice, it's not copyrighted.

This was true in the past, but today almost all major nations follow the Berne copyright convention. For example, in the U.S., almost everything created privately and originally after April 1, 1989 is copyrighted and protected, whether it has a notice or not. The default you should assume for other people's works is that they are copyrighted and may not be copied unless you *know* otherwise. There are some old works that lost protection without notice, but frankly you should not risk it unless you know for sure.

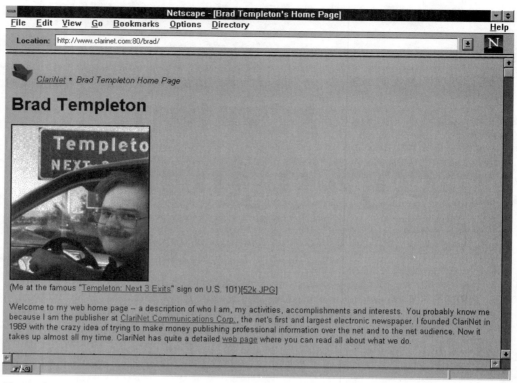

Figure A-1

It is true that a notice strengthens the protection, by warning people and by allowing one to get more and different damages, but it is not necessary. If it looks copyrighted, you should assume it is.

This applies to pictures, too. You may not scan pictures from magazines and post them to the Internet, and if you come upon something unknown, you shouldn't post that either.

The correct form for a copyright notice is:

"Copyright (dates) by (copyright holder)."

You can use the copyright symbol © instead of the word "Copyright," but "(C)" has never been given legal force. The phrase "All Rights Reserved" used to be required in some nations, but is now not needed.

2. If I don't charge for it, it's not a violation.

Absolutely false. Whether you charge can affect the damages awarded in court, but that's essentially the only difference. It's still a violation if you give it away— and there can still be heavy damages if you hurt the commercial value of a protected property.

3. If it's posted to Usenet it's in the public domain.

False. Nothing is in the public domain anymore unless the owner explicitly puts it in the public domain. Explicitly, as in you have a note from the copyright holder stating, "I grant this to the public domain." If not those exact words, then words very much like them.

Some argue that posting to the Usenet implicitly grants permission to everybody to copy the posting within fairly wide bounds, and others feel that Usenet is an automatic store-and-forward network where all the thousands of copies made are done at the command (rather than the consent) of the poster. This is a matter of some debate, but even if the former is true (and in this writer's opinion we should all pray it isn't true), it simply would suggest posters are implicitly granting permissions "for the sort of copying one might expect when one posts to Usenet" and in no case is this a placement of material into the public domain. Furthermore it is very difficult for an implicit license to supersede an explicitly stated license of which the copier was aware.

Note that all this assumes that the poster had the right to post the item in the first place. If the poster didn't, then all the copies are pirate, and no implied license or theoretical reduction of the copyright can take place.

Copyrights can expire after a long time, putting something into the public domain, and there are some fine points on this issue regarding older copyright law versions. However, none of this applies to an original article posted to Usenet.

Note that granting something to the public domain (PD) is a complete abandonment of all rights. You can't make something "PD for noncommercial use." If your work is PD, other people can even modify one byte and put their name on it.

4. My posting was just fair use!

The "fair use" exemption to copyright law was created to allow things such as commentary, parody, news reporting, research and education about copyrighted works without the permission of the author. Intent and damage to the commercial value of the work are important considerations. Are you reproducing an article from the New York Times because you needed to in order to criticize the quality of the New York Times, or because you couldn't find time to write your own story, or didn't want your readers to have to pay to log onto the online services with the story or buy a copy of the paper? The first probably is fair use, the others are not.

Fair use is almost always a short excerpt and almost always attributed. (One should not use more of the work than is necessary to make the commentary.) It should not harm the commercial value of the work—in the sense of people no longer needing to buy it (which is another reason why reproduction of the entire work generally is forbidden.)

Note that most inclusion of text in Usenet follow-ups is for commentary and reply, it doesn't damage the commercial value of the original posting (if it has any), and as such it is fair use. Fair use isn't an exact doctrine, either. The court decides if the right to comment overrides the copyright on an individual basis in each case.

There have been cases that go beyond the bounds of what's been covered here, but in general they don't apply to the typical Internet misclaim of fair use. It's a risky defense to attempt.

5. If you don't defend your copyright you lose it.

False. Copyright is effectively never lost these days, unless explicitly given away. You may be thinking of trademarks, which can be weakened or lost if not defended.

6. Somebody has that name copyrighted.

You can't copyright a name or anything short like a name. Titles usually don't qualify, but you could not write a song titled: "Everybody's got something to hide except for me and my monkey." (J.Lennon/P.McCartney)

You can't copyright words, but you can trademark them, generally by using them to refer to your brand of a generic type of product or service: Like an "Apple" computer. Apple Computer "owns" that word as applied to computers, even though it is also an ordinary word. Apple Records owns it when applied to music. Neither owns the word on its own, only in context, and owning a mark doesn't mean complete control—see a more detailed treatise on this law for details.

You can't use somebody else's trademark in a way that would unfairly hurt the value of the mark, or in a way that might make people confuse you with the real owner of the mark, or which might allow you to profit from the mark's good name. For example, if I were giving advice on music videos, I would be very wary of trying to label my works with a name like "MTV."

7. They can't get me; defendants in court have powerful rights!

Copyright law is mostly civil law. If you violate a copyright you usually would get sued, not charged with a crime. "Innocent until proven guilty," is a principle of criminal law, as is "proof beyond a reasonable doubt." In copyright suits these don't apply the same way, if at all. It's mostly which side and which set of evidence the judge or jury accepts or believes more, though the rules vary based on the type of infringement. In civil cases you can even be made to testify against your own interests.

8. Copyright violation isn't a crime.

Actually, recently in the U.S., commercial copyright violation involving more than 10 copies and a value of more $2500 was made a felony. So use caution. (At least you get the protections of criminal law.) On the other hand, don't think you're going to get people thrown in jail for posting your E-mail. The courts have much better things to do than that. This is a fairly new, untested statute.

9. It doesn't hurt anybody—in fact it's free advertising.

It's up to the owner to decide if they want the free ads or not. If they want them, they will be sure to contact you. Don't rationalize whether it hurts the owner or not, ask them. Usually that's not too hard to do. In times past, ClariNet published the very funny Dave Barry column to a large and appreciative Usenet audience for a fee, but some person didn't ask, forwarded it to a mailing list, got caught, and the newspaper chain that employs Dave Barry pulled the column from the Internet. Even if you can't think of how the author or owner gets hurt, think about the fact that piracy on the Internet hurts everybody who wants a chance to use this wonderful new technology to do more than read other people's flamewars.

10. They e-mailed me a copy, so I can use it.

To have a copy is not to have the copyright. All the E-mail you write is copyrighted. However, E-mail is not, unless previously agreed, secret. So you can certainly report on what E-mail you are sent, and reveal what it says. You can even quote parts of it to demonstrate. Frankly, somebody who sues over an ordinary message might well get no damages, because the message has no commercial value, but if you want to stay strictly in the law, you should seek permission.

On the other hand, don't go nuts if somebody posts your E-mail. If it was an ordinary, nonsecret personal letter of minimal commercial value with no copyright notice (like 99.9% of all E-mail), you probably won't get any damages if you sue.

In summary

Almost everything written today is copyrighted the moment it's written and no copyright notice is required.

Copyright is still violated whether you charged money or not, though damages usually increase if you charge money.

Postings to the Internet are not granted to the public domain, and don't grant you any permission to do further copying except perhaps the sort of copying the poster might have expected in the ordinary flow of the Internet.

Fair use is a complex doctrine meant to allow certain valuable social purposes. Ask yourself why you are republishing what you are posting, and why you didn't rewrite it in your own words.

Copyright is not lost because you don't defend it; that's a concept from trademark law. The ownership of names is also from trademark law, so don't say somebody has a name copyrighted.

Copyright law is mostly civil law where the special rights of criminal defendants you hear so much about don't apply. Watch out, however, as new laws are moving copyright violation into the criminal realm.

Don't rationalize that you are helping the copyright holder; the Internet has made it easier that ever to secure permission.

Posting E-mail is technically a violation, but revealing facts from E-mail isn't, and for almost all typical E-mail, nobody could wring any damages from you for posting it.

Continuing Education

U.S. Copyright Office Automated Information Service
gopher://marvel.loc.gov/11/copyright

This is an actual connection to a directory listing within the U.S. copyright office in Washington, D.C. Begin by clicking on the first document on the list, titled "Introduction to the Copyright Office." After reading it, return to the first page and click on any of the directory folders that you need to access.

Figure A-2

The United States Patent and Trademark Office (USPTO)
http://www.uspto.gov

The USPTO (see Figure A-2) provides a Web page titled "Basic Facts About Registering A Trademark." Topics include securing trademark rights, submitting applications, who may apply, how to search for conflicting previously registered trademarks, and rules for using TM and "circled R" symbols. Some of the information here can help your organization sort out the relationship (or lack thereof) between Internet domain names and registered trademarks.

Electronic Freedom Frontier's intellectual property law primer

http://www.eff.org/pub/CAF/law/ip-primer

This is a primer written by J. Diane Brinson and Mark F. Radcliffe to help you understand intellectual property law issues as they apply to the development and distribution of multimedia works. The information was derived from the Multimedia Law Handbook (Ladera Press, 340 pages, 1-800-523-3721).

Cornell University

http://www.law.cornell.edu/topics/copyright.html

This is a comprehensive Web page with hypertext links to just about every aspect of intellectual property law you could ask for. It includes a hypertext version of U.S. copyright law from the Legal Information Institute (LII), and a hypertext version of the Berne international copyright convention.

Copyright Clearance Center Online

http://www.openmarket.com/copyright/

The online version of the Copyright Clearance Center, a nonprofit organization that provides collective copyright licensing services. They help ease the permissions burdens and consolidate payments rights for organizations of all sizes and types.

Ohio State

http://www.cis.ohio-state.edu/hypertext/faq/usenet/Copyright-FAQ/top.html

A detailed listing of copyright Frequently-Asked-Questions (FAQ) covering many issues, including compilation copyright, the intricacies of fair use, and international copyright issues.

Computer ergonomics

THE OVER-INFORMATION Age is enough to give anyone a brain cramp—don't let it cramp your health, too. If computers and the Internet are adversely affecting your body as well as your mind, check out these sites for a world of information about computer ergonomics.

Continuing Education

University of Virginia

http://www.virginia.edu/~enhealth/ERGONOMICS/toc.html

This home page (see Figure B-1) is entitled, "Avoiding a Painful Desk Job!!!" You'll find links that lead to educational hypermedia and information about defining and evaluating ergonomic risks, creating ergonomically-appropriate video-display terminal (VDT) workstations and preventing work-related musculoskeletal disorders (CTDs). Be sure and click on the link entitled, "Stretch Breaks" for a series of graphic images that depict stretching exercises designed for computer users.

University of California, San Francisco and Berkeley

http://www.me.berkeley.edu/ergo/

The home page of this site describes its vision as being "To understand the mechanisms leading to upper extremity musculoskeletal disorders, such as tendonitis and carpal tunnel syndrome, and identify and evaluate equipment designs and work practices that reduce excessive stresses on tissues in order to prevent these disorders from developing."

Typing injury/keyboard alternative archive

http://alumni.caltech.edu/~dank/typing-archive.html

This site specializes in Carpal Tunnel Syndrome, Repetitive Stress Injury, Cumulative Trauma Disorder and such innovations as "DragonDictate," a voice-activated computer command system that enables you to issue WordPerfect for

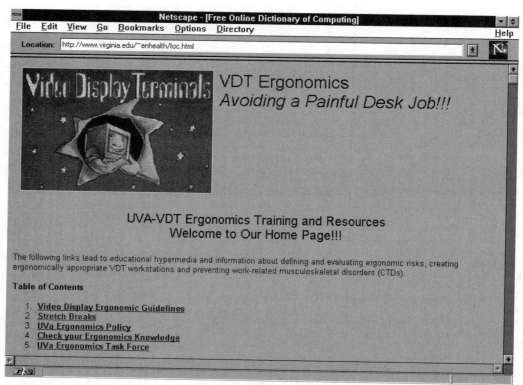

Figure B-1

Windows commands by speaking them. For example, to save a document, you could speak, "File, Save."

Typing injury FAQs

http://www.cs.princeton.edu/~dwallach/tifaq/

This is the home page for the Typing Injury FAQ and Typing Injury Archive. Clicking below should lead you to all kinds of documents and resources. One feature is entitled, "Keyboard Alternatives" and includes more than 30 alternatives to regular keyboards—some obscure and expensive, others surprisingly affordable. Another feature profiles furniture information and proves that specially designed desks and chairs can increase comfort and boost productivity.

Computer related repetitive strain injury (RSI)

http://engr-www.unl.edu/ee/eeshop/rsi.html

This site defines RSI, lists symptoms for which you can be on guard, doles out prevention advice and can help you if you already are suffering from the effects of RSI (see Figure B-2). This site includes a slew of MPEG desktop exercise videos courtesy of David Brown & the New Zealand Occupational Safety and Health Service as well as references to several good books on RSI afflictions.

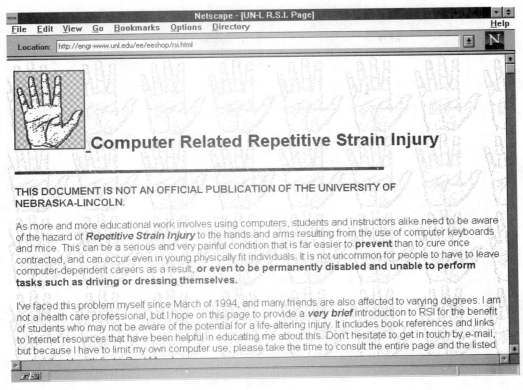

Figure B-2

Ergonomics mailing list

http://www.cs.cmu.edu/afs/cs.cmu.edu/help/www/06-Miscellaneous/RSI/m_lists.html

This address will get you information on subscribing to a mailing list for people with sore hands. This mailing list discusses carpal tunnel syndrome, tendonitis, etc. This page also has a more general mailing list intended to help solve health issues related to using computers in general. Both are listserv-style mailing lists.

312

How we created this book

THE MCGRAW-HILL INTERNET TRAINING GUIDE would not have been produced on time without the productivity and speed benefits of online communications. The book was begun online and now lives online.

The book began with an e-mail message to Ron Wagner from his literary agent, Bill Adler, Jr., telling Ron about a conversation Bill had had with Brad Schepp at McGraw-Hill. Bill's office is in Washington, D.C., Ron's office is in Herndon, Virginia (a Washington suburb), and Brad is based in Blue Ridge Summit, Pennsylvania.

Ron agreed to write the book, and most of the early coordination was done via e-mail—the distance between Ron, Bill, and Brad made no difference, of course. Because of a short time-line—and to improve technical accuracy—all three of us agreed that a co-author would be a good idea.

Ron sought out some top Internet experts and was fortunate to find Eric Engelmann. Eric's office is in Olney, Maryland, but he spends a lot of time in Washington at the World Bank. Ron and Eric had one face-to-face meeting in Olney to go over the book's outline, but everything else between them was coordinated via the Internet—except for one pool party in Ron's backyard to celebrate the contract signing.

Once the project was underway, Ron used the Internet extensively to contact resources for the book. A lot of the resources were found locally, but that's not surprising when you consider that Northern Virginia is a rapidly-growing high-tech center— something of a Silicon Valley East. Nonetheless, reams of information was made available from across the country—the Internet made it seem that everyone was local.

Michael Morrison, president of a local Internet service provider, Internext, set up a PPP account for Ron and included an FTP site. The FTP site became the book's home (see Figure C-1). Ron put the book's chapters on the FTP site as each reached the rough draft stage and Eric would download them. Eric then made revisions, additions, and technical enhancement and then put the chapters back

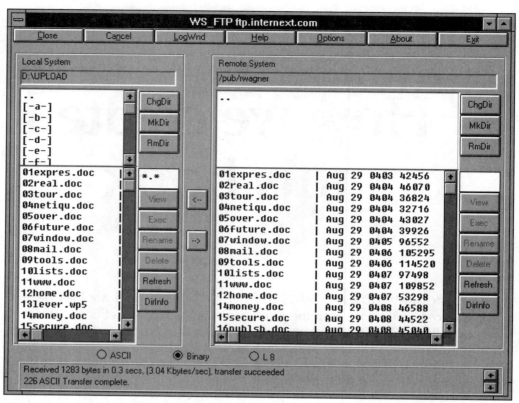

Figure C-1

up on the site. We were able to freely go back and forth with the chapters at any time. The site always had the latest version of each chapter—saved with password protection—as it became available.

Two other authors, both based in North Carolina, contributed substantially to the book. Jeff Davidson, founder of The Breathing Space Institute, helped with chapter 5, "The over-information age," from his office in Chapel Hill, North Carolina. Chapter 5 is based on Jeff's material, but Ron rewrote it specifically to apply to the Internet. The chapter went back and forth several times between Ron and Jeff in electronic format.

Dick Connor, the father of "Client-centered Marketing," helped with chapter 13, "Client-centered Interneting," from his office in Riverbend, North Carolina. Chapter 13 is a rewrite of some of Dick's Client-centered Marketing material, modified to apply to the Internet. Dick did not have any stand-alone FTP software, so he couldn't upload the chapter. But Ron uploaded versions of the chapter using WS_FTP, and Dick was able to download them with Netscape. When Dick was ready to send a version back to Ron, he e-mailed it with Eudora as a MIME attachment. Dick, Jeff, and Ron all work in WordPerfect for Windows, so this was an easy solution that preserved all WordPerfect formatting and gave us each a file that we could open directly in WordPerfect.

Along the way another associate, Fran Exley, offered to go over a couple of the chapters. Because the chapters were just sitting at an FTP site, Ron gave Fran the password to open the documents and Fran was able to download them at his convenience.

In the acknowledgments at the front of the book you'll see a long list of people who helped with the book. Many of these people directly contributed some text. The usual pattern was that the input arrived via e-mail, Ron rewrote it to fit into the book, Ron sent it back for approval, then the contributor e-mailed a response. When the text was ready to move into the manuscript, Ron simply dragged his mouse across it, hit CTRL+C to copy it, hit ALT+TAB to switch to WordPerfect, then hit CTRL+V to paste it in. Very fast, very productive.

Sometimes Ron would find that the text on a Web page was all he needed as input. In those cases, he simply dragged his mouse across the text he wanted and did the same CTRL+C, ALT+TAB, CTRL+V combination. The contributors didn't have to write a single additional word. Ron then used ALT+TAB to return to the Web page, found a link to e-mail for permission, and quickly secured the rights to use the text he had copied.

Your Internet service provider should easily be able to set up an FTP site for your organization from which you, too, can manage projects that need to coordinate input from people who are scattered all over the world.

Also, you likely will find a lot of text on the Web that you can use in a report, a letter, a newsletter, or even on your own Web page. Just use your mouse and the Windows clipboard to grab whatever you need, then jump back to the Web page and e-mail for permission. No one refused us reprint rights. You will find that almost everyone will be happy to contribute to your project if you maintain their copyright notice and include their URL with the text. If you have to rewrite the piece, most people will want you to e-mail them a copy of the revised text, but that too is a simple copy-and-paste procedure.

Both authors now are working on other Internet projects. Eric is helping the World Bank to complete its coverage of Africa. Ron is working with Dick Connor to promote Client-centered Interneting, and with Jeff Davidson to help Jeff bring some Breathing Space to all of us who use the Internet. Ron also has begun writing *The McGraw-Hill Web Training Guide*, due out in mid-1996.

Glossary

NET TIP This glossary is available online at the book's Web page: *http://www.marketing-coach.com/mh-guide*, then click on **Glossary**. The online version contains additional definitions, as well as links to several other online glossaries and technical dictionaries.

anonymous FTP—Using the FTP function of the Internet anonymously; not logging in with an actual login ID and password. Anonymous FTP is often permitted by large host computers who are willing to openly share some of the files on their system with outside users who otherwise would not be able to log in.

Archie—An ancient Internet search tool, not used much since way back in the good old days of 1994. It's an archive of filenames maintained at Internet FTP sites. Don't pine its passing; you didn't miss anything fun—the Web is much more fun.

bandwidth—The transmission capacity of the lines that carry the Internet's electronic traffic. Historically it has imposed severe limitations on the ability of the Internet to deliver all that we are demanding it deliver, but fiber-optic cables will ensure that bandwidth soon will be essentially limitless and free.

browser—Software that enables users to browse through the cyberspace of the World Wide Web. Netscape is the primary Internet browser today.

ClariNet—A commercial news service that provides tailored news reports via the Internet. You can access ClariNet news within Usenet newsgroups. There is a whole series of them, dedicated to a wide range of broad topics. In general, you can find them on news servers at *clari.**.

client/server—Computer technology that separates computers and their users into two categories: clients and servers. When you want information from a computer on the Internet, you are a client. The computer that delivers the information is the server. A server both stores information and makes it available to any authorized client who requests the information. You may hear this one frequently, especially if someone says, "You can't contact us today because our Web server is down."

dial-in—A modem-based Internet account that can connect any PC directly to the Internet. The account is used by having a PC-based (usually Windows-based) software application dial in to an Internet service provider (ISP). The software connects with the ISP and establishes a TCP/IP link to the Internet that enables your software to access Internet information.

e-mail—(Electronic mail) Messages transmitted over the Internet from user to user. E-mail can contain text, but also can carry with it files of any type as attachments.

FAQs—(Frequently Asked Questions) Files that commonly are maintained at Internet sites to answer frequently asked questions so that experienced users don't have to bear the annoying burden of hearing newbies repeatedly ask the same questions. It's good netiquette to check for FAQs and read them. It's extremely poor netiquette—and a good way to get flamed—to post questions that already are answered in the FAQ.

Finger—An Internet function that enables one user to query (finger) the location of another Internet user. Finger can be applied to any computer on the Internet, if set up properly. For example, the most famous finger site of all was a Coke machine at Carnegie-Mellon that students wired to the Internet so they could finger it and track such important information as how many bottles of which beverage remained, and how long the bottom bottle in each stack had been in the machine—so they wouldn't walk all the way to the machine and find it empty, or purchase a warm soda. You won't use this, but it was fun while it lasted. Most sites on which you could use Finger are shutting it down because it helps hackers crack a system.

flames—Insulting, enraged Internet messages; the equivalent of schoolyard brawls in cyberspace. Unfortunately, a good schoolyard brawl would be preferable, because at least then the only people who suffer are the dummies who fight. On the Internet, everyone suffers as resources are squandered on ridiculous, infantile behavior. As a representative of a business organization, you won't be using flames, of course.

FQDN—(Fully Qualified Domain Name) The "official" name assigned to a computer. Organizations register names, such as "ibm.com" or "utulsa.edu." They then assign unique names to their computers, such as "watson5.ibm.com" or "hurricane.cs.utulsa.edu."

FTP—(File Transfer Protocol) The basic Internet function that enables files to be transferred between computers. You can use it to download files from a remote host computer, as well as to upload files from your computer to a remote host computer. (See Anonymous FTP.)

gateway—A host computer that connects networks that communicate in different languages. For example, a gateway connects a company's local area network to the Internet.

GIF—(Graphics Interchange Format) A graphics file format that is commonly used on the Internet to provide graphics images in Web pages.

Gopher—An information-retrieval tool that was the primary tool for finding Internet resources before the World Wide Web became popular. Gopher now is buried under mountains of WWW pages—don't bother learning how to use this directly. You sometimes will find a Web link that takes you to a Gopher site, but at that point, if you're using Netscape, its usage will be obvious and actually will look a great deal like the Web.

host—A computer that "hosts" outside computer users by providing files and services or by sharing its resources.

HTML—(Hypertext Markup Language) The basic language that is used to build hypertext documents on the World Wide Web. It is used in basic, plain ASCII-text documents, but when those documents are interpreted (called rendering) by a Web browser such as Netscape, the document can display formatted text, color, a variety of fonts, graphic images, special effects, hypertext jumps to other Internet locations, and information forms.

HTTP—(Hypertext Transfer Protocol) The protocol (set of rules) that computers use to transfer hypertext documents.

hypertext—Text in a document that contains a hidden link to other text. You can click a mouse on a hypertext word and it will take you to the text designated in the link. Hypertext is used in Windows help programs and CD encyclopedias to jump to related references elsewhere within the same document. The wonderful thing about hypertext, however, is its ability to link—using http over the World Wide Web—to any Web document in the world, yet still require only a single mouse click to jump clear around the world.

IP—(Internet Protocol) The rules that provide basic Internet functions. (See TCP/IP.)

IRC—(Internet Relay Chat) Currently an Internet tool with a limited use that lets users join a "chat" channel and exchange typed, text messages. Few people have used IRC, but it is going to create a revolution in communication when the Internet can provide the bandwidth to carry full-color, live-action video and audio. Once that occurs, the IRC will provide full video-conferencing. Even today, while limited for all practical purposes only to text, the IRC can be a valuable business conferencing tool, already providing adequate voice communication.

ISDN—(Integrated Services Digital Network) A set of communications standards that enable a single phone line or optical cable to carry voice, digital network services, and video. ISDN is intended to eventually replace our standard telephone system.

JPEG—(Joint Photographic Experts Group) The name of the committee that designed the photographic image-compression standard. JPEG is optimized for compressing full-color or gray-scale photographic-type digital images. It doesn't work well on drawn images such as line drawings, and it does not handle black-and-white images or video images.

Kbps—(kilobits per second) A speed rating for computer modems that measures (in units of 1,024 bits) the maximum number of bits the device can transfer in one second under ideal conditions.

KBps—(kilobytes per second). Remember, one byte is eight bits.

leased line—A leased phone line that provides a full-time, dedicated, direct connection to the Internet.

listserv—An Internet application that automatically "serves" mailing lists by sending electronic newsletters to a stored database of Internet user addresses. Users can handle their own subscribe/unsubscribe actions without requiring anyone at the server location to personally handle the transaction.

MIME—(Multipurpose Internet Mail Extensions) A set of Internet functions that extends normal e-mail capabilities and enables computer files to be attached to e-mail. Files sent by MIME arrive at their destination as exact copies of the original so that you can send fully-formatted word processing files, spreadsheets, graphics images and software applications to other users via simple e-mail.

modem—An electronic device that lets computers communicate electronically. While modems historically have been used to connect computers via telephone lines, you soon will see "cable modems" that will connect computers via cable television lines that will provide speed improvements in the range of one thousand times faster than today's telephone-line modems.

POP—(Post Office Protocol) An Internet protocol that enables a single user to read e-mail from a mail server.

PoP—(Point of Presence) A site that has an array of telecommunications equipment: modems, digital, leased lines, and Internet routers. An Internet access provider may operate several regional PoPs to provide Internet connections within local phone service areas. An alternative is for access providers to employ virtual PoPs (virtual Points of Presence) in conjunction with third party providers.

protocols—Computer rules that provide uniform specifications so that computer hardware and operating systems can communicate. It's similar to the way that mail, in countries around the world, is addressed in the same basic format so that postal workers know where to find the recipient's address, the sender's return address and the postage stamp. Regardless of the underlying language, the basic "protocols" remain the same.

router—A network device that enables the network to reroute messages it receives that are intended for other networks. The network with the router receives the message and sends it on its way exactly as received.

shell account—A software application that lets you use someone else's Internet connection. It's not the same as having your own direct Internet connection, but it's pretty close. You connect to a host computer and use the Internet through the host computer's connection.

signature file—An ASCII text file, maintained within e-mail programs, that contains a few lines of text for your signature. The programs automatically attach the file to your messages so you don't have to repeatedly type a closing.

SLIP/PPP—(Serial Line Internet Protocol/Point-to-Point Protocol) The basic rules that enable PCs to connect, usually by dial-up modem, directly to other computers that provide Internet services.

SMTP—(Simple Mail Transfer Protocol) The basic programming language behind the Internet's e-mail functions.

spam—Anything that nobody wants. It applies primarily to commercial messages posted across a large number of Internet newsgroups, especially when the ad contains nothing of specific interest to the posted newsgroup.

T1—An Internet backbone line that carries up to 1.536 million bits per second (1.536Mbps).

T3—An Internet backbone line that carries up to 45 million bits per second (45Mbps).

TCP/IP—(Transmission Control Protocol/Internet Protocol) The basic programming foundation that carries computer messages around the globe via the Internet. TCP/IP was co-created by Vinton G. Cerf, former president of the Internet Society, and Robert E. Kahn.

Telnet—An Internet protocol that lets you connect your PC as a remote workstation to a host computer anywhere in the world, and to use that computer as if you were logged on locally. You often have the ability to use all of the software and capability on the host computer, even if it's a huge mainframe.

UNIX—The computer operating system that was used to write most of the programs and protocols that built the Internet. The need for UNIX is rapidly waning, and mainstream users will never need to use a UNIX command-line prompt.

URL—(Uniform Resource Locator) A critical term. It's your main access channel to Internet sites; the equivalent to having the phone number of a place you want to call. You constantly will use URLs with your Internet software applications.

Usenet—Another name for Internet Newsgroups. A distributed bulletin board system running on news servers, UNIX hosts, online services, and bulletin board systems. Collectively, all the users who post and read articles to newsgroups. The Usenet is international in scope, and is the largest decentralized information utility. The Usenet includes government agencies, universities, high schools, organizations of all sizes, as well as millions of stand-alone PCs. Some estimates we found say that there were 15,000 public newsgroups in 1996, collecting more than 100 megabytes of data daily; but no one really knows.

Veronica—Archie's companion—not really, because Veronica actually helps you find information on Gopher menus and within the text of Gopher documents. It's an acronym for "Very Easy Rodent-Oriented Net-wide Index to Computerized

Archives." You probably never will use it, because Web searches are faster and more extensive.

WAIS—(Wide Area Information Servers) A distributed information retrieval system that is sponsored by Apple Computer, Thinking Machines, and Dow Jones, Inc.. Users can locate documents using keyword searches that return a list of documents ranked according to the frequency of occurrence of the search criteria.

WinVN—The most widely used stand-alone Windows-based Internet Usenet newsgroup reader application, WinVN is a powerful program with many useful functions. Now that Netscape includes built-in newsgroup functions, however, the use of WinVN is waning except for users with advanced Newsgroup needs. In many ways, Netscape is a better newsgroup reader for mainstream users.

World Wide Web—(WWW) (W3) (the Web) An Internet client-server distributed information and retrieval system based upon the hypertext transfer protocol (http), which transfers hypertext documents across a varied array of computer systems. The Web was created by the CERN High-Energy Physics Laboratories in Geneva, Switzerland in 1991. CERN boosted the Web into international prominence on the Internet.

Index

About the authors

Ron Wagner

This is Ron's eighth book. His first two were computer guide books, one on "Turbo Pascal" and one on "Electric Desk" (later called "LotusWorks"). Ron also wrote three software applications for Software Express/Direct that were advertised nationally in PC Magazine. That same year—1986, the first year he owned a PC—Ron also wrote a column for a computer magazine called "Uptime."

Ron switched in 1989 from programming to training and became WordPerfect Corporation's 129th "Certified Instructor." PC-computer training and writing have been his primary revenue source since then. Before 1989, Ron spent 16 years as a professional pilot, flying VIP transports for the U.S. Air Force in the Presidential Wing at Andrews AFB in Washington and flying Boeing 727s for Eastern Air Lines out of Washington National.

In 1991, Ron became an international trainer for Group1 Software's "ArcList" and "AccuMail" packages, which got him back in the air again, training coast-to-coast in the U.S. and overseas to London, Madrid, Mexico City, Buenos Aires and Johannesburg. Ron wrote four books in 1991—all were ghost-writing projects for people such as founders of well-known (but nameless here) corporations.

In 1993, he co-authored *The Weather Sourcebook* with Bill Adler, Jr. It sold out its first printing in four months and has gone into its third printing.

Ron expanded his computer business again with Internet training and consulting and now is working with Dick Connor to develop their "Client-centered Interneting" system. They are planning to co-author a new book titled *Net Profit: Client-centered Interneting* and to develop the supporting software *Your Marketing Coach* (see *http://www.marketing-coach.com*).

Eric Engelmann

Eric Engelmann, the president of EMS Consulting Services, has 18 years of experience in computing, networks and training. He is a graduate of John Hopkins University with post-graduate studies in computer and electronics engineering at George Mason University. He's worked as a programmer, systems engineer and technical trainer for several companies.

Eric develops and trains all levels of Internet courses: introduction, applications, browsers, advanced Netscape, WinVN, publishing, Internet Assistant, advanced mail applications, finding resources and using multimedia on the Internet. He also teaches courses on how to build effective World Wide Web pages as well as consulting on Internet business opportunities.

Eric has served a variety of industries throughout the U.S. and internationally. He now is the primary Internet trainer for the Africa region at the World Bank. He also teaches the Internet through a Washington-area training center (CPSI@http://www.cpsi.com) and through EMS Consulting Services. Eric has established a presence on the Web for many retail, nonprofit, and professional organizations, giving him some exciting success stories as follow-ups to the "how-to" expertise he provides (see *http://www.wdn.com/ems*). He now is establishing the World Bank's World Wide Web presence (see *http://www.worldbank.org*), concentrating on Africa. He'll be helping the World Bank establish Web servers, database publishing strategies, and Internet support for their offices throughout Africa.